TH

of JUSTIFICATION

Books by John Piper

THE FUTURE
of JUSTIFICATION

A Response to N. T. Wright

JOHN PIPER

CROSSWAY BOOKS
WHEATON, ILLINOIS

Library of Congress Cataloging-in-Publication Data
Piper, John, 1946–
    The Future of Justification : a response to N.T. Wright / John Piper.
       p. cm.
    Includes index.
    ISBN 978-1-58134-964-1 (tpb)
    1. Justification (Christian theology)—History of doctrines—20th century.
2. Wright, N. T. (Nicholas Thomas) II. Title.
BT764.3.P57   2007
234'.7—dc22   2007029481

BP		17	16	15	14	13	12	11	10	09	08	07
15	14	13	12	11	10	9	8	7	6	5	4	3	2	1

In memory of my father

WILLIAM SOLOMON HOTTLE PIPER

*who preached the gospel of Jesus Christ
for seventy years*

Contents

ACKNOWLEDGMENTS

THIS IS THE YEAR (2007) that my father died. Who can estimate the debt we owe our fathers? Bill Piper preached the gospel of grace for over seventy years, if you count the songs and testimonies at the nursing home. He was an evangelist—the old southern, independent, fundamentalist sort, without the attitude. He remains in my memory the happiest man I ever knew.

In the last chapter of his ministry one of his favorite and most fruitful sermons was titled "Grace for the Guilty." As I read it even today I realize again why, under God, my father must be acknowledged first at the beginning of this book. That great sermon comes toward its end with these simple words, "God clothes you with his righteousness when you believe, giving you a garment that makes you fit for heaven." We all knew what he meant. He was a lover of the great, deep, power-laden old truths. He wielded them in the might of the Spirit to see thousands—I dare say tens of thousands—of people profoundly converted. For my father, the gospel of Christ included the news that there is a righteousness—a perfect obedience of Jesus Christ—that is offered freely to all through faith alone. And when faith is given, that righteousness is imputed to the believer once and for all. Together with the sin-forgiving blood of Jesus, this is our hope. From the moment we believed until the last day of eternity God is 100 percent for us on this basis alone—the sin-bearing punishment of Christ, and the righteousness-providing obedience of Christ. This my father preached and sang, and I believed with joy.

> O let the dead now hear Thy voice;
> Now bid Thy banished ones rejoice;
> Their beauty this, their glorious dress,
> Jesus, Thy blood and righteousness. [1]

---

[1] John Wesley, "Jesu, Thy Blood and Righteousness."

This book took its origin from the countless conversations and e-mails with those who are losing their grip on this great gospel. This has proved to be a tremendous burden for my soul over the past ten years. But I thank God for it. And I acknowledge him for any clarity and faith and worship and obedience that might flow from this effort.

The book began to take shape while I was on sabbatical in the spring and summer of 2006 at Tyndale House in Cambridge, England. This is a very fruitful place to study, write, and interact with thoughtful scholars. The book was put in its final form during a month-long writing leave in May, 2007. Without the support of the Council of Elders of Bethlehem Baptist Church I could not have done this work. I am writing these acknowledgments on the first day of my twenty-eighth year as pastor of Bethlehem, and my heart is full of thanks for a people that love the great truths of the gospel and commission me to study and write and preach these truths.

Also indispensable were my assistants David Mathis and Nathan Miller. Reading the manuscript repeatedly, and making suggestions, and finding resources, and tracking down citations, and certifying references, and lifting dozens of practical burdens from my shoulders, they made this work possible.

More than any other book that I have written, this one was critiqued in the process by very serious scholars. I received detailed critical feedback to the first draft from Michael Bird, Ardel Caneday, Andrew Cowan, James Hamilton, Burk Parsons, Matt Perman, Joseph Rigney, Thomas Schreiner, Justin Taylor, Brian Vickers, and Doug Wilson. Most significant of all was the feedback I received from N. T. Wright. He wrote an 11,000-word response to my first draft that was very helpful in clarifying issues and (I hope) preventing distortions. The book is twice the size it was before all of that criticism arrived. If it is not a better book now, it is my fault, not theirs.

Thanks again to Carol Steinbach and her team for providing the indexes. The only other person who has touched more of my books more closely than Carol is my wife, Noël. Nothing of this nature would happen without her support.

As usual it has been a deeply satisfying partnership to work with Justin Taylor, Ted Griffin, Lane Dennis, and the entire team at Crossway Books.

It should not go unmentioned that besides my father there are other "fathers" who have shaped my understanding of the doctrine of justification. Martin Luther, John Calvin, John Owen, Jonathan Edwards, Daniel Fuller, George Ladd, John Murray, Leon Morris—not that I have agreed with them all on every point, but I have learned so much from them. I would be happy if it was said of this book what John Erskine said in 1792 of Solomon Stoddard's book, *The Safety of Appearing at the Day of Judgment, in the Righteousness of Christ*: "The general tendency of this book is to show that our claim to the pardon of sin and acceptance with God is not founded on any thing wrought in us, or acted by us, but only on the righteousness of Christ."[2]

---

[2]Solomon Stoddard, *The Safety of Appearing at the Day of Judgment, in the Righteousness of Christ* (Morgan, PA: Soli Deo Gloria Publications, 1995, orig. 1687), vii.

INTRODUCTION

THE FINAL JUDGMENT feels too close for me to care much about scoring points in debate. Into my seventh decade, the clouds of time are clearing, and the prospect of wasting my remaining life on gamesmanship or one-upmanship is increasingly unthinkable. The ego-need to be right has lost its dominion, and the quiet desire to be a faithful steward of the grace of truth increases. N. T. Wright is about three years younger than I am, and I assume he feels the same.

The risen Lord Jesus sees through all our clever turns of phrase—I am preaching to myself. He knows perfectly when we have chosen words to win, but not to clarify. He has planted a banner on the pulpit of every preacher and on the desk of every scholar: "No man can give the impression that he himself is clever and that Christ is mighty to save."[1] We will give an account to the all-knowing, all-ruling Lord of the universe in a very few years—or days. And when we do, what will matter is that we have not peddled God's word but "as men of sincerity, as commissioned by God, in the sight of God we speak in Christ" (2 Cor. 2:17).

THE FRAGRANCE FROM DEATH TO DEATH AND FROM LIFE TO LIFE

Those of us who are ordained by the church to the Christian ministry have a special responsibility to feed the sheep (John 21:17). We have been made "overseers, to shepherd the church of God which He purchased with His own blood" (Acts 20:28, NASB). We bear the burden of being not only teachers, who "will be judged with greater strictness" (James 3:1), but also examples in the way we live, so that our people may "consider the outcome of [our] way of life, and imitate [our] faith" (Heb. 13:7). The apostle Paul charges us: "Keep a close watch on your-

---

[1]These are the words of James Denney, quoted in John Stott, *Between Two Worlds: The Art of Preaching in the Twentieth Century* (Grand Rapids, MI: Eerdmans, 1982), 325.

self and on the teaching" (1 Tim. 4:16). We are "servants of Christ and stewards of the mysteries of God. Moreover, it is required of stewards that they be found trustworthy" (1 Cor. 4:1–2)—trustworthy in *life*, "in step with the truth of the gospel" (Gal. 2:14), and trustworthy in *teaching*, "rightly handling the word of truth" (2 Tim. 2:15).

The seriousness of our calling comes from the magnitude of what is at stake. If we do not feed the sheep in our charge with "the whole counsel of God," their blood is on our hands. "I am innocent of the blood of all of you, for I did not shrink from declaring to you the whole counsel of God" (Acts 20:26–27). If we do not equip the saints by living in a way that exalts Christ, and by teaching what accords with the gospel, it will be laid to our account if our people are like "children, tossed to and fro by the waves and carried about by every wind of doctrine" (Eph. 4:12, 14).

More importantly, eternal life hangs in the balance: "We are the aroma of Christ to God among those who are being saved and among those who are perishing, to one a fragrance from death to death, to the other a fragrance from life to life. Who is sufficient for these things?" (2 Cor. 2:15–16). How we live and what we teach will make a difference in whether people obey the gospel or meet Jesus in the fire of judgment, "when the Lord Jesus is revealed from heaven with his mighty angels in flaming fire, inflicting vengeance on those who do not know God and on those who do not obey the gospel of our Lord Jesus" (2 Thess. 1:7–8).

This is why Paul was so provoked at the false teaching in Galatia. It was another gospel and would bring eternal ruin to those who embraced it. This accounts for his unparalleled words: "Even if we or an angel from heaven should preach to you a gospel contrary to the one we preached to you, let him be accursed" (Gal. 1:8). Getting the good news about Jesus right is a matter of life and death. It is the message "by which you are being saved" (1 Cor. 15:2).

IF RIGHTEOUSNESS WERE THROUGH THE LAW, THEN CHRIST DIED FOR NO PURPOSE

Therefore, the subject matter of this book—justification by faith apart from works of the law—is serious. There is as much riding on this truth as could ride on any truth in the Bible. "If righteousness were through the law, then Christ died for no purpose" (Gal. 2:21). And if Christ died for no purpose, we are still in our sins, and those who have died in Christ have perished. Paul called down a curse on those who bring a different gospel because "all who rely on works of the law are under a curse" (Gal. 3:10), and he would spare us this curse. "You are severed from Christ, you who would be justified by the law" (Gal. 5:4). And if we are severed from Christ, there is no one to bear our curse, because "Christ redeemed us from the curse of the law by becoming a curse for us" (Gal. 3:13). I hope that the mere existence of this book will raise the stakes in the minds of many and promote serious study and faithful preaching of the gospel, which includes the good news of justification by faith apart from works of the law (Rom. 3:28; Gal. 2:16).

N. T. WRIGHT

My conviction concerning N. T. Wright is not that he is under the curse of Galatians 1:8–9, but that his portrayal of the gospel—and of the doctrine of justification in particular—is so disfigured that it becomes difficult to recognize as biblically faithful. It may be that in his own mind and heart Wright has a clear and firm grasp on the gospel of Christ and the biblical meaning of justification. But in my judgment, what he has written will lead to a kind of preaching that will not announce clearly what makes the lordship of Christ good news for guilty sinners or show those who are overwhelmed with sin how they may stand righteous in the presence of God.

Nicholas Thomas Wright is a British New Testament scholar and the Anglican Bishop of Durham, England. He is a remarkable blend of weighty academic scholarship, ecclesiastical leadership, ecumenical involvement, prophetic social engagement, popular Christian advocacy, musical talent, and family commitment.[2] As critical as this book is of Wright's understanding of the gospel and justification, the seriousness and scope of the book is a testimony to the stature of his scholarship and the extent of his influence. I am thankful for his strong commitment to Scripture as his final authority, his defense and celebration of the resurrection of the Son of God, his vindication of the deity of Christ, his belief in the virgin birth of Jesus, his biblical disapproval of homosexual conduct, and the consistent way he presses us to see the big picture of God's

---

[2]An abundance of information about Dr. Wright—as well as written, audio, and video materials by him—are available at http://www.ntwrightpage.com.

universal purpose for all peoples through the covenant with Abraham—
and more. In this book, my hope, most remotely, is that Wright might
be influenced to change some of what he thinks concerning justification
and the gospel. Less remotely, I hope that he might clarify, in future writings, some things that I have stumbled over. But most optimistically, I
hope that those who consider this book and read N. T. Wright will read
him with greater care, deeper understanding, and less inclination to find
Wright's retelling of the story of justification compelling.

"THIS WHOLE THING IS GOING TO FLY"

For the last thirty years, Wright has been rethinking and retelling the
theology of the New Testament. He recalls an experience in the mid-
seventies when Romans 10:3[3] became the fulcrum of a profoundly new
way of looking at Paul's theology. He was trying to make sense of Paul
on the basis of the inherited views of the Reformation but could not.

> I was reading C.E.B. Cranfield on Romans and trying to see how it
> would work with Galatians, and it simply doesn't work. Interestingly,
> Cranfield hasn't done a commentary on Galatians. It's very difficult.
> But I found then, and this was the mid-seventies before E. P. Sanders
> was published, before there was such a thing as a "new perspective,"
> that I came out with this reading of Romans 10:3 which is really the
> fulcrum for me around which everything else moved: "Being ignorant
> of the righteousness of God and seeking to establish their own."
>
> In other words, what we have here is a covenant status which is for
> Jews and Jews only. I have a vivid memory of going home that night,
> sitting up in bed, reading Galatians through in Greek and thinking, "It
> works. It really works. This whole thing is going to fly." And then all
> sorts of things just followed on from that.[4]

What he means by "this whole thing" is a top-to-bottom rethinking of Paul's theology in categories largely different from the way most
people have read their New Testament in the last fifteen hundred years
(see chapter 1, note 6). When someone engages in such a thorough
reconstruction of New Testament theology, critics must be extremely

---

[3] "For, being ignorant of the righteousness of God, and seeking to establish their own, they did not
submit to God's righteousness."
[4] Travis Tamerius, "An Interview with N. T. Wright," *Reformation & Revival Journal* 11, Nos.
1 and 2 (Winter and Spring 2003). Available online at http://www.hornes.org/theologia/content/
travis_tamerius/interview_with_n_t_wright.htm.

careful. Their job is almost impossible. The temptation is to hear a claim about justification or about the gospel that sounds so wrongheaded that a quick critical essay contrasting the "wrongheaded" claim with the traditional view seems like a sufficient response. Wright is understandably wearied with such rejoinders.

WHEN GLOBAL PARADIGMS COLLIDE

However, in Wright's reconstruction, he has recast the old definitions and the old connections. This may or may not mean that the old reality is lost. It may or may not mean that the new way of saying things is more faithful to the apostles' intentions. It may or may not mean that the church will be helped by this new construction. But what is clear is that criticism of such global reconstructions requires a great deal of effort to get inside the globe and see things from there. Whether I have succeeded at this or not, I have tried.

We all wear colored glasses—most wear glasses colored by tradition; some wear glasses colored by anti-tradition; and some wear glasses colored by our emerging, new reconstruction of reality. Which of these ways of seeing the world is more seductive, I don't know. Since they exist in differing degrees, from one time to the next, probably any of them can be overpowering at a given moment. I love the gospel and justification that I have seen in my study and preaching over the last forty years. N. T. Wright loves the gospel and justification he has seen in that same time. My temptation is to defend a view because it has been believed for centuries. His temptation is to defend a view because it fits so well into his new way of seeing the world. Public traditions and private systems are both very powerful. We are agreed, however, that neither conformity to an old tradition nor conformity to a new system is the final arbiter of truth. Scripture is. And we both take courage from the fact that Scripture has the power to force its own color through any human lens.

WHAT IS BEHIND THIS BOOK?

For those who wonder what Wright has written that causes a response as long and as serious as this book, it may be helpful to mention a few of the issues that I will try to deal with in the book. These are some of those head-turners that tempt the critic to say, "He can't be serious."

But remember, the shock may only be because we are, as he would say, looking at things in the old way and not in the way he has redefined them. On the other hand, there may be real problems.

The Gospel Is Not about How to Get Saved?

First, it is striking to read not just what Wright says the gospel *is*, but what he says it *isn't*. He writes, "'The gospel' itself refers to the proclamation that Jesus, the crucified and risen Messiah, is the one, true and only Lord of the world."[5] For Paul, this imperial announcement was "that the crucified Jesus of Nazareth had been raised from the dead; that he was thereby proved to be Israel's Messiah; that he was thereby installed as Lord of the world."[6] Yes. That is an essential announcement of the gospel. But Wright also says, "'The gospel' is not an account of how people get saved."[7] "Paul's gospel to the pagans was not a philosophy of life. Nor was it, even, a doctrine about how to get saved."[8] "My proposal has been that 'the gospel' is not, for Paul, a message about 'how one gets saved.'"[9] "The gospel is not . . . a set of techniques for making people Christians."[10] "'The gospel' is not an account of how people get saved. It is . . . the proclamation of the lordship of Jesus Christ."[11]

These are striking denials in view of 1 Corinthians 15:1–2, "Now I would remind you, brothers, of *the gospel* I preached to you . . . by which you are being *saved*." But be careful. Perhaps this only means that salvation *results* from believing the gospel, not that the gospel message tells how to be saved. Perhaps. But one wonders how the death and resurrection of Jesus could be heard as good news if one had spent his life committing treason against the risen King. It seems as though one would have to be told how the death and resurrection of Christ actually saves sinners, if sinners are to hear them as good news and not as a death sentence. There is so much more to say (see especially chapter 5). I am only illustrating the flash points.

---

[5]N. T. Wright, "Paul in Different Perspectives: Lecture 1: Starting Points and Opening Reflections," at the Pastors Conference of Auburn Avenue Presbyterian Church, Monroe, Louisiana (January 3, 2005). Accessed 5-11-07 at http://www.ntwrightpage.com/Wright_Auburn_Paul.htm.
[6]N. T. Wright, *What Saint Paul Really Said* (Grand Rapids, MI: Eerdmans, 1997), 46.
[7]Ibid., 133.
[8]Ibid., 90.
[9]Ibid., 60.
[10]Ibid., 153.
[11]Ibid., 133.

Justification Is Not How You Become a Christian?

Second, Wright says, "Justification is not how someone becomes a Christian. It is the declaration that they have become a Christian."[12] Or again, "'Justification' in the first century was not about how someone might establish a relationship with God. It was about God's eschatological definition, both future and present, of who was, in fact, a member of his people."[13] "[Justification] was not so much about 'getting in', or indeed about 'staying in', as about 'how you could tell who was in'. In standard Christian theological language, it wasn't so much about soteriology as about ecclesiology; not so much about salvation as about the church."[14] So the divine act of justification does not constitute us as Christians or establish our relationship with God. It informs or announces. "The word *dikaioō* [justify] is, after all, a declarative word, declaring that something is the case, rather than a word for making something happen or changing the way something is."[15]

This is startling because we are used to reading Romans 5:1 as if justification had in fact altered our relationship with God. "Therefore, since we have been justified by faith, we have peace with God through our Lord Jesus Christ." We thought that justification had brought about this fundamentally new and reconciled relationship with God. (For further discussion, see especially chapter 6.)

Justification Is Not the Gospel?

Third, it follows then that Wright would say that the message of justification is not the gospel. "I must stress again that the doctrine of justification by faith is not what Paul means by 'the gospel.'"[16] "If we come to Paul with these questions in mind—the questions about how human beings come into a living and saving relationship with the living and saving God—it is not justification that springs to his lips or pen. The message about Jesus and his cross and resurrection—'the gospel' . . . is announced to them; through this means, God works by his Spirit upon their hearts."[17]

---

[12]N. T. Wright, *What Saint Paul Really Said* (Minneapolis: Fortress, 2005), 125.
[13]Ibid., 119.
[14]Ibid.
[15]N. T. Wright, "New Perspectives on Paul," in *Justification in Perspective: Historical Developments and Contemporary Challenges*, ed. Bruce L. McCormack (Grand Rapids, MI: Baker Academic, 2006), 258.
[16]Wright, *What Saint Paul Really Said*, 132.
[17]Ibid., 116.

This is astonishing in view of the fact that Paul brought his sermon in Pisidian Antioch to a gospel climax by saying, "Let it be known to you therefore, brothers, that through this man forgiveness of sins is proclaimed to you, and by him everyone who believes is *justified* [δικαιοῦται] from everything from which you could not be *justified* [δικαιωθῆναι] by the law of Moses" (Acts 13:38–39, my translation). And again it is difficult to know how a sinner could hear the announcement of the cross and resurrection as good news without some explanation that by faith it makes a person forgiven and righteous before God. (See more on this in chapter 6.)

We Are Not Justified by Believing in Justification?

Fourth, part of the implication of what Wright has said so far is that we are not justified by believing in justification by faith but by believing in Jesus: "We are not justified by faith by believing in justification by faith. We are justified by faith by believing in the gospel itself—in other words, that Jesus is Lord and that God raised him from the dead."[18] This sounds right. Of course, we are not saved by doctrine. We are saved by Christ. But it is misleading, because it leaves the meaning of "believing in the gospel" undefined. Believing in the gospel *for what*? Prosperity? Healing? A new job? If we are going to help people believe the gospel in a saving way (not the way the demons believe, and not the way Simon the magician believed, James 2:19; Acts 8:13, 21–23), we will have to announce the good news that Christ died *for them*; that is, we will have to announce why this death and resurrection are good news *for them*.

There is more than one way to say it. Many people have been saved without hearing the language of justification. The same is true with regard to the words and realities of "regeneration" and "propitiation" and "redemption" and "reconciliation" and "forgiveness." A baby believer does not have to understand all of the glorious things that have happened to him in order to be saved. But these things do all have to happen to him. And if he comes to the settled conviction, when he hears about them, that he will not trust Christ for any one of them, there is a serious question mark over his salvation. Therefore, it is misleading to say that we are not saved by believing in justification by faith. If we

---

[18]Wright, "New Perspectives on Paul," 261.

hear that part of the gospel and cast ourselves on God *for this divine gift*, we are saved. If we hear that part of the gospel and reject it, while trying to embrace Christ on other terms, we will not be saved. (There is more on this in chapter 5.)

The Imputation of God's Own Righteousness Makes No Sense At All?
Fifth, Wright's construction of Paul's theology appears to have no place for the imputation of divine righteousness to sinners.

> If we use the language of the law-court, it makes no sense whatever to say that the judge imputes, imparts, bequeaths, conveys or otherwise transfers his righteousness to either the plaintiff or the defendant. Righteousness is not an object, a substance or a gas which can be passed across the courtroom. . . . If and when God does act to vindi-cate his people, his people will then, metaphorically speaking, have the status of 'righteousness' . . . . But the righteousness they have will not be God's own righteousness. That makes no sense at all.[19]

But Wright would protest that if we leave it there, we quibble with words and miss the substance. With his new definitions and connections, he believes he has preserved the substance of what the Reformation theologians meant by imputation:

> [Jesus'] role precisely *as* Messiah is not least to draw together the iden-tity of the whole of God's people so that what is true of him is true of them and vice versa. Here we arrive at one of the great truths of the gospel, which is that the accomplishment of Jesus Christ is *reckoned* to all those who are "in him". This is the truth which has been expressed within the Reformed tradition in terms of "imputed righteousness", often stated in terms of Jesus Christ having fulfilled the moral law and thus having accumulated a "righteous" status which can be shared with all his people. As with some other theological problems, I regard this as saying a substantially right thing in a substantially wrong way, and the trouble when you do that is that things on both sides of the equation, and the passages which are invoked to support them, become distorted.[20]

I doubt that this is the case. But we will save the argument for chapter 8.

[19]Wright, *What Saint Paul Really Said*, 98–99.
[20]Wright, "Paul in Different Perspectives: Lecture 1." Emphasis in original.

Future Justification Is on the Basis of the Complete Life Lived?

Sixth, Wright makes startling statements to the effect that our future justification will be on the basis of works. "The Spirit is the path by which Paul traces the route from justification by faith in the present to justification, *by the complete life lived*, in the future."[21] "Paul has . . . spoken in Romans 2 about the final justification of God's people *on the basis of their whole life*."[22] "Present justification declares, on the basis of faith, what future justification will affirm publicly (according to [Rom.] 2:14–16 and 8:9–11) *on the basis of the entire life*."[23] That he means future "justification by works" is seen in the following quote:

> This declaration, this vindication, occurs twice. It occurs in the future, as we have seen, *on the basis of the entire life a person has led in the power of the Spirit*—that is, it occurs *on the basis of "works"* in Paul's redefined sense. And near the heart of Paul's theology, it occurs in the present as *an anticipation of that future verdict*, when someone, responding in believing obedience to the call of the gospel, believes that Jesus is Lord and that God raised him from the dead.[24]

Again, beware of thinking this means what you might think it means. Remember that Wright has redefined "justification." It is not what makes you a Christian or saves you. Therefore, it may be that Wright means nothing more here than what I might mean when I say that our good works are the necessary evidence of faith in Christ at the last day. Perhaps. But it is not so simple. (I return to this topic in chapter 7.)

First-century Judaism Had Nothing of the Alleged Self-Righteous and Boastful Legalism?

Seventh, Wright follows the New Perspective watchword that Paul was not facing "legalistic works-righteousness" in his churches. The warnings against depending on the law are not against legalism but ethnocentrism. Wright is by no means a stereotypical New Perspective scholar and goes his own way on many fronts. But he does embrace the fundamental claim of the New Perspective on Paul as articulated by E. P. Sanders:

---

[21]Wright, *Paul in Fresh Perspective*, 148. Emphasis added.
[22]Ibid., 121. Emphasis added.
[23]Wright, *What Saint Paul Really Said*, 129. Emphasis added.
[24]Wright, "New Perspectives on Paul," 260. First two emphases added.

[Sanders's] major point, to which all else is subservient, can be quite simply stated. Judaism in Paul's day was not, as has regularly been supposed, a religion of legalistic works-righteousness. If we imagine that it was, and that Paul was attacking it as if it was, we will do great violence to it and to him. . . . The Jew keeps the law out of gratitude, as the proper response to grace—not, in other words, in order to *get* into the covenant people, but to *stay* in. Being "in" in the first place was God's gift. This scheme Sanders famously labeled as "covenantal nomism" (from the Greek *nomos*, law).[25]

When Wright did his own research, for example, into the mind of the Qumran sect represented in 4QMMT, he concluded that these documents "reveal nothing of the self-righteous and boastful 'legalism' which used to be thought characteristic of Jews in Paul's day."[26] In chapters 9 and 10, I will examine whether 4QMMT sustains this judgment. More importantly, I will try to dig out the implications of the fact that a common root of self-righteousness lives beneath both overt legalism and Jewish ethnocentrism. Something was *damnable* in the Galatian controversy (Gal. 1:8–9). If it was ethnocentrism, it is hard to believe that the hell-bound ethnocentrists were "keeping the law out of gratitude, as a proper response to grace." But again, I will have much more to say on this in chapters 9 and 10.

God's Righteousness Is the Same as His Covenant Faithfulness?

Eighth, I will mention one more thing that I think *should* be startling but no longer *is*. Wright understands "the righteousness of God" generally as meaning God's "covenant faithfulness." It does include "his impartiality, his proper dealing with sin and his helping of the helpless."[27] But chiefly it is "his faithfulness to his covenant promises to Abraham."[28] I am going to argue in chapter 3 that these descriptions stay too much on the surface. They denote some of the things righteousness *does*, but do not press down to the common root beneath these behaviors as to what God's righteousness *is*. When Paul says,

---

[25]Wright, *What Saint Paul Really Said*, 18–19.
[26]N. T. Wright, "4QMMT and Paul: Justification, 'Works,' and Eschatology," in *History and Exegesis: New Testament Essays in Honor of Dr. E. Earle Ellis for His 80th Birthday*, ed. Aang-Won (Aaron) Son (New York and London: T&T Clark, 2006), 106.
[27]N. T. Wright, *The Climax of the Covenant: Christ and the Law in Pauline Theology* (Edinburgh: T&T Clark, 1991), 36.
[28]Ibid.

"For our sake he made him to be sin who knew no sin, so that in him we might become *the righteousness of God*" (2 Cor. 5:21), one must break the back of exegesis to make this mean, "We become *the covenant faithfulness of God.*" This is exactly what Wright does—in one of the most eccentric articles in all his work.[29] Chapter 11 is my effort to show that this unprecedented reinterpretation of 2 Corinthians 5:21 does not stand.

THE FUTURE OF JUSTIFICATION

For these eight reasons, and more that will emerge along the way, I am not optimistic that the biblical doctrine of justification will flourish where N. T. Wright's portrayal holds sway. I do not see his vision as a compelling retelling of what Saint Paul really said. And I think, as it stands now, it will bring great confusion to the church at a point where she desperately needs clarity. I don't think this confusion is the necessary dust that must settle when great new discoveries have been made. Instead, if I read the situation correctly, the confusion is owing to the ambiguities in Wright's own expressions, and to the fact that, unlike his treatment of some subjects, his paradigm for justification does not fit well with the ordinary reading of many texts and leaves many ordinary folk not with the rewarding "ah-ha" experience of illumination, but with a paralyzing sense of perplexity.[30]

---

[29]N. T. Wright, "On Becoming the Righteousness of God," in *Pauline Theology*, Vol. II: *1 & 2 Corinthians*, ed. David M. Hay (Minneapolis: Fortress, 1993), 203.

[30]I do not infer Wright's defective view of justification to mean that he is not himself justified. Jonathan Edwards and John Owen give good counsel on this point even if the debates then were not identical to ours. Edwards wrote during one of his controversies:

How far a wonderful and mysterious agency of God's Spirit may so influence some men's hearts, that their practice in this regard may be contrary to their own principles, so that they shall not trust in their own righteousness, though they profess that men are justified by their own righteousness—or how far they may believe the doctrine of justification by men's own righteousness in general, and yet not believe it in a particular application of it to themselves—or how far that error which they may have been led into by education, or cunning sophistry of others, may yet be indeed contrary to the prevailing disposition of their hearts, and contrary to their practice—or how far some may seem to maintain a doctrine contrary to this gospel-doctrine of justification, that really do not, but only express themselves differently from others; or seem to oppose it through their misunderstanding of our expressions, or we of theirs, when indeed our real sentiments are the same in the main—or may seem to differ more than they do, by using terms that are without a precisely fixed and determinate meaning—or to be wide in their sentiments from this doctrine, for want of a distinct understanding of it; whose hearts, at the same time, entirely agree with it, and if once it was clearly explained to their understandings, would immediately close with it, and embrace it: — how far these things may be, I will not determine; but am fully persuaded that great allowances are to be made on these and such like accounts, in innumerable instances; though it is manifest, from what has been said, that the teaching and propagating [of] contrary doctrines and schemes, is of a pernicious and fatal tendency. (Jonathan Edwards, "Justification by Faith Alone," in

The future of justification will be better served, I think, with older guides rather than the new ones.[31] When it comes to the deeper issues of how justification really works both in Scripture and in the human soul, I don't think N. T. Wright is as illuminating as Martin Luther or John Owen or Leon Morris. But that remains to be shown.

I end the Introduction where I began. My little earthly life is too far spent to care much about the ego gratification of scoring points in debate. I am still a sinner depending on Christ for my righteousness before God. So I am quite capable of fear and pride. But I do hope that, where I have made mistakes, I will be willing to admit it. There are far greater things at stake than my fickle sense of gratification or regret. Among these greater things are the faithful preaching of the gospel, the care of guilt-ridden souls, the spiritual power of sacrificial deeds of love, the root of humble Christian political and social engagement, and the courage of Christian missions to confront all the religions of the world with the supremacy of Christ as the only way to escape the wrath to come. When the gospel itself is distorted or blurred, everything else is eventually affected. May the Lord give us help in these days to see the word of his grace with clarity, and savor it with humble and holy zeal, and spread it without partiality so that millions may believe and be saved, to the praise of the glory of God's grace.

Sermons and Discourses, 1734-1738, The Works of Jonathan Edwards, Vol. 19 [New Haven, CT: Yale University Press, 2001], 242)

Owen wrote: "Men may be really saved by that grace which *doctrinally they do deny*; and they may be justified by the imputation of that righteousness which *in opinion they deny to be imputed.*" But I would add: the clearer the knowledge of the truth and the more deep the denial, the less assurance one can have that the God of truth will save him. Owen's words are not meant to make us cavalier about the content of the gospel, but to hold out hope that men's hearts are often better than their heads. John Owen, *The Doctrine of Justification by Faith*, chapter VII, "Imputation, and the Nature of It," Banner of Truth, *Works*, Vol. 5, 163-164.

[31]In a sobering review of Mark A. Noll and Carolyn Nystrom, *Is the Reformation Over? An Evangelical Assessment of Contemporary Roman Catholicism*, Scott Manetsch wisely writes, "Now more than ever, there is urgent need for evangelical Protestants in North America to 'protest' against theological superficiality, to eschew cultural faddishness and myopic presentism, and recover *their* historic roots, not only in the religious awakenings of colonial America, but in the Christian renewal movements of sixteenth-century Europe. Evangelicals who make this journey to Wittenberg and Geneva, to Zurich and Edinburgh and London will discover a world of profound biblical and theological insight, a rich deposit of practical wisdom, a gift given by God to his church for life and ministry in the twenty-first century." Scott Manetsch, "Discerning the Divide: A Review Article," in *Trinity Journal*, 28NS (2007): 62–63.

ON CONTROVERSY

I AM A PASTOR FIRST. Polemics are secondary and serve that. Part of our pastoral responsibility is what Paul calls "the defense and confirmation of the gospel" (Phil. 1:7). Virtually all of Paul's letters serve the church by clarifying and defending doctrinal truth and its practical implications.

The reason I take up controversy with N. T. Wright and not, say, J. D. G. Dunn or E. P. Sanders (all notable for their relationship to the so-called New Perspective on Paul) is that none of my parishioners has ever brought me a thick copy of a book by Dunn or Sanders, wondering what I thought about them. But Wright is a popular and compelling writer as well as a rigorous scholar. Therefore, he exerts significant influence both in the academic guild and among the wider public. If he is mistaken on the matter of justification, he may do more harm than others. In addition, Wright loves the apostle Paul and reverences the Christian Scriptures. That gives me hope that engaging with him will be fruitful. I know I have learned from him, and I hope that our common ground in Scripture will enable some progress in understanding and agreement.

HOW THEN SHALL WE CONDUCT THE CONTROVERSY?

In his essay called "Polemic Theology: How to Deal with Those Who Differ from Us," Roger Nicole begins,

> We are called upon by the Lord to contend earnestly for the faith (Jude 3). That does not necessarily involve being contentious; but it involves avoiding compromise, standing forth for what we believe, standing forth for the truth of God—without welching at any particular moment.[1]

---

[1]Roger Nicole, "Polemic Theology: How to Deal with Those Who Differ from Us," http://www.founders.org/FJ33/article3.html.

When we are arguing about the meaning of the gospel, it is important to do it "in step with the truth of the gospel" (Gal. 2:14). If Bible-believers are going to disagree about the meaning of the Bible, we should try to do so biblically. To that end, I offer the following encouragements.[2]

WISE WORDS FROM OLD TIMES

In 1655 John Owen published *The Mystery of the Gospel Vindicated and Socinianism Examined*. It contains one of my favorite exhortations, namely, that "we have communion with God in the doctrine we contend for." In other words, arguing for the truth of God should never replace enjoyment of the God of truth.

> [More important than all is] *a diligent endeavor to have the power of the truths professed and contended for abiding upon our hearts*, that we may not contend for notions, but that we have a practical acquaintance within our own souls. When the heart is cast indeed into the mould of the doctrine that the mind embraceth—when the evidence and necessity of the truth abides in us—when not the sense of the words only is in our heads, but the sense of the thing abides in our hearts—when we have communion with God in the doctrine we contend for—then shall we be garrisoned by the grace of God against all the assaults of men.[3]

But is it really necessary? Must we contend? Cannot we not simply be positive, rather than trying to show that others are wrong? On June 17, 1932, J. Gresham Machen delivered an address before the Bible League of Great Britain in London titled "Christian Scholarship and the Defense of the Faith." In it he said,

> Men tell us that our preaching should be positive and not negative, that we can preach the truth without attacking error. But if we follow that advice we shall have to close our Bible and desert its teachings. The New Testament is a polemic book almost from beginning to end.

---

[2] What follows is not new. The fullest statements I have made about controversy among Christians are found in "Charity, Clarity, and Hope: The Controversy and the Cause of Christ," in *Recovering Biblical Manhood and Womanhood: A Response to Evangelical Feminism*, ed. John Piper and Wayne Grudem (Wheaton, IL: Crossway Books, 1991; 2006), 403–422, and *Contending for Our All: Defending Truth and Treasuring Christ in the Lives of Athanasius, John Owen, and J. Gresham Machen* (Wheaton, IL: Crossway Books, 2006), especially the Introduction and Conclusion.
[3] John Owen, *Vindiciae Evangelicae; or, The Mystery of the Gospel Vindicated and Socinianism Examined*, Vol. 12, The Works of John Owen, ed. William Goold (Edinburgh: Banner of Truth, 1966), 52.

Some years ago I was in a company of teachers of the Bible in the colleges and other educational institutions of America. One of the most eminent theological professors in the country made an address. In it he admitted that there are unfortunate controversies about doctrine in the Epistles of Paul; but, said he in effect, the real essence of Paul's teaching is found in the hymn to Christian love in the thirteenth chapter of I Corinthians; and we can avoid controversy today, if we will only devote the chief attention to that inspiring hymn.

In reply, I am bound to say that the example was singularly ill-chosen. That hymn to Christian love is in the midst of a great polemic passage; it would never have been written if Paul had been opposed to controversy with error in the Church. It was because his soul was stirred within him by a wrong use of the spiritual gifts that he was able to write that glorious hymn. So it is always in the Church. Every really great Christian utterance, it may almost be said, is born in controversy. It is when men have felt compelled to take a stand against error that they have risen to the really great heights in the celebration of truth.[4]

Machen also reminds us that not just the heights of celebration in the truth but also the salvation of souls may well come through controversy for the cause of the gospel:

During the academic year, 1924–25, there has been something like an awakening. Youth has begun to think for itself; the evil of compromising associations has been discovered; Christian heroism in the face of opposition has come again to its rights; a new interest has been aroused in the historical and philosophical questions that underlie the Christian religion; true and independent convictions have been formed. Controversy, in other words, has resulted in a striking intellectual and spiritual advance. Some of us discern in all this the work of the Spirit of God. . . . Controversy of the right sort is good; for out of such controversy, as Church history and Scripture alike teach, there comes the salvation of souls.[5]

LONGING FOR THE DAY OF UNITY IN THE TRUTH

The heart-wrenching truth of our day, and every day, is that Christians often disagree with each other—sometimes about serious matters.[6]

---

[4]J. Gresham Machen, "Christian Scholarship and the Defense of the Faith," in *J. Gresham Machen: Selected Shorter Writings*, ed. D. G. Hart (Phillipsburg, NJ: P&R, 2004), 148–149.
[5]J. Gresham Machen, *What Is Faith?* (1925; reprint Edinburgh: Banner of Truth, 1991), 42–43.
[6]This sentence and the remainder of this note on controversy are adapted from the Conclusion of *Contending for Our All* (cited in note 2).

Therefore, we rejoice that it is God himself who will fulfill his plan for the church: "My counsel shall stand, and I will accomplish all my purpose" (Isa. 46:10). We take heart that, in spite of all our blind spots and bungling and disobedience, God will triumph in the earth: "All the ends of the earth shall remember and turn to the LORD, and all the families of the nations shall worship before you. For kingship belongs to the LORD, and he rules over the nations" (Ps. 22:27–28).

Yet one of the groanings of this fallen age is controversy, and most painful of all, controversy with brothers and sisters in Christ. We resonate with the apostle Paul—our joy would be full if we could all be "of the same mind, having the same love, being in full accord and of one mind" (Phil. 2:2). But for all his love of harmony and unity and peace, it is remarkable how many of Paul's letters were written to correct fellow Christians. One thinks of 1 Corinthians. It begins with Paul's thanks (1:4) and ends with his love (16:24). But between those verses he labors to set the Corinthians straight in their thinking and behavior.[7]

The assumption of the entire New Testament is that we should strive for peace. Peace and unity in the body of Christ are exceedingly precious. "Behold, how good and pleasant it is when brothers dwell in unity!" (Ps. 133:1). "Seek peace and pursue it" (1 Pet. 3:11). "So then let us pursue what makes for peace and for mutual upbuilding" (Rom. 14:19). But just as clear is that we are to pursue peace by striving to come to agreement in the truth. "The wisdom from above is first pure, then peaceable" (James 3:17). It is *first* pure. Peace is not a first thing. It is derivative. It comes from hearty agreement in truth.

For example, Paul tells us to set our minds on what is true, and honorable, and just; and the God of peace will be with us (Phil. 4:8–9). Peace is a wonderful by-product of heartfelt commitments to what is true and right. Hebrews speaks of the "peaceful fruit of righteousness" (12:11). Paul tells Timothy to "pursue *righteousness* . . . and peace" (2 Tim. 2:22). The unity we strive for in the church is a unity in knowledge and truth and righteousness. We grow up into the one body "joined and held together" as we "attain to the unity of the faith and *of the knowledge of the Son of God*" (Eph. 4:13, 16). "Grace and peace"

---

[7]He addresses the danger of boasting in leaders (1:10–3:23), the limits of sexual freedom (5:1–8), the extent of true separation (5:9–13), the proper handling of lawsuits (6:1–8), the goodness of sexual relations in marriage (7:1–16), the nature of Christian freedom (8:1–13), the proper demeanor for men and women in worship (11:2–16), how to behave at the Lord's Supper (11:17–34), the use of spiritual gifts (chaps. 12–14), and the nature and the reality of the resurrection (chap. 15).

are multiplied to us *"in the knowledge of God* and of Jesus our Lord"
(2 Pet. 1:2). And paradoxically, the weaponry with which we wage war
for "the gospel of peace" begins with "the belt of *truth*" (Eph. 6:14–15)
and ends with "the sword of the Spirit," the *Word of God* (6:17).

WHY TRUE UNITY FLOWS FROM TRUTH

The reason for this is that truth frees us from the control of Satan,
the great deceiver and destroyer of unity: "you will know the truth,
and the truth will set you free" (John 8:32; cf. 2 Tim. 2:24–26). Truth
serves love, the bond of perfection. Paul prays for the Philippians that
their "love [may] abound more and more, with knowledge and all dis-
cernment" (Phil. 1:9). Truth sanctifies, and so yields the righteousness
whose fruit is peace: "Sanctify them in the truth; your word is truth"
(John 17:17; cf. 2 Pet. 1:3, 5, 12).

For the sake of unity and peace, therefore, Paul labors to set the
churches straight on numerous issues—including quite a few that do
not in themselves involve heresy. He does not exclude controversy from
his pastoral writing. And he does not limit his engagement in controversy to first-order doctrines, where heresy threatens. He is like a par-
ent to his churches. Parents do not correct and discipline their children
only for felonies. Good parents long for their children to grow up into
all the kindness and courtesy of mature adulthood. And since the fabric
of truth is seamless, Paul knows that letting minor strands continue to
unravel can eventually rend the whole garment.

Thus Paul teaches that elders serve the church, on the one hand, by
caring for the church without being pugnacious (1 Tim. 3:3, 5), and, on
the other hand, by rebuking and correcting false teaching. "He must hold
firm to the trustworthy word as taught, so that he may be able to give
instruction in sound doctrine and also to rebuke those who contradict it"
(Titus 1:9; cf. 1:13; 2:15; 1 Tim. 5:20). This is one of the main reasons
we have the Scriptures: they are "profitable for teaching, for reproof, for
correction, and for training in righteousness" (2 Tim. 3:16).

"BY THE OPEN STATEMENT OF THE TRUTH WE COMMEND OURSELVES"

Faithful Christians do not love controversy; they love peace. They love
their brothers and sisters who disagree with them. They long for a

common mind for the cause of Christ. But for this very reason they are bound by their conscience and by the Word of God to try to persuade the church concerning the fullness of the truth and beauty of God's word.

We live in a day of politicized discourse that puts no premium on clear assertions. Some use language to conceal where they stand rather than to make clear where they stand. One reason this happens is that clear and open statements usually result in more criticism than ambiguous statements do. Vagueness will win more approval in a hostile atmosphere than forthrightness will.

But we want nothing to do with that attitude. Jesus refused to converse with religious leaders who crafted their answers so as to conceal what they thought (Mark 11:33). Our aim (if not our achievement) is always to be like Paul when he said, "But we have renounced disgraceful, underhanded ways. We refuse to practice cunning or to tamper with God's word, but by the open statement of the truth we would commend ourselves to everyone's conscience in the sight of God" (2 Cor. 4:2).[8]

---

[8]These final paragraphs are based on what I wrote earlier in "Clarity, Charity, and Hope," 404–406.

CHAPTER ONE

CAUTION: NOT ALL
BIBLICAL-THEOLOGICAL METHODS
AND CATEGORIES ARE ILLUMINATING

A COMMON CAUTION

Most scholars are aware that methods and categories of thought taken from *historical* and *systematic* theology may control and distort the way one reads the Bible. But we don't hear as often the caution that the methods and categories of *biblical* theology can do the same. Neither systematic nor biblical theology *must* distort our exegesis. But both *can*.

For example, suppose one took the category of "eschatology" from a traditional systematic theology textbook. It typically would be treated in a final chapter as "the doctrine of last things"—events that are yet future and will happen during and after the end of this age. If someone takes that understanding of eschatology and makes it the lens through which one reads the New Testament, it is possible that it would conceal or distort the truth that in the New Testament the end of the ages has *already* arrived in the coming of Jesus the Messiah, so that the "end times" began with the first coming of Christ.[1]

---

[1]See 1 Corinthians 10:11: "Now these things happened to them as an example, but they were written down for our instruction, on whom *the end of the ages has come.*" Hebrews 1:1–2a: "Long ago, at many times and in many ways, God spoke to our fathers by the prophets, but *in these last days* he has spoken to us by his Son." First Peter 1:20: "He was foreknown before the foundation of the world but was made manifest *in the last times* for your sake." This emphasis on the eschatological nature of the whole New Testament is expressed in the title and substance of George Ladd's book, *The Presence of the Future* (Grand Rapids, MI: Eerdmans, 1974).

Biblical theology, as over against *systematic theology*, is sometimes acclaimed as the discipline that has set us free from these possible distortions of systematic theology. Biblical theology aims to read
the authors of Scripture along the trajectory of redemptive history in
light of the authors' own categories that are shaped by the historical
milieu in which they lived. Done properly, this is an essential part of
responsible exegesis and theology. Those who submit their minds to the
authority of Scripture, as N. T. Wright readily confesses that he does,[2]
will want to understand what the authors originally intended to say—
not what they can be made to say by later reinterpretation.

A NOT-SO-COMMON CAUTION

But, as far as I can see in these days, a similar caution about the possible
distorting effect of the categories of *biblical theology* is not commonly
sounded. The claim to interpret a biblical author in terms of the first
century is generally met with the assumption that this will be illuminating. Some today seem to overlook that this might result in bringing
ideas to the text in a way that misleads rather than clarifies. But common sense tells us that first-century ideas can be used (inadvertently)
to distort and silence what the New Testament writers intended to say.
There are at least three reasons for this.

Misunderstanding the Sources

First, the interpreter may *mis*understand the first-century idea. It is
remarkable how frequently there is the tacit assumption that we can
be more confident about how we interpret secondary first-century
sources than we are of how we interpret the New Testament writers themselves. But it seems to me that there is a *prima facie* case for
thinking that our interpretations of extra-biblical literature are *more
tenuous* than our interpretations of the New Testament. In general,

---

[2]"Out of sheer loyalty to the God-given text, particularly of Romans, I couldn't go back to a
Lutheran reading. (Please note, my bottom line has always been, and remains, not a theory, not
a tradition, not pressure from self-appointed guardians of orthodoxy, but the text of scripture.)"
N. T. Wright, "The Shape of Justification" (2001), accessed 6-24-06 at http://www.thepaulpage.
com/Shape.html. For a fuller statement of Wright's view of Scripture, see also N. T. Wright, *The
Last Word: Beyond the Bible Wars to a New Understanding of the Authority of Scripture* (San
Francisco: HarperSanFrancisco, 2005), which has been helpfully reviewed and critiqued by D. A.
Carson in *Trinity Journal*, Spring (2006): 1–63. Carson's review also was made available at http://
www.reformation21.org/Past_Issues/2006_Issues_1_16_/2006_Issues_1_16_Shelf_Life/May_2006/
May_2006/181/vobId__2926/.

this literature has been less studied than the Bible and does not come with a contextual awareness matching what most scholars bring to the Bible. Moreover, the Scripture comes with the added hope that there is coherency because of divine inspiration and that the Holy Spirit will illumine Scripture through humble efforts to know God's mind for the sake of the glory of Christ.

Yet there seems to be an overweening confidence in the way some scholars bring their *assured* interpretations of extra-biblical texts to illumine their *less sure* reading of biblical texts. Thankfully, there always have been, and are today, competent scholarly works that call into question the seemingly assured interpretations of extra-biblical sources that are sometimes used to give biblical texts meanings that their own contexts will not bear.[3]

We all need to be reminded that the last two hundred years of biblical scholarship is the story not just of *systematic* categories obscuring the biblical text, but, even more dramatically, of a steady stream of *first-century ideas* sweeping scholarship along and then evaporating in the light of the stubborn clarity of the biblical texts.[4]

Assuming Agreement with a Source When There Is No Agreement

A second reason why an external first-century idea may distort or silence what the New Testament teaches is that while it may accurately reflect certain first-century documents, nevertheless it may reflect only one among many first-century views. Whether a New Testament writer embraced the particular way of thinking that a scholar has found in

---

[3]For example, specifically in regard to matters relating to justification, see especially D. A. Carson, Peter O'Brien, and Mark A. Seifrid, eds., *Justification and Variegated Nomism: The Complexities of Second Temple Judaism*, Vol. 1 (Grand Rapids, MI: Baker Academic, 2001); see also Simon Gathercole, *Where Then Is Boasting? Early Jewish Soteriology and Paul's Response in Romans 1–5* (Grand Rapids, MI: Eerdmans, 2002); Mark Elliott, *The Survivors of Israel: A Reconsideration of the Theology of Pre-Christian Judaism* (Grand Rapids, MI: Eerdmans, 2000); A. Andrew Das, *Paul, the Law, and the Covenant* (Peabody, MA: Hendrickson, 2001); Friedrich Avemarie, *Tora und Leben: Untersuchungen zur Heilsbedeutung der Tora in der frühen rabbinischen Literatur* (Tübingen: J.C.B. Mohr, 1996); Timo Laato, *Paul and Judaism: An Anthropological Approach* (Atlanta: Scholars, 1996).

[4]N. T. Wright documents this story in part with regard to the interpretation of Paul. *What Saint Paul Really Said: Was Saul of Tarsus the Real Founder of Christianity?* (Grand Rapids, MI: Eerdmans, 1997), 12–19. The same story can be told of the ever-changing interpretation of the quest for the historical Jesus. For example, see the surveys in Ben Witherington III, *The Jesus Quest: The Third Search for the Jew of Nazareth* (Downers Grove, IL: InterVarsity Press, 1995); Larry Hurtado, "A Taxonomy of Recent Historical-Jesus Work," in *Whose Historical Jesus?* ed. William E. Arnal and Michel Desjardins (Waterloo, Ontario: Wilfrid Laurier University Press, 1997), 272–295; Jonathan Knight, *Jesus: An Historical and Theological Investigation* (London: T&T Clark International, 2004), 15–56; *The Historical Jesus in Recent Research*, ed. James D. G. Dunn and Scot McKnight (Winona Lake, IN: Eisenbrauns, 2005).

the first century is not obvious from the mere existence of that way of thinking.

As an analogy, one may only think about all that flies under the banner "evangelical" in our own day—and hope that no historian in a thousand years will assign any of those meanings to us simply because we bore that label. Therefore, one must be cautious in saying on the basis of one's interpretation of extra-biblical texts that this is "how first-century Jews understood the world."[5] Sweeping statements about worldviews in first-century Judaism are precarious.

Misapplying the Meaning of a Source

A third reason why external first-century ideas may distort or silence what the New Testament teaches is that while the New Testament writer may embrace the external idea in general, a scholar may *misapply* it to the biblical text. For example, Paul may agree that one important meaning for *gospel* (εὐαγγέλιον) is the announcement that God is king over all the universe (Isa. 52:7) but not intend for this meaning to govern or dominate what he means by *the gospel* in every context. Indeed, Paul (or any other biblical writer) may also intend to go precisely beyond the common use of any term and expand its meaning in light of the fuller revelation of God in Christ Jesus.

It will be salutary, therefore, for scholars and pastors and laypeople who do not spend much of their time reading first-century literature to have a modest skepticism when an overarching concept or worldview from the first century is used to give "new" or "fresh" interpretations to biblical texts that in their own context do not naturally give rise to these interpretations.

---

[5]N. T. Wright gives his understanding of the *covenant* and the *law-court* images of Israel's future judgment and then says, "Learning to 'see' an event in terms of two great themes like these is part of learning how first-century Jews understood the world." *What Saint Paul Really Said*, 33. This seems too sweeping. He gives the impression that there was a monolithic standpoint. But Wright *does* agree with the principle that the biblical context of the New Testament writer must *confirm* any interpretation suggested by external sources. Yet his esteem for the importance of the extra-biblical context seems to give it a remarkably controlling role for his interpretation of the New Testament. Within this context, the New Testament writers may build in "nuances and emphases." He writes, "We can never, in other words, begin with the author's use of a word; we must begin with the wider world he lived in, the world we meet in our lexicons, concordances, and other studies of how words were used in that world, and must then be alive to the possibility of a writer building in particular nuances and emphases of his or her own." "The Shape of Justification." The problem with that emphasis is that it obscures the facts (1) that "the author's use of the word" is *the* most crucial evidence concerning its meaning and (2) that all other uses of the word are themselves other instances that are as vulnerable to misunderstanding as is the biblical use. There is no access to "how words were used in that world" other than particular uses like the one right there in the Bible.

ENERGIZED BY WHAT IS NEW

N. T. Wright is explicitly energized by finding "new" and "fresh" interpretations of Paul. But one does not find in Wright an appreciation and celebration of the insights of older interpretation that glows with similar exuberance. It is sobering to hear him say, for example, "The discussions of justification in much of the history of the church, certainly since Augustine, got off on the wrong foot—at least in terms of understanding Paul—and they have stayed there ever since."[6]

Wright's confidence that the church (Catholic, Protestant, and Orthodox) has not gotten it right for fifteen hundred years explains in part his passion for seeing things in a fresh way. Thus he says:

> It is, I think, a time for exploration and delighted innovation rather than simply for filling in the paradigms left by our predecessors. . . . I have to say that for me there has been no more stimulating exercise, of the mind, the heart, the imagination and the spirit, than trying to think Paul's thoughts after him and constantly to be stirred up to fresh glimpses of God's ways and purposes with the world and with us strange human creatures. The church and the academy both urgently need a new generation of teachers and preachers who will give themselves totally to the delighted study of the text and allow themselves to be taken wherever it leads, to think new thoughts arising out of the text and to dare to try them out in word and deed.[7]

That last sentence is a way of writing that summons us to something good while in the same breath commending something that may not be good. To be sure, we need preachers who (1) give themselves to the text and (2) allow themselves to be taken wherever it truly leads. But when Wright continues the sentence by saying we need pastors who "think new thoughts" and "dare to try them out," he implies that this will be the result of allegiance to the text. In fact, allegiance to the text may as often awaken joyful gratitude and worship over and confirmation of insights that have been seen clearly and cherished for centuries.

My own assessment of the need of the church at this moment in history is different from Wright's: I think we need a new generation of preachers who are not only open to new light that God may shed upon

---

[6]Wright, *What Saint Paul Really Said*, 115.
[7]Wright, *Paul in Fresh Perspective*, ix–x.

his word, but are also suspicious of their own love of novelty and are eager to test all their interpretations of the Bible by the wisdom of the centuries.[8] Of course, Wright and I would agree that the final authority must be the biblical text itself, not novelty or tradition, but there is *in our time* a profound ignorance of the wisdom of the centuries and a facile readiness to be "fresh." N. T. Wright is certainly not facile. He is a disciplined, thoughtful, rigorous handler of biblical texts and lover of the church. The point here is simply to caution that his celebration of "delighted innovation" may confirm a neophilia of our culture that needs balancing with the celebration of the wisdom of the centuries precisely for the sake of faithfulness to the biblical text.[9]

Do the Large Frameworks Illumine Justification?

One of the impressions one gets in reading N. T. Wright is that large conceptual frameworks are brought to the text of the New Testament from outside and are providing a lens through which the meaning is seen. Wright would say that these larger frameworks *illumine* the text because they are faithful to the historical context and to the flow of thought in the New Testament. That is possible. But I have offered the caution above so that there may be a careful weighing of this claim. This book exists because of my own concern that, specifically in the matter of justification by faith, Wright's approach has not been as illuminating as it has been misleading, or perhaps, confusing. I hope that the interaction that follows will help readers make wise judgments in this regard.

---

[8]See John Piper, "Preaching as Expository Exultation for the Glory of God," in *Preaching the Cross*, ed. Mark Dever et al. (Wheaton, IL: Crossway Books, 2007), 103–115.
[9]Wright would want it pointed out that this assessment of his bent toward newness would be news to most of his colleagues in the Church of England who see him as "a dyed-in-the wool traditionalist on everything from the Trinity to sexual ethics" (his own words from personal correspondence). Indeed we may be thankful that Wright has defended great doctrines of the historic Christian faith. That is not inconsistent with our observations of the new way he has constructed Paul's teaching—new, he would say, over against tradition, not over against Paul.

CHAPTER TWO

THE RELATIONSHIP BETWEEN COVENANT AND LAW-COURT IMAGERY FOR JUSTIFICATION

JUSTIFICATION: DECLARING ONE TO BE A MEMBER OF THE FAMILY

For N. T. Wright, God's covenant with Israel is the dominant concept for understanding Paul and justification.[1] This covenant is part of an even larger picture of the fallenness of creation and God's glorious purpose to rescue his creation from sin and its effects.

> The point of election always was that humans were sinful, that the world was lapsing back into chaos, and that God was going to mount a rescue operation. That is what the covenant was designed to do, and that is why "belonging to the covenant" means, among other things, "forgiven sinner".[2]

Justification must be seen in this larger picture. *"Justification, for Paul, is a subset of election*, that is, it belongs as a part of his doctrine of the people of God."[3] Wright is recognized for his unusual definition of justification as *the declaration that a person is in the covenant family.*

---

[1]What he means by "covenant" is not any particular manifestation of covenant (Mosaic, Davidic, New, etc.) over against the others, but rather the Creator's purpose to make a people his own (beginning with the family of Abraham) for the sake of the entire broken world. In other words, when he speaks of "covenant," he speaks of the reason for why there is a chosen Israel at all—namely, finally to deal with sin and to set the whole world right. "The covenant was there in the first place to deal with the sin of the world." *What Saint Paul Really Said*, 33.
[2]Wright, *Paul in Fresh Perspective*, 121.
[3]Ibid.

For example, he says, "Those who hear the gospel and respond to it in faith are then declared by God to be his people. . . . They are given the status *dikaios*, 'righteous', 'within the covenant.'"[4] Or again, and more sweepingly, "'Justification' in the first century[5] was not about how someone might establish a relationship with God. It was about God's eschatological definition, both future and present, of who was, in fact, a member of his people."[6]

Is Wright true to the apostle Paul's thought when he makes covenant membership the *denotation* (as opposed to implication) of the divine act of justification? It seems to stretch Paul's language to the breaking point. We will deal with Wright's use of the concept of justification more fully in later chapters, but it may be helpful to register an initial objection[7] here. Will Paul's use of δικαιόω (I justify) bear the weight of Wright's meaning? I doubt it for at least two reasons.

One reason is that there are uses of δικαιόω in Paul where the meaning "declaring one as a covenant member" does not work. For example, it does not work in Romans 3:4 where God is the one who is justified: "Let God be true though every one were a liar, as it is written, 'That you may be *justified* in your words, and prevail when you are judged.'" The usual meaning of "reckon one to be just or innocent" fits

---

[4]Ibid., 122.

[5]Here is one of those statements about the "first century" that seems too sweeping (see chapter 1).

[6]Wright, *What Saint Paul Really Said*, 119. This statement (and others like it) make it difficult to see how Wright's way of saying things can be described as a fresh and helpful way of preserving the essence of the historic view of justification as the imputation of God's righteousness in Christ as some have suggested to me. (Chapter 8 is a response to this objection.) Wright's way of speaking about justification will be virtually unintelligible to the average person in the pew as he or she tries to conceive how the word *justify* corresponds to family membership. They can certainly grasp that the justified sinner is *also* in the family and that *only* justified sinners are in the family, and that being in the family is an *implication* of being justified. But to say that justification was *about who was a member of God's family* is going to mislead. It will obscure the denotative meaning of the word *justify* by calling one of its attendant implications a denotative meaning.

[7]An objection that was pointed out to me by Andrew Cowan, who makes every effort to be fair to Wright, is expressed here in a quote from personal correspondence, with permission:

Defining "righteousness" as "covenant membership" seems inadequate. "Covenant membership" only implies that one is bound by the stipulations of a covenant. In terms of the Mosaic covenant, it seems that all Jews were covenant members, but on the basis of their conduct they either received the blessings promised in the covenant or the curses threatened by the covenant. Covenant membership was never a guarantee that one would participate in the covenant's blessings. "In the covenant" as a salvific category is inadequate. Of course, to be in the *new* covenant is salvific; but . . . Wright rarely makes a clear distinction between the covenants, and this can hardly be what God meant when he counted *Abraham's* faith for righteousness. Perhaps Wright's claim that justification is a declaration of "covenant membership" is simply shorthand for being credited as one who has been covenantally faithful (this would fit with his understanding of the justification of God in Romans 3), but he is not very forthright about this, and this way of speaking is misleading at best. He does, though, usually offer a number of parallel terms (i.e., Abraham's true family) that make his point more understandable.

in Romans 3:4, but "declare to be a member of the covenant" does not. Similarly, in 1 Timothy 3:16, Christ himself is said to be justified: "He was manifested in the flesh, *vindicated* [ἐδικαιώθη = *justified*] by [or in] the Spirit, seen by angels, proclaimed among the nations, believed on in the world, taken up in glory." That is, Christ was shown to be, or declared to be, in the right, just, vindicated.

Another reason that δικαιόω will not bear the weight of Wright's meaning is that Paul's use of the word regularly signifies a definite action that *accomplishes* something now. It is not simply a *declaration* of a person's covenant membership that came about decisively through *another* prior action (e.g., God's effectual call).[8] This is contrary to Wright's construal. He explains his view of justification in relation to how a person passes from unbelief to renewal of life:

> The point is that the *word* 'justification' does not itself *denote* the process whereby, or the event in which, a person is brought by grace from unbelief, idolatry and sin into faith, true worship and renewal of life. Paul, clearly and unambiguously, uses a different word for that, the word 'call'. The word 'justification', despite centuries of Christian misuse, is used by Paul to denote that which happens immediately after the 'call': 'those God called, he also justified' (Romans 8:30). In other words, those who hear the gospel and respond to it in faith are then declared by God to be his people, his elect, 'the circumcision', 'the Jews', 'the Israel of God'. They are given the status δίκαιος, 'righteous', 'within the covenant'.[9]

One of the problems with this is that it does not come to terms with the possibility that the divine act of justification, which Wright admits is "*immediately* after the call," is, *along with the call*, determinative and constitutive of the new relation to God. This can be true without defining justification as "the event in which a person is brought by grace from unbelief, idolatry and sin into faith." I'm not sure who has ever taught that. The historic teaching is that justifica-

---

[8]Wright says that δικαιόω is "a declarative word, declaring that something is the case, rather than a word for making something happen or changing the way something is." Wright, "New Perspectives on Paul," in *Justification in Perspective*, 258. "'Justification' is not about 'how I get saved' but 'how I am declared to be a member of God's people.' *Paul in Fresh Perspective*. "Justification is not how someone becomes a Christian. It is the declaration that they have become a Christian." *What Saint Paul Really Said*, 122, 125. "Justification, for Paul, is not (in Sanders's terminology) how one 'gets into' God's people but about God's declaration that someone is in." Wright, "New Perspectives on Paul," 261.
[9]Wright, *Paul in Fresh Perspective*, 121–122.

tion is "by faith," not the process of coming to faith. Wright does not express an understanding of the historic view—namely, that immediately upon the call of God and the awakening of faith God does something essential to a person's right standing with God—that is, essential to their acceptance and their membership in the family. He counts them as perfectly fulfilling all his requirements (= righteousness) because by their call-awakened faith they are united to Christ who is their righteousness. This counting as righteous—this justification—is not the event by which a person moves from unbelief to faith. It is the divine act without which a person cannot be a member of God's family. But Wright seems to want to limit the meaning of justification to a declaration that a covenant membership has already come into being because of *something else*, namely, God's call. The act of justification has no part in determining or constituting that new relationship with God. But does this fit with what Paul says?

It has seemed to most interpreters of Paul that something decisive and once-for-all *happens* at justification. Justification is not a mere declaration that something *has* happened or *will* happen. For example, in Romans 5:1, Paul says, "Therefore, since *we have been justified by faith*, we have peace with God through our Lord Jesus Christ." In other words, something decisive happened that resulted in peace with God. It does *not* say that since we have been justified we may "know" that we have peace with God. A declaration that something (like God's call) *has* happened might result in our *knowing* that we have peace with God. But Paul's words more naturally mean that the justification does not bring about our *knowing* but our *having* peace with God. In fact, it seems that the divine act of justification actually *establishes* the peace because in it God does not just declare but determines our new identity. Thus Simon Gathercole writes, "God's act of justification is not one of recognition but is, rather, closer to creation. It is God's determination of our new identity rather than a recognition of it."[10]

The meaning of justification is fleshed out by Paul in Romans 4 with the language of "counting" or "reckoning." One simple and very important insight about Paul's meaning of justification by faith apart from works of law is that he defines his own use of "justify"

---

[10]Simon Gathercole, "The Doctrine of Justification in Paul and Beyond: Some Proposals," in *Justification in Perspective*, 229.

(δικαιόω) by the use of the phrase "reckon righteousness" (λογίζομαι δικαιοσύνην). Thus, for example, Romans 3:28 is most naturally interpreted in light of the parallel in Romans 4:6. "One is *justified* by faith apart from works of the law" (δικαιοῦσθαι πίστει ἄνθρωπον χωρὶς ἔργων νόμου, Romans 3:28) is explained by "God *credits righteousness* apart from works" (ὁ θεὸς λογίζεται δικαιοσύνην χωρὶς ἔργων, Romans 4:6, NASB). Therefore, "to justify" (δικαιοῦσθαι, 3:28) is parallel with "to credit righteousness" (λογίζεται δικαιοσύνην, 4:6). And "apart from works of law" (χωρὶς ἔργων νόμου, 3:28) is parallel with "apart from works" (χωρὶς ἔργων, 4:6).

> One is justified by faith
> apart from works of the law
> God credits righteousness
> apart from works

This reckoning righteous (justification) is not synonymous with declaring that one has already become a covenant member. It is larger and deeper. It makes covenant membership possible. Thus, Gathercole observes:

> By divine decision, this [faith] is reckoned as righteousness. That is to say, the believer is reckoned as having accomplished all that God requires. Justification, then, is not merely a reckoning as being in covenant membership. It is something bigger—God's creative act whereby, through divine determination, the believer has done everything that God requires.[11]

This divine act of justification determines or constitutes an essential aspect of the new relationship with God. Without it there would be no saving covenant membership. Therefore, justification is not a declaration that one has become a covenant member by virtue of God's prior call. Rather, together with the call, justification is an essentially saving act. Wright seems to have things backward: first covenant membership, then justification. In fact, justification is part of the ground, not the declaration, of saving covenant membership. Wright has a good bit more to say about the relationship between

---

[11]Ibid., 240.

justification and how one gets saved. (We will wrestle again with this issue in chapter 5.)

So, on the face of it, Wright's definition of justification as "God's eschatological definition, both future and present, of who was, in fact, a member of his people" does not fit well with Paul's use of justification language. In and of itself, this may not be a devastating mistake, because it may simply conflate denotation and implication. In other words, justification does not *denote* or *mean* covenant membership, but it does *imply* covenant membership. Indeed, justified people *are* members of the covenant of grace. And, as we will see immediately below, Wright also uses the word *justification* in more traditional ways. He has his reasons for talking the way he does about justification, which we will come to later.

COVENANT AND LAW-COURT, NOT *EITHER-OR*

This unprecedented way of defining justification (as the declaration of a believer's covenant membership) has led some critics to accuse Wright of missing or minimizing the forensic or "law-court" dimension of justification. But this is not a fair accusation. Wright has labored hard to clarify that it is *both-and*—covenant *and* law-court—not *either-or*. One of the most important paragraphs for helping me see how he thinks is the following:

> The law-court metaphor was vital to the underlying meaning of the covenant. The covenant was there in the first place to deal with the sin of the world, and (to the Hebrew mind) you dealt with sin through the law-court, condemning the sinner and "justifying", i.e. acquitting or vindicating, the righteous. It was therefore utterly appropriate that this great event, the final sorting-out of all things, should be described in terms drawn from the law-court. God himself was the judge; evildoers (i.e. the Gentiles, and renegade Jews) would finally be judged and punished; God's faithful people (i.e. Israel, or at least the true Israelites) would be vindicated.[12]

The Covenant Is for the World

The first crucial thing we see in this paragraph is that Wright starts with the *global* purpose of God's covenant with Israel. From the very

---

[12]Wright, *What Saint Paul Really Said*, 33–34.

beginning in Genesis 12:3, the covenant that God made with Israel was intended to bless *the world*: "I will bless those who bless you, and him who dishonors you I will curse, and in you all the families of the earth shall be blessed." This insight has a profound effect on Wright's understanding of God's covenant-keeping work in Christ and his understanding of the gospel. The covenant, as he says, "was there in the first place to deal with the sin of the world." So the Jewish categories of covenant and redemption turn out not to be limited, ethnic categories but globally relevant categories for all peoples. God's covenant-keeping includes making *the world* right. This happens through Jesus, the Jewish Messiah and Lord of the universe.[13] "The death and resurrection of Jesus were themselves the great eschatological events, revealing God's covenant faithfulness, his way of putting the world to rights."[14]

This British phrase, "putting the world to rights," means for Wright that "in Jesus of Nazareth [God] had overcome evil and was creating a new world in which justice and peace would reign supreme."[15] The global, social, and political note is often struck by Wright, who laments "the disastrous dichotomy that has existed in people's minds between 'preaching the gospel' on the one hand and what used to be called loosely 'social action' or 'social justice' on the other."[16]

REDEMPTION: GLOBAL, SOCIAL, AND PERSONAL

But it would be wrong to say that Wright stresses redemption as social and political to the exclusion of redemption as the personal forgiveness of sins. His way of saying this involves some provocative denials about how the gospel relates to getting saved. For example, he says, "Paul's gospel to the pagans was not a philosophy of life. Nor was it, even, a doctrine about how to get saved."[17] "[The gospel] is not . . . a system

---

[13]"[Paul's] announcement was that the crucified Jesus of Nazareth had been raised from the dead; that he was thereby proved to be Israel's Messiah; that he was thereby installed as *Lord of the world*." Wright, *What Saint Paul Really Said*, 46. Emphasis added.
[14]Ibid., 37.
[15]Ibid.
[16]Ibid., 154.
[17]Ibid., 90. This way of understanding the gospel will be discussed further in chapter 4. What puzzles me is that Wright seems to be able to speak of the gospel without explicitly showing what makes it good news *for me*. If the death and resurrection and lordship of Jesus over the world is true, but not good news *for me* (saving me from and for whatever I need saving from and for), then how is it gospel?

of how people get saved."[18] "My proposal has been that 'the gospel' is not, for Paul, a message about 'how one gets saved.'"[19] "But 'the gospel' is not an account of how people get saved. It is . . . the proclamation of the lordship of Jesus Christ."[20] "The gospel is not . . . a set of techniques for making people Christians."[21]

Wright does not deny that God uses the gospel of Christ's death and resurrection and lordship over the world to save people. He wants to stress that there is a difference between one of the *effects* of the gospel—namely, personal salvation—and the proclamation of the gospel itself. My concern is that, in expressing this the way he does, he confuses people because unless those great gospel announcements do in fact include news about personal salvation, they are *not* good news. That Jesus died, rose, and reigns as King of the universe may be terrible news in view of my treason, unless that announcement includes some news about how and why I personally will not be destroyed by the risen Christ.

But we will leave aside for the moment those provocative statements about how the gospel is not "about how to get saved" and deal with what he affirms. He affirms that the covenant is not only about rescuing the cosmos from spiraling further into chaos, but about providing forgiveness of sin through the death of Jesus.

> The point of election [of a covenant people] always was that humans were sinful, that the world was lapsing back into chaos, and that God was going to mount a rescue operation. That is what the covenant was designed to do, and that is why "belonging to the covenant" means, among other things, "forgiven sinner."[22]

PROPITIATION AND EXPIATION

The forgiveness of the sins of the world is based on the death of Christ who is both a *propitiation* of God's wrath and an *expiation* of our sins

---

[18]Ibid., 45.
[19]Ibid., 60.
[20]Ibid., 133.
[21]Ibid., 153. It is not easy to discern whether the emphasis falls on the apparently pejorative words "doctrine," "system," and "techniques" or whether he really means to say that the preaching of the gospel does not herald the way of personal salvation from everlasting perishing. See more on the relationship between the gospel and justification in chapter 5.
[22]Wright, *Paul in Fresh Perspective*, 121. "'Justification', as seen in [Romans] 3:24–26, means that those who believe in Jesus Christ are declared to be members of the true covenant family; which of course means that their sins are forgiven, since that was the purpose of the covenant." "Membership in this family cannot be played off against forgiveness of sins: the two belong together." Wright, "The Shape of Justification."

(Wright's terms). Wright makes this foundation of forgiveness clear in his exposition of Romans 3:25–26. To appreciate the boldness and significance of what he says in these wishy-washy days when pastors and scholars are afraid to teach with forthrightness and clarity the whole truth of the work of Christ, we should quote the text and let Wright interpret it for us:

> *God put [Christ] forward as a propitiation by his blood, to be received by faith. This was to show God's righteousness, because in his divine forbearance he had passed over former sins. It was to show his righteousness at the present time, so that he might be just and the justifier of the one who has faith in Jesus. (Rom. 3:25–26)*

We will come back later to the meaning of God's righteousness in this text. But for now, the focus is on the death of Jesus as the basis for the forgiveness of sins. What God did in the death of Jesus, Wright says, is "deal properly, i.e. *punitively*, with sins."[23] "Whatever Paul is saying in the first half of v. 25, it must be such as to lead to the conclusion that now, at last God has *punished sins as they deserved*."[24]

In punishing sins as they deserve, God satisfied the demands of the situation: he had passed over former sins in such a way that it looked as if he were not a righteous judge. He seemed to be sweeping sins under the rug. Indeed, the entire undertaking of justifying the ungodly created an evident problem for the righteousness of God. This problem was solved by God putting Jesus forward to die. "Whatever precisely Paul intends to say, it must have to do with the means by which the righteous God could, without compromising that righteousness, find in favor of the ungodly"[25] (Rom. 4:5).

A Regrettable Endorsement: Steve Chalke's The Lost Message of Jesus

Wright realizes he is treading on very controversial ground. He wrote a blurb[26] for Steve Chalke's book, *The Lost Message of Jesus*, even

---

[23]N. T. Wright, *The Letter to the Romans*, in *The New Interpreter's Bible*, Vol. X (Nashville: Abingdon Press, 2002), 476. Emphasis added.
[24]Ibid., 473. Emphasis added.
[25]Ibid.
[26]Quoted on the first page of the book (see next footnote) are his words: "Steve Chalke's new book is rooted in good scholarship, but its clear, punchy style makes it accessible to anyone and everyone. Its message is stark and exciting: Jesus of Nazareth was far more challenging in his own day, and remains far more relevant to ours, than the church has dared to believe, let alone preach."

though Chalke makes the claim—which, at least on the face of it, is blasphemous—that God the Father's "punishing his Son for an offence he has not even committed" would have been a form of "cosmic child abuse." Chalke goes on, "If the cross is a personal act of violence perpetrated by God towards humankind but borne by his Son, then it makes a mockery of Jesus' own teaching to love your enemies and to refuse to repay evil with evil."[27] These sentiments are tragically widespread today and, if taken with full seriousness, amount to an abandonment of the foundation of the gospel.

There is nothing unclear about Wright's commitment to penal substitution.

> I am the author of the longest ever exposition and defense, certainly in modern times, of the view that Jesus himself made Isaiah 53, the greatest atonement-chapter in the Old Testament, the clearest statement of penal substitution in the whole of the Bible, central to his own self-understanding and vocation,[28] and I have spelled out the meaning of that, in the sustained climax of my second longest book, in great detail. I have done my NT scholarship in a world where battle-lines were drawn up very clearly on this topic: those who want to avoid penal substitution at all costs have done their best to argue that Jesus did not refer to Isaiah 53, and I have refuted that attempt at great length and, I trust, with proper weight.[29]

On Eastertide, 2007, Wright published an article that explained the circumstances surrounding the endorsement of Steve Chalke's book. In a review of *Pierced for Our Transgressions: Rediscovering the Glory of Penal Substitution* by Mike Ovey, Steve Jeffrey, and Andrew Sach (Inter-Varsity [UK], 2007), Wright attempted to vindicate Chalke from the charges of unbelief in penal substitution. However, it seems to me that to rescue Steve Chalke from the denial of this basic Christian doctrine, Wright obscured the way God's wrath is expressed in the

---

[27]Here is the whole quotation in context: "The fact is that the cross isn't a form of cosmic child abuse—a vengeful Father, punishing his Son for an offence he has not even committed. Understandably, both people inside and outside of the Church have found this twisted version of events morally dubious and a huge barrier to faith. Deeper than that, however, is that such a concept stands in total contradiction to the statement: God is love. If the cross is a personal act of violence perpetrated by God towards humankind but borne by his Son, then it makes a mockery of Jesus' own teaching to love your enemies and to refuse to repay evil with evil." Steve Chalke and Alan Mann, *The Lost Message of Jesus* (Grand Rapids, MI: Zondervan, 2003), 182–183.

[28]He is referring primarily to his lengthy argument in *Jesus and the Victory of God* (Minneapolis: Fortress, 1996), 579–611.

[29]Wright, "Paul in Different Perspectives: Lecture 1."

atonement, with the result that the biblical doctrine of penal substitution in Chalke's understanding remains invisible. Nevertheless, we will let Wright make his own case in the following excursus.

EXCURSUS: N. T. WRIGHT ON STEVE CHALKE

In a 2007 Internet post Wright explains:

> One of the most lively and effective Christian leaders in the UK in recent years is Steve Chalke of Oasis Trust and Faithworks. When I was myself working in London Steve came to see me a couple of times, with an assistant. They had been reading my books on Jesus and wanted to be sure they had understood what I was getting at; clearly they were excited by the way I was reading the gospels and by the portrait of Jesus and his kingdom-bringing work that I was advancing. Steve then (together with Alan Mann) produced a short, sharp, clear and challenging little book called *The Lost Message of Jesus* (Zondervan 2003). He sent me an advance copy. Since—almost embarrassingly at times—the book follows quite closely several of the lines of thought I have myself advanced, though giving them a good deal more energy through shrewd use of anecdote and illustration, I could do no other than write a strong commendation. What I said was this:
>
> > Steve Chalke's new book is rooted on good scholarship, but its clear, punchy style makes it accessible to anyone and everyone. Its message is stark and exciting: Jesus of Nazareth was far more challenging in his own day, and remains far more relevant to ours, than the church has dared to believe, let alone preach.
>
> Part of that was quoted prominently on the front cover. I stand by every word I wrote.
>
> Imagine my puzzlement, then, when I heard that a great storm had broken out because 'Steve Chalke has denied substitutionary atonement'. After all, the climax of my book *Jesus and the Victory of God*, upon which Steve had relied to quite a considerable extent, is the longest ever demonstration, in modern times at least, that Jesus' self-understanding as he went to the cross was rooted in, among other Old Testament passages, Isaiah 53, the clearest and most uncompromising statement of penal substitution you could find. I shall return to this below, and to the puzzle that many of the new right-wing (so-called 'conservative') evangelicals have turned their back on the deepest and richest statement of the doctrine they claim to cherish, namely the one lived and announced by Jesus himself. But back to Steve Chalke. I was puzzled, as I say, when I heard about the fuss, because I hadn't remembered Steve

denying at that point something I had been affirming, and since I had
been strongly and deeply affirming the substitutionary (and, yes, penal)
nature of Jesus' death I wasn't sure whether I had missed something. I
was prepared to say, in effect, 'Well, I obviously missed that bit when I
read the book, and if he said that I disagree with him,' and to write it off
as a warning to read a book extremely carefully before commending it.
And so it might have rested, at least for me; I have been far too busy in
the last three years to take any part in what I gather have been ongoing
and at times acrimonious inter-evangelical discussions.

But, faced with the Oak Hill book, and its angry denunciation of
Steve Chalke (pp 25f., 327f.), I thought I ought to take another look.
(The show now runs and runs: on the day that I am writing this [April
20], the *Church of England Newspaper* has a letter from someone saying, casually, that Steve Chalke, like Jeffrey John, 'denies penal substitution' and thus undermines more or less everything else in the Bible.) I
have just re-read Steve's short chapter on the meaning of the cross within
the mission of Jesus. He says many things I agree with, and, though
he doesn't actually make the main point that I made in *Jesus and the
Victory of God* ch. 12, drawing on Isaiah 53 in particular, he does say,

> Just as a lightning-conductor soaks up powerful and destruc-
> tive bolts of electricity, so Jesus, as he hung on that cross, soaked
> up all the forces of hate, rejection, pain and alienation all around
> him. (*The Lost Message of Jesus* p. 179).

Earlier on in the chapter he had expressed puzzlement at how 'basic
statements of the gospel' in ordinary churches would focus mainly on
sin and judgment rather than with the love of God, and at the way in
which the cross, seen as the answer to the punishment due for our sin,
was becoming the sum and substance of the gospel to the exclusion
even of the resurrection (except in the sense of a 'happy ending'). Steve
is not alone in this puzzlement, and with good reason. As we shall see,
the Bible and the gospel are more many-sided than that. It is in that
context that Steve makes his now notorious statement:

> The fact is that the cross isn't a form of cosmic child abuse—a
> vengeful Father, punishing his Son for an offence he has not even
> committed. Understandably, both people inside and outside of
> the Church have found this twisted version of events morally
> dubious and a huge barrier to faith. Deeper than that, however, is
> that such a concept stands in total contradiction to the statement
> that "God is Love". If the cross is a personal act of violence per-
> petrated by God towards humankind but borne by his Son, then
> it makes a mockery of Jesus' own teaching to love your enemies
> and to refuse to repay evil with evil. (p. 182f.)

Now, to be frank, I cannot tell, from this paragraph alone, which of two things Steve means. You could take the paragraph to mean (a) on the cross, as an expression of God's love, Jesus took into and upon himself the full force of all the evil around him, in the knowledge that if he bore it we would not have to; but this, which amounts to a form of penal substitution, is quite different from other forms of penal substitution, such as the mediaeval model of a vengeful father being placated by an act of gratuitous violence against his innocent son. In other words, there are many models of penal substitution, and the vengeful-father-and-innocent-son story is at best a caricature of the true one. Or you could take the paragraph to mean (b) because the cross is an expression of God's love, there can be no idea of penal substitution at all, because if there were it would necessarily mean the vengeful-father-and-innocent-son story, and that cannot be right.

Clearly, Steve's critics have taken him to mean (b), as I think it is clear Jeffrey John and several others intend. I cannot now remember what I thought when I read the book four years ago and wrote my commendation, but I think, since I had been following the argument through in the light of the arguments I myself have advanced, frequently and at length, about Jesus' death and his own understanding of it, that I must have assumed he meant (a). I have now had a good conversation with Steve about the whole subject and clarified that my initial understanding was correct: he does indeed mean (a). The book, after all, wasn't about atonement as such, so he didn't spell out his view of the cross in detail; and it is his experience that the word 'penal' has put off so many people, with its image of a violent, angry and malevolent God, that he has decided not to use it. *But the reality that I and others refer to when we use the phrase "penal substitution" is not in doubt,* for Steve any more than for me. 'There is therefore now no condemnation' in Romans 8.1 is explained by the fact, as in Romans 8.3, that God condemned sin in the flesh of his Son: he bore sin's condemnation in his body, so we don't bear it. That, I take it, is the heart of what the best sort of 'penal substitution' theory is trying to say, and Steve is fully happy with it. And this leads to the key point: *there are several forms of the doctrine of penal substitution, and some are more biblical than others.* What has happened since the initial flurry of debate about *The Lost Message of Jesus* has looked, frankly, like a witch-hunt, with people playing the guilt-by-association game: hands up anyone who likes Steve Chalke; right, now we know who the bad guys are.[30]

---

[30]N. T. Wright, "The Cross and the Caricatures: A Response to Robert Jenson, Jeffrey John, and a New Volume Entitled *Pierced for Our Transgressions,*" http://www.fulcrum-anglican.org.uk/news/2007/20070423wright.cfm?doc=205.

Attempts like this to show Chalke as a believer in penal substitution do not bode well for the firmness and clarity of Wright's own view. It seems to me to be wishful thinking to construe Chalke's own words in a way that would portray him as comfortable thinking of the personal God making his own personal Son bear the Father's own legal retribution for my sin. It has not been shown that what Chalke rejects in the "traditional" portrayals of penal substitution is not in part what the Bible actually teaches. But N. T. Wright's own words concerning penal substitution seem clear and strong. Here is what we see:

> The idea of punishment as part of atonement is itself deeply controversial; horrified rejection of the mere suggestion has led on the part of some to an unwillingness to discern any reference to Isaiah 40–55 in Paul.[31] But it is exactly that idea that Paul states, clearly and unambiguously, in [Romans] 8:3, when he says that God *"condemned sin in the flesh"*—i.e., *the flesh of Jesus.*[32]
>
> Dealing with wrath or punishment is *propitiation*; with sin, *expiation*. You propitiate a person who is angry;[33] you expiate a sin, crime, or stain on your character. Vehement rejection of the former idea in many quarters has led some to insist that only "expiation" is in view here. But the fact remains that in [Romans] 1:18–3:20 Paul has declared that the wrath of God is revealed against all ungodliness and wickedness and that despite God's forbearance this will finally be meted out; that in 5:8, and in the whole promise of 8:1–30, *those who are Christ's are rescued from wrath.*[34]

---

[31]Such as Isaiah 53:4–5, 10: "Surely he has borne our griefs and carried our sorrows; yet we esteemed him stricken, smitten by God, and afflicted. But he was wounded for our transgressions; he was crushed for our iniquities; upon him was the chastisement that brought us peace, and with his stripes we are healed. . . . Yet it was the will of the LORD to crush him; he has put him to grief." Wright observes, "Although the attempt to read Paul, and particularly Romans, in the light of these chapters [Isa. 40–55] has been controversial . . . there is a good deal to be said for such an allusion as at least part of the explanation of the present passage." He draws out the following allusions in Paul: Romans 4:25 = Isaiah 53:6, 12; Romans 5:15, 19 = Isaiah 53:11–12; Romans 15:21 = Isaiah 52:15; Romans 10:16 = Isaiah 53:1. Wright, *The Letter to the Romans*, 475–476.
[32]Ibid., 476.
[33]In view of this assertion that God propitiated the anger of God, it is mystifying that Wright would construct the following sentence in this context: "It should go without saying that this in no way implies, what the start of the verse has already ruled out, that God is an angry malevolent tyrant who demands someone's death, or someone's blood, and is indifferent as to whose it is." Ibid., 476. What is subtle and misleading about this sentence is that it starts with the denial of pejorative things about God and then ends up denying, with no distinction, things that Wright himself has affirmed. The sentence is written in such a way as to make Wright's own true view almost unrecognizable. What is to be denied and what is not? Is God angry? Yes. Is he malevolent? No. Is he a tyrant? No (too many false connotations), but he is certainly totally in charge. Does he demand someone's death? Yes. Blood? Yes. Is he indifferent as to whose it is? No. This is *not* a helpful way to explain what one thinks. It seems to me that he undercuts with this sentence the force of what he has spent great effort defending from the text of Romans.
[34]Ibid. Emphasis added.

So God's purpose in the covenant with Israel was to bring redemption to the world, including not only global restoration of peace and justice, but also the forgiveness of sins for all who are members of the covenant by faith in Jesus.[35] This forgiveness implies that the wrath of God against us has been removed. This happened through God's own act[36] in punishing our sin in the flesh of Jesus.

LAW-COURT IMAGERY SUBORDINATE AND INTEGRAL TO THE COVENANT

Now we return to the earlier point that it is a mistake to say Wright's stress on the covenantal context of justification overlooks the importance of the forensic or law-court context. In other words, it is wrong to claim that since Wright says justification is the declaration that we are part of the covenant people, therefore he does not say that justification is the declaration that we have the law-court status of being in the right (i.e., acquitted). He is clear that it is *both-and*: "'Justification' is thus the declaration of God, the just judge, that someone is (a) in the right, that their sins are forgiven, and (b) a true member of the covenant family, the people belonging to Abraham."[37]

The reason Wright weaves covenant and law-court together is because he believes the covenant is the overarching category for understanding the great story of redemption, and the law-court metaphor is a subordinate but integral part of it. The reason it is integral is that "the covenant was there in the first place to deal with the sin of the world," but "you dealt with sin through the law-court condemning the sinner and 'justifying', i.e. acquitting or vindicating, the righteous."[38] So the law-court serves to accomplish the goal of the covenant—"putting the world to rights."

This explains why Wright speaks of justification as the declaration that people are in the covenant.

---

[35]"'The gospel' is the announcement of Jesus' lordship, which works with power to bring people into the family of Abraham, now redefined around Jesus Christ and characterized solely by faith in him. 'Justification' is the doctrine which insists that all those who have this faith belong as full members of his family, on this basis and no other." Wright, *What Saint Paul Really Said*, 133.

[36]"Jesus' self-giving faithfulness to death, seen as *the act of God*, not of humans operating toward God, had the effect of turning away the divine wrath that otherwise hung over not only Israel but also the whole world." Wright, *The Letter to the Romans*, 477. Thus, God turned away the wrath of God.

[37]Wright, "The Shape of Justification."

[38]Wright, *What Saint Paul Really Said*, 33.

Justification is part of Paul's picture of the family God promised (i.e. covenanted) to Abraham. When God, as judge, finds in favor of people on the last day, they are declared to be part of this family (Rom. 4; cf. Gal. 3). This is why law-court imagery is appropriate: the covenant was there, from Genesis onwards, so that through it God could deal with sin and death, could (in other words) put his creation to rights.[39]

Justification was the means by which the covenant would accomplish its goal—that sinners from all nations be justified, given the status of a forgiven sinner[40] and "in the right" before God,[41] and welcomed into the world-transforming family of faith in Christ.

"CASHING OUT" LAW-COURT IMAGES IN COVENANTAL TERMS

Therefore, Wright feels warranted to "translate" law-court language for justification back into covenantal categories. "To say that they are 'righteous' means that the judge has found in their favor; or, *translating back into covenantal categories*, that the covenant God has declared them to be the covenant people."[42] Or to put it another way, Wright feels warranted to "cash out" law-court language in terms of covenantal language: "They are given the status of being 'righteous' in the metaphorical law-courts. When this is *cashed out in terms of the underlying covenantal theme*, it means that they are declared, in the present, to be what they will be seen to be in the future, namely, the true people of God."[43]

As I said above, even though this "translation" of law-court language into covenantal language causes terminological confusion and clouds the interpretation of specific texts and stretches the language of justification (δικαιόω) to the breaking point, it is not in itself a devas-

---

[39]Wright, "The Shape of Justification."

[40]"That is what the covenant was designed to do, and that is why 'belonging to the covenant' means, among other things, 'forgiven sinner.'" *Paul in Fresh Perspective*, 121. You can already see what I mentioned earlier: that Wright begins to use justification language in a more traditional sense that seems in tension with membership language. How can "justified" mean "*given* the status of a forgiven sinner" (emphasis added) if justification is the declaration that someone is a member of the covenant? Does not forgiveness determine and constitute the passage from outside to inside the saving covenant? So is justification God's act of determining and constituting membership? Or is it the subsequent declaration of the membership, which was constituted earlier by the call of God?

[41]"God's justifying activity is the declaration that this people are 'in the right,' in other words, announcing the verdict in their favor." Wright, *The Letter to the Romans*, 473.

[42]Ibid., 473. If this sounds strange, read the first word *covenant* as an adjective modifying *God*: "that the *covenant* God has declared them to be the covenant people."

[43]Wright, *What Saint Paul Really Said*, 129.

tating mistake. It conflates implication and definition, but this is not where the most serious criticism of Wright's treatment of justification should focus. We move closer to the heart of things if we go into the law-court with him and hear him lay out the parameters for understanding justification there.

CHAPTER THREE

THE LAW-COURT DYNAMICS OF JUSTIFICATION AND THE MEANING OF GOD'S RIGHTEOUSNESS

INDISPENSABLE IN WRIGHT'S explanation of the law-court under-standing of justification is the fact that the law-court scene in view is the *final* judgment.

> It's best to begin at the end, with Paul's view of the *future*. . . . The one true God will finally judge the whole world; on that day, some will be found guilty and others will be upheld (Rom. 2.1–16). God's vindication of these latter on the last day is his act of final 'justifica-tion' (Rom. 2.13).[1]

Wright's assumption that "'Justification' . . . in its Jewish context . . . refers to the greatest lawsuit of all: that which will take place on the great day when the true God judges all the nations"[2] seems a bit too sweeping. He is aware that the term "justification" referred in Paul's day to more simple, diverse, and immediate realities without any con-notation, let alone denotation, of the final judgment.[3]

---

[1]Wright, "The Shape of Justification."
[2]The quote goes on: "God will, at least, find in favor of his people: he will judge the pagan nations and rescue his true people. 'Justification' thus describes the coming great act of redemption and salvation, *seen from the point of view* of the covenant (Israel is God's people) on the one hand and the law-courts on the other (God's final judgment will be like a great law-court scene, with Israel winning the case)." Wright, *What Saint Paul Really Said*, 33.
[3]See his article on "Righteousness" in *New Dictionary of Theology*, ed. David F. Wright et al. (Downers Grove, IL: InterVarsity Press, 1988), 590–592.

The term "justification" refers to what happens in ordinary court-rooms, not just at the end of the age (Deut. 25:1; 1 Kings 8:32). It refers to Elihu wanting to justify Job (Job 33:32); to the evil of justifying the wicked for a bribe (Isa. 5:23; cf. 1:17); to the wisdom of God being justified (Matt. 11:19); to God's being justified now by the crowds (Luke 7:29); to a man's trying to justify himself and save face (Luke 10:29; cf. 16:15). And in the theological sense in the New Testament, it far more often refers to the *present* reality of justification, not the future. There are references in the future tense; however, not even all these are obviously a reference to the last judgment (Rom. 2:13; 3:20; Gal. 2:16; Matt. 12:37). The future tense may refer to the immediate future or the distant future. Thus if I say, "Walk in the light and you will be blessed," I might mean you will be blessed now as you walk in the light, or I might mean you will be blessed in heaven. It is misleading to create the impression that when the word *justification* is used, the first or main thought coming to anyone's mind would be *final, eschatological* judgment. That is not proved, and I think not likely for most instances in Paul. This is not to deny the reality of a future court scene in which God will judge on behalf of his people. It is rather a caution that justification in the writings of Paul may not be as controlled by the future, eschatological conception as Wright says it is. But let's leave that to the side and press on with his explanation.

THE JUDGMENT HAS ALREADY HAPPENED IN CHRIST

Having pointed out that the climactic event of justification happens in the future at the last judgment, Wright moves from the future to the past and shows that in a profound sense the judgment has already happened in the death and resurrection of Jesus.

> God's action in Jesus forms Paul's template for this final justifica-tion. . . . Jesus has been faithful, obedient to God's saving purposes right up to death (Rom. 5.12–21; Phil. 2.6–9); God has now declared decisively that he is the Son of God, the Messiah, in whom Israel's destiny has been summed up (Rom. 1.3f.). . . . Jesus' resurrection was, for Paul, the evidence that God really had dealt with sin on the cross (1 Cor. 15.12–19). In the death of Jesus God accomplished what had been promised to Abraham, and 'what the law could not do' (Rom.

8.3): for those who belong to the Messiah, there is 'no condemnation' (Rom. 8.1, 8.31–9).[4]

Because God has already condemned sin in the flesh of Jesus (Rom. 8:3), it is possible for Jew and Gentile in the present to put their faith in what Jesus has done and share in his vindication in advance of their final vindication at the last judgment. "Justification in the present is based on God's past accomplishment in Christ, and anticipates the future verdict. . . . God vindicates in the present, in advance of the last day, all those who believe in Jesus as Messiah and Lord (Rom. 3.21–31; 4.13–25; 10.9–13)."[5]

How the Righteousness of Judge and Defendant Differ

To grasp how justification works in this law-court context according to Wright, we need to see how he clarifies the difference between the righteousness of the judge and the righteousness of the plaintiff and defendant. Wright says that God the Judge is righteous in four senses: "his faithfulness to his covenant promises to Abraham, his impartiality, his proper dealing with sin and his helping of the helpless."[6] This is distinct from what righteousness means for the plaintiff and the defendant:

> For the plaintiff or defendant to be 'righteous' in the biblical sense *within the law-court setting* is for them to have that status *as a result*

[4]Wright, "The Shape of Justification."
[5]Ibid.
[6]Wright, *The Climax of the Covenant*, 36. For the working out of the distinctions between judge and plaintiff and defendant in the law-court, see *What Saint Paul Really Said*, 97–98. In general, and most importantly, Wright treats the righteousness of God as God's faithfulness to his covenant. "Romans [is] Paul's exposition of God's faithfulness to his covenant (in technical language, his righteousness')." Ibid., 48. "For a reader of the Septuagint, the Greek version of the Jewish scriptures, 'the righteousness of God' would have one obvious meaning: God's own faithfulness to his promises, to the covenant." Ibid., 96. "In this context [Rom. 3:1–8] 'God's righteousness' most naturally means 'God's covenant faithfulness.'" Ibid., 106. "The gospel—the announcement of the lordship of Jesus the Messiah—reveals God's righteousness, his covenant faithfulness." Ibid., 126. It seems to me that this way of describing the righteousness of God falls under the same criticism as Wright's treatment of justification—that it forces an *implication* of God's righteousness (that he keeps his promises) into the *definition* of God's righteousness (that he is the kind of God who always does what is right). What righteousness *is* does not equal what righteousness *does*. Defining righteousness as covenant-keeping is like defining integrity as contract-keeping. Yes, integrity keeps the terms of its contracts, but integrity also tells the truth about where you were last night—and a hundred other things. I will argue later that God keeps his promises, judges impartially, deals with sin properly, and helps those who are unjustly oppressed *because* he is righteous. These actions *are not* his righteousness. They *flow from* his righteousness (and other attributes). I will try to show that the failure to make this distinction hinders Wright from focusing on the heart of God's righteousness and distorts the way he sees justification in Paul.

of the decision of the court. . . . This doesn't necessarily mean that
he or she is good, morally upright or virtuous; simply that he or she
has, in this case, been vindicated against the accuser; in other words,
acquitted.[7]

IMPUTATION IN THIS COURT "MAKES NO SENSE AT ALL"

Now, with these definitions and conceptions set up, Wright draws out
the deeply controversial implication concerning the historic doctrine
of imputation.

> The result of all this should be obvious, but is enormously important for
> understanding Paul. If we use the language of the law-court, *it makes
> no sense whatever to say that the judge imputes, imparts, bequeaths,
> conveys or otherwise transfers his righteousness to either the plaintiff
> or the defendant.* Righteousness is not an object, a substance or a gas
> which can be passed across the courtroom. For the judge to be righ-
> teous does not mean that the court has found in his favour. For the
> plaintiff or defendant to be righteous does not mean that he or she has
> tried the case properly or impartially. To imagine the defendant some-
> how receiving the judge's righteousness is simply a category mistake.
> That is not how the language works. . . . If and when God does act
> to vindicate his people, his people will then, metaphorically speaking,
> have the status of "righteousness." . . . *But the righteousness they have
> will not be God's own righteousness.* That makes no sense at all.[8]

ON THE WRONG FOOT FOR FIFTEEN HUNDRED YEARS?

If Wright is correct here, then the entire history of the discussion of
justification for the last fifteen hundred years—Catholic, Protestant,
and Orthodox—has been misguided. Virtually everyone has been committing a "category mistake," and the entire debate between Roman
Catholics and Protestants about imputing versus imparting divine
righteousness "makes no sense at all." This is a remarkable claim to
make about church history. But Wright is ready to play the man. "The

---

[7]Wright, *What Saint Paul Really Said*, 98. "'Justification' . . . is God's declaration that the person
is now in the right, which confers on them the status 'righteous'. (We may note that, since 'righteous' here, within the law-court metaphor, refers to 'status', not 'character', we correctly say that
God's declaration makes the person 'righteous', i.e. in good standing.)" Wright, "The Shape of
Justification."
[8]Ibid., 98–99. Emphasis added.

discussions of justification in much of the history of the church, *certainly since Augustine*, got off on the wrong foot—at least in terms of understanding Paul—and they have stayed there ever since."[9]

A MODERN-DAY LUTHER?

It is no final argument against what Wright says, but only a caution, to observe that he sees himself methodologically in the same role as Martin Luther—rediscovering what the New Testament originally meant over against fifteen centuries of misguided tradition.

> What I am doing, often enough, is exactly parallel, in terms of method, to what Martin Luther did when he took the gospel word *metanoeite* and insisted that it didn't mean 'do penance', as the Vulgate indicated, but "repent" in a much more personal and heartfelt way. *The only way* to make that sort of point is to show that that's what the word would have meant at the time. That's the kind of serious biblical scholarship the Protestant Reformation was built on, and I for one am proud to carry on that tradition—if need be, against those who have turned the Reformation itself into a tradition to be set up over scripture itself.[10]

Whether we should follow Wright as a new Luther over against the Reformation and fifteen hundred years of wrong-footed conceptuality is open to question. I don't think so. One of the differences between Wright and the Reformers is that the latter labored to link their thinking to the writings of the church fathers (hence the Reformers' adoption of the slogan, *ad fontes*, "back to the sources"). In his recurrent reminders that he is a Protestant-like, Scripture-only man, Wright does not communicate the kind of respect for history and careful treatment of it that wins our confidence.[11]

Moreover, I do not think it is accurate to say that "the only way" to demonstrate a new meaning like Luther's (or Wright's) is to show that it is "what the word would have meant at the time." *"At the time"* is too general. Words mean different things at any given time depending on how they are used in different contexts. Wright, of course, knows this and would, I think, agree that the final court of appeal is the context of an author's own argument.

---

[9]Ibid., 115.
[10]Wright, "The Shape of Justification." Emphasis added.
[11]See the section in chapter 1 entitled "Energized by What Is New," 37-38.

I see at least three problems with the way Wright arrives at the conclusion that imputing God's righteousness to a defendant is a "category mistake" and "makes no sense."

Wright's Definition of Righteousness Does Not Go Deep Enough

First, Wright's definition of the righteousness of God does not go to the heart of the matter, but stays at the level of what divine righteousness *does* rather than what it *is*. He defines God's righteousness by saying that it *keeps* covenant, *judges* impartially, *deals* properly with sin, and *advocates* for the helpless.[12] None of those is what righteousness *is*, but they are some of the things righteousness *does*. This limited way of treating God's righteousness distorts Wright's reading of Paul. Thus, he has defined the righteousness of God, in part, in terms of God's acting impartially—and then he portrays the imputation of divine righteousness as if it would mean that God imputes to a plaintiff the impartial way he tried the case. Wright claims this "makes no sense at all"—it's "a category mistake."

Since this is not a whole book focused only on the righteousness of God, I can only give a summary statement here of what I think is a more faithful reading of Paul and the wider Scripture concerning God's righteousness. I content myself that I devoted most of an entire book to this issue—a book that is still in print and that I still believe is compelling. *The Justification of God*[13] contains chapters titled "The Righteousness of God in the Old Testament," "The Righteousness of God in Romans 3:1–8," "The Righteousness of God in Romans 3:25–26," and "The Rights and Purposes of the Creator in Romans 9:19–23."

Not in the least do I want to question that God's righteousness impels him to be faithful to his covenant promises, to judge without partiality, to deal with sin "properly," and to stand up for those who are unjustly oppressed. But God's love (*hesed*) and his faithfulness (*emet*) and his goodness (*tov*) could also be said to produce these actions. Yet

---

[12]See footnote 6 above.
[13]John Piper, *The Justification of God: An Exegetical and Theological Study of Romans 9:1–23*, 2nd ed. (Grand Rapids, MI: Baker, 1993). A side note that I find interesting is that I was writing this book at the same time N. T. Wright was writing his D.Phil. thesis for Oxford in 1980. As I read his section on the righteousness of God in this unpublished thesis, I was struck by how in those days he and I were dealing with the same issues and quoting the same people (Käseman, Ziesler, etc.). But the conclusions we came to and the direction we have gone are very different.

God's righteousness and love and faithfulness and goodness are not all synonyms. So the crucial question in defining the righteousness of God is: *What is it about God's righteousness that inclines him to act in these ways?* Behind each of those actions is the assumption that there is something about God's righteousness that explains why he acts as he does. What is that? That is the question, so far as I can see, that Wright does not ask.

I do not ask it for speculative reasons but exegetical ones. Paul's use of the righteousness language in Romans begs for this question to be asked. The δικαι- word group is used over seventy times in Romans. Paul's profound argument in answer to the question "Is there injustice [ἀδικία] on God's part?" (Rom. 9:14) pushes us deeper into God beneath and before the covenant. And the development of his argument in Romans 1–3 regarding man's "unrighteousness" [ἀδικίαν] (Rom. 1:18) apart from the covenant presses us behind the covenant for the ultimate meaning of righteousness as Paul conceived of it.

HOW DOES GOD DECIDE WHAT IS RIGHT TO DO?

There is a simple way to say the answer to this question and a more complex and profound way. The simple way is to say that God's righteousness consists in his unswerving commitment to do what is right. In other words, behind his doing what is right is a knowledge and love of what is right that is so full and so strong that it consists in an inviolable allegiance or commitment or faithfulness to do what is right. If I limited myself to this simple way of describing God's righteousness, it would be simple, straightforward, and true. The only reason I press beyond the more simple way is that it proves remarkably illuminating exegetically.

It is not very satisfying simply to say that God's righteousness is his commitment to do what is right, because it leaves the term "right" undefined. We don't feel like we have gained very much in defining "righteousness" if we use the word "right" to define it. To be sure, it is not an insignificant thing to say to a child, "God is the kind of Person who always knows and loves and does what is right." That is a wise and true thing to say. But someday that child is going to become a teenager and ask, "How does God decide what is right? Who tells God what is right? Is there a book of laws or rules that God has to obey?"

Answering those questions gets at the deeper meaning of *righteousness*. What is the "right" to which God is unswervingly committed?

The answer is that there is no book of laws or rules that God consults to know what is right. He wrote the book. What we find therefore in the Old Testament and in Paul is that God defines "right" in terms of *himself*. There is no other standard to consult than his own infinitely worthy being. Thus, what is right, most ultimately, is what upholds the value and honor of God—what esteems and honors God's glory.

The reasoning goes like this: The ultimate value in the universe is God—the whole panorama of all his perfections. Another name for this is God's holiness (viewed as the intrinsic and infinite worth of his perfect beauty) or God's glory (viewed as the out-streaming manifestation of that beauty). Therefore, "right" must be ultimately defined in relation to this ultimate value, the holiness or the glory of God—this is the highest standard for "right" in the universe. Therefore, what is right is what upholds in proper proportion the value of what is infinitely valuable, namely, God. "Right" actions are those that flow from a proper esteem for God's glory and that uphold his glory as the most valuable reality there is. This means that the essence of the righteousness of God is his unwavering faithfulness to uphold the glory of his name. And human righteousness is the same: the unwavering faithfulness to uphold the glory of God.

BEHIND GOD'S COVENANT-KEEPING IS ALLEGIANCE TO HIS GLORY

On pages 111–119 of *The Justification of God*, I present this argument on the basis of dozens of Old Testament texts. The reasoning may sound speculative until one reads the Old Testament with this question in mind and then reads Paul with a view to the relationship between the glory of God and the righteousness of God. What is the highest value that God and the authors of Scripture continually go back to in accounting for the actions of God? The answer is: the glory of God, or the sacred and infinite value of his holiness, or sometimes simply his *name*. There is something far deeper in God than covenant faithfulness. God was not unrighteous before there was a covenant. He was righteous before there was any covenant to keep. "The LORD is righteous in *all* his ways" (Ps. 145:17), not just in keeping the covenant. "He will judge *the world* with righteousness" (Ps. 98:9). Something creates the covenant. Behind the making and keeping of the covenant, and behind all other divine actions, is this ultimate allegiance to his glory, his holiness, his name.

> For my name's sake *I defer my anger,*
> for the sake of my praise *I restrain it for you,*
> *that I may not cut you off.*
> *Behold, I have refined you, but not as silver;*
> *I have tried you in the furnace of affliction.*
> For my own sake, for my own sake, *I do it,*
> *for* how should my name be profaned?
> My glory I will not give to another. *(Isa. 48:9–11)*

> *I, I am he who blots out your transgressions* for my own sake,
> *and I will not remember your sins. (Isa. 43:25)*

> *Help us, O God of our salvation,* for the glory of your name;
> *deliver us, and atone for our sins,* for your name's sake! *(Ps. 79:9)*

> *But when they came to the nations, wherever they came, they profaned*
> *my holy name. . . . But I had concern for my holy name, which the*
> *house of Israel had profaned among the nations to which they came.*
> *Therefore say to the house of Israel, Thus says the Lord* GOD: *It is not*
> *for your sake, O house of Israel, that I am about to act, but for the sake*
> *of my holy name, which you have profaned among the nations to which*
> *you came. And I will vindicate the holiness of my great name, which*
> *has been profaned among the nations. (Ezek. 36:20–23)*

In these contexts, the motivation for God's saving action is something deeper than covenant faithfulness. It is God's faithfulness—his unwavering commitment—to act for the value of his glory.[14] "He remains faithful—for he cannot deny *himself*" (2 Tim. 2:13).

This is part of his nature. It is part of what it means to be God. This is the deeper foundation for covenant-keeping (and all other divine action). Coming from this deepest allegiance of God is what makes a divine action "right" or "righteous."

---

[14]See 1 Samuel 12:22 for one example of how God's commitment to his people is rooted most deeply in his allegiance to his own name: "For the LORD will not forsake his people, for his great name's sake, because it has pleased the LORD to make you a people for himself."

> For your name's sake, O LORD, preserve my life!
> In your righteousness bring my soul out of trouble! (Ps. 143:11)

Notice that "in your righteousness" is parallel to "for your name's sake." From this and similar lines of textual argument in the Old Testament, I conclude, "The *righteousness of God* consists most basically in God's unswerving commitment to preserve the honor of his name and display his glory."[15]

DOES PAUL SHARE THIS UNDERSTANDING OF THE RIGHTEOUSNESS OF GOD?

All of this would not matter much for interpreting Paul if there were no clear internal evidence that he thought this way about the righteousness of God. But, in fact, we find abundant evidence, especially in the book of Romans, where the righteousness of God is a major theme. Paul sets up the deepest problem of humankind in terms of human unrighteousness and our failure to glorify God. He describes the "*unrighteousness of men*" (ἀδικίαν ἀνθρώπων, Rom. 1:18) in terms of how they "did not *glorify* him as God" (οὐχ ὡς θεὸν ἐδόξασαν, Rom. 1:21, author's translation) and how they "exchanged the *glory* of the immortal God" (ἤλλαξαν τὴν δόξαν τοῦ ἀφθάρτου θεοῦ) for his creatures (Rom. 1:23, author's translation). All of this is described without any reference to a covenant.

Paul describes the Jewish participation in this global *unrighteousness* as the dishonoring of God and the blaspheming of his *name*. "You who boast in the law dishonor God (τὸν θεὸν ἀτιμάζεις) by breaking the law. For, as it is written, 'The name of God is blasphemed (ὄνομα τοῦ θεοῦ δι' ὑμᾶς βλασφημεῖται) among the Gentiles because of you'" (Rom. 2:23–24). Hence, "None is *righteous* (δίκαιος), no, not one" (Rom. 3:10), neither Jew nor Gentile.

Then Paul confirms that this is the essential problem by explaining sin in terms of this exchange of God's glory for created things: "All have *sinned* and fall short of the *glory* of God" (πάντες γὰρ ἥμαρτον καὶ ὑστεροῦνται τῆς δόξης τοῦ θεοῦ, Rom. 3:23). The word for "fall short of" (ὑστεροῦνται) means "to lack." This is a reiteration of Romans 1:23. The point is that we "lack" the glory of God because we

---
[15]Piper, *The Justification of God*, 119.

"exchanged" it. We have suicidally traded it for the poisonous pleasure of idols. Thus, for Paul, sin is essentially preferring and embracing other things and other people as more to be desired than the infinitely valuable and all-satisfying glory of God. This is the essence of sin and (as we saw in the Old Testament) the essence of unrighteousness.

RIGHTEOUSNESS *CREATES* THE PROBLEM FOR COVENANT FAITHFULNESS (ROM. 3:25)

Now, with this understanding of how Paul has described the situation of the world, we are able to understand more clearly the problem he is dealing with when he says two verses later in Romans 3:25 that "God put [Christ] forward as a propitiation by his blood . . . to show God's *righteousness* because in his divine forbearance he had passed over former sins." What this enormously important text shows is that God's righteousness was called into question by God's "passing over sins" (τὴν πάρεσιν τῶν . . . ἁμαρτημάτων). He has just explained that the problem with humanity is that we are "unrighteous" in that we belittle the glory of God (1:23; 3:10) and that this belittling of the glory of God is what "sin" is (cf. 3:23 and 1:23).

But now we find God "passing over sin"—that is, treating sin in a way that makes it look less outrageous than it is. This makes God look as though he does not properly esteem his own glory that sin belittles. Therefore, we can see that the reason God "shows [his] righteousness" is that his glory has been dishonored and yet God seems to have treated this lightly and thus acted unrighteously. In passing over countless belittlings of his glory (sins), he looks as though he counts his glory as a small thing. This would be unrighteousness in God—the very essence of unrighteousness. Therefore, he puts Christ forward to vindicate his righteousness, that is, to show that he does not take lightly the scorning of his glory. When he justifies the "ungodly" (who have treated his glory with contempt, Rom. 1:18, 23; 4:5), he is not unrighteous, because the death of Christ exhibits God's wrath against God-belittling sin.

Wright says on Romans 3:25, "The first question at issue, then—the aspect of God's righteousness that might seem to have been called into question and is now demonstrated after all—is

God's proper dealing with sins—i.e., punishment."[16] This is a telling sentence. Wright's most common definition of God's righteousness—God's covenant faithfulness—does not, it seems, fit easily into Romans 3:25–26. On the contrary, in these verses God's righteousness *creates a problem for covenant faithfulness* and must be satisfied in order that his covenant faithfulness may continue. Wright sees this and speaks of "the aspect of God's righteousness that is called into question." Yes. And this "aspect" is *not* most naturally, in this context, God's covenant faithfulness. God's passing over sin would seem to be not a *problem* for God's covenant faithfulness, but an *expression* of it.

Wright calls the aspect of God's righteousness that is called into question "God's proper dealing with sin—i.e., punishment."[17] He may indeed prefer to say that God's "righteousness" all the way through this text refers to covenant faithfulness, but even if so, notice that something in God other than covenant commitment determines what the "proper" stipulations of the covenant are in the first place. That is implied in calling punishment a "proper" dealing with sin. God's righteousness, before there was a covenant, determined that punishment for sin would be part of what happens in the covenant (and outside it!). And notice also that the flow of the context from Romans 3:9ff. suggests that the "passing over of sins" in Romans 3:25 was not just the passing over of the sins of the covenant people Israel (see also Acts 14:16; 17:30), but of the nations as well. Therefore, limiting the "righteousness of God" in this context to covenantal categories is too narrow.

My point is that Paul operates with the Old Testament understanding that the deepest meaning of God's righteousness is his unwavering commitment to act for the sake of his glory. The belittling of his glory by all humanity is the problem Paul sets up in Romans 1–3. Then, as he presents God's solution, he describes sin in terms of belittling God's glory (3:23), restates the problem as the passing over of these God-belittling sins, and gives the glorious answer in the vindication of God's righteousness, that is, his unwavering commitment to act for the glory of his name.

---

[16]Wright, *The Letter to the Romans*, 473.
[17]I do not think the problem is solved for Wright by saying that punishment in this context is one aspect of covenant faithfulness.

IT IS RIGHTEOUS TO SHOW WRATH FOR HIS OWN GLORY (ROM. 3:1–8)

In addition to this line of thought, there is more evidence for how Paul understood God's righteousness in Romans 3:1–8. In these verses Paul shows that, while God is faithful to his covenant promises, he would not be "unrighteous" to inflict wrath on unrighteous Israel. The most fundamental reason he would not be unrighteous to punish them is that in his judgment "God's truth abounds to his *glory*" (Rom. 3:7). This link between God's glory being vindicated and God being shown righteous confirms again that Paul saw God's righteousness most fundamentally as his unwavering faithfulness to uphold the glory of his name. Here are the key verses (Rom. 3:5–7):

> But if our unrighteousness serves to show the righteousness of God, what shall we say? That God is unrighteous to inflict wrath on us? (I speak in a human way.) By no means! For then how could God judge the world? But if through my lie God's truth abounds to his glory [ἐπερίσσευσεν εἰς τὴν δόξαν αὐτοῦ], why am I still being condemned as a sinner?

Notice the parallel between verses 5 and 7.

VERSE 5	VERSE 7
But if our unrighteousness serves to show the *righteousness of God,* what shall we say? That God is unrighteous to inflict wrath on us?	But if through my lie God's truth abounds to his *glory,* why am I still being condemned as a sinner?

The middle parallel shows that the demonstration of God's glory and the demonstration of God's righteousness are interpreting each other. In other words, Paul's underlying assumption is that vindicating God's glory is what righteousness does. Righteousness is God's inviolable faithfulness to uphold the value of his glory. Paul is echoing the *conclusions* of his opponents in the third parallel in verses 5 and 7—both of which he disagrees with—that it would be unrighteous of God to inflict wrath on someone whose unrighteousness brought down God's judgment (v. 5), and that persons should not be condemned as sinners if their falsehood highlighted God's glory when he condemned them (v. 7). Both conclusions are wrong. But the premises are true: Unfaithful Israelites will be judged, and this shows the righteousness of God because it magnifies his glory. What his opponents try to conclude from these true premises is that it is impossible for God to judge Israel. They are mistaken.[18]

UPHOLDING GOD'S GLORY IN THE FREEDOM OF MERCY (ROM. 9:14–23)

Consider one more illustration of Paul's understanding of the righteousness of God as God's unwavering commitment to his glory. Romans 9:14–23 (NASB) deals with the question raised in verse 14, "What shall we say then? There is no unrighteousness with God, is there [μὴ ἀδικία παρὰ τῷ θεῷ]?" The question was raised by God's freedom in choosing Jacob over Esau, "though they were not yet born and had done nothing either good or bad" (Rom. 9:11).

Paul's answer moves from the self-revelation of God at Mount Sinai where he says God's *name and glory* consist in his freedom to have mercy on whom he will (Rom. 9:15 = Ex. 33:19), to the Exodus where God raised up Pharaoh "that I might show my power in you, and that *my name* might be proclaimed in all the earth" (Rom. 9:17 = Ex. 9:16), to the conclusion in Romans 9:23 that God's freedom in election is not capricious but aims at a definite global purpose—"to make known the riches of *his glory* for vessels of mercy, which he has prepared beforehand *for glory*." In other words, Paul's answer to the question of whether there is unrighteousness with God is no. And the reason is that he has acted in a way that most fully upholds and displays the supreme worth of his *glory*.

The upshot of this evidence is that God's righteousness, in the mind of Paul, as in the Old Testament, is most fundamentally his unwavering allegiance to uphold the value of his glory. It is also plain that this is the righteousness he demands from his creatures—that they forsake their "unrighteousness" and "glorify him as God or give thanks to him" (Rom. 1:18, 21, author's translation). When he says that "none is righteous" (Rom. 3:10), he means that all of us have failed to glorify God as

---

[18]For the full argument of the verses and a more extended defense of Paul's understanding of the glory of God in relation to his righteousness in Romans 3:1–8, see *The Justification of God*, 123–134. Wright, it seems, does not take note of the parallel between God's glory (v. 7) and his righteousness (v. 5). So he settles for the statement, "In this context [Rom. 3:1–8] 'God's righteousness' most naturally means 'God's covenant faithfulness.'" Wright, *What Saint Paul Really Said*, 106. But this will not work. Try putting "covenant faithfulness" in the place of "righteousness of God" in verse 5. It will not work because the righteousness of God is the warrant *not* for covenant faithfulness but for God's wrath being inflicted on Israel.

we should. We do not "seek God" (Rom. 3:11). Instead, we exchange the glory of God and seek what his creation can offer (Rom. 1:23). And, in the case of Israel, "the name of God is blasphemed among the Gentiles because of you" (Rom. 2:24). "All have sinned"—that is, all have bartered away the glory of God for false substitutes. The aim of creation and redemption is that God be glorified—treasured and displayed as infinitely glorious. "Christ became a servant to the circumcised . . . in order that the Gentiles might *glorify God* for his mercy" (Rom. 15:8–9).

WHAT RIGHTEOUSNESS MEANS IN GOD'S LAW-COURT

Therefore, it seems to me that when Wright sets up God's law-court scene in such a way that the righteousness of the Judge and the righteousness of the defendant cannot be the same, he has done something artificial. When he says that the righteousness of the Judge is his "trying the case impartially" and the righteousness of the defendant is his "being declared in the right," his framework fails to get at the meaning of righteousness behind these different expressions. Therefore, he forces a portrayal of historic imputation that "makes no sense at all."[19] But this is not because imputation itself makes no sense, but because Wright has set things up in a way that makes it *look* nonsensical. And this is because he treats the righteousness of God merely in terms of the actions of the Judge, not in terms of his deeper attribute of righteousness. The power of Wright's paradigm to explain Paul turns out to limit and distort rather than clarify.

There is a very different way to look at things. For both the defendant and the judge, righteousness is "an unwavering allegiance to treasure and uphold the glory of God." This is what makes God and humans "righteous." Therefore, it may turn out in this law-court that it is indeed conceivable for the Judge's righteousness to be shared by the defendant. It may be that when the defendant lacks moral righteousness, the Judge, who is also Creator and Redeemer, may find a way to make his righteousness count for the defendant, since it is exactly the righteousness he needs—namely, an unwavering and flawless and acted-out allegiance to the glory of the Judge. We will return to this possibility in chapter 11. But first there are two more problems with Wright's law-court scene that I will try to address in the following chapter.

---

[19]Wright, *What Saint Paul Really Said*, 99.

CHAPTER FOUR

THE LAW-COURT DYNAMICS OF JUSTIFICATION AND THE NECESSITY OF REAL MORAL RIGHTEOUSNESS

IN THE PREVIOUS CHAPTER, we looked at the law-court setting that Wright develops to illumine the dynamics of justification. I have tried to address one problem with that scene, namely, that Wright's definition of the righteousness of God does not go to the heart of the matter but stays at the level of what divine righteousness *does* rather than what it *is*.

The second problem I see in Wright's way of setting up the law-court imagery is that it does not seem to come to terms with the fact that the judge is omniscient. The omniscience of the judge implies that the defendant must have a different righteousness than Wright would concede, that is, a righteousness that is more than the mere status of being acquitted, regardless of innocence or guilt. Wright stresses that for the defendant, righteousness is not a character quality (i.e., not a moral righteousness) but a status, namely, that the court has found in the defendant's favor. The defendant may or may not have committed the crime with which he was charged. Regardless, if the court finds in his favor, he is "righteous." He has that *status*.

This definition of "righteous" may work in ordinary human law-courts where judges are fallible and their judgments must stand, whether they are right or wrong. But there's a catch. In God's court-room, the Judge is omniscient and just. Now everyone in the first

century would agree that in a courtroom where the Judge knows
everything and is just, there can never be a case where there is a discrepancy between the truth of the charge and the truth of the verdict.
In *this* court, what would be the basis of saying, "I bestow on you the
status of *righteous*, and I find you *guilty as charged*"? How could such
a finding be intelligible, not to mention just? One right answer that I
think Wright would agree with is that this is what the atonement is all
about. Christ died for our sins to provide a basis for this finding, and
therefore, though guilty, the court can exercise clemency (or in God's
case, forgiveness) because of Christ and we go free.[1]

BUT CLEMENCY AND FORGIVENESS ARE NOT EQUIVALENT TO JUSTIFICATION

God's clemency in the courtroom and his personal forgiveness are
certainly true and glorious. We will sing of it to all eternity. But the
question is whether Paul has something to add—an even wider basis
for our justification—something that makes our salvation even more
wonderful and brings more glory to our Savior. I think he does. It
emerges when we realize that in the first-century courtroom, treating as innocent a defendant who is known in the court to be guilty
(letting him go free without condemnation) *on the basis of clemency*
(or forgiveness) would not have been described as "justifying" him.
Commenting on Romans 4:6–8, Wright says,

> Paul can assume that "reckoning righteousness apart from works" and
> "not reckoning sin against someone" *are equivalents*. The covenant, we
> must always remind ourselves, was there to deal with sin; when God
> forgives sin, or reckons someone within the covenant [=justifies], these
> are *functionally equivalent*. They draw attention to different aspects of
> the same event.[2]

But, as we will see below, when the charge in the court is "none
is *righteous*" and the context is *immorality* ("no one does good, not

---

[1]For example, he says, "The death of Jesus has explained why it is that God was right to pass over
former sins. That which was unjust in the human law-court is now contained within a higher justice." Wright, *The Letter to the Romans*, 492. I do not bring in at this point anything about what the
defendant must do to enjoy this finding of the court. That is, I leave until later the question: What is
Wright's view of "by faith alone"? And: What is the role, if any, of our Spirit-transformed behavior
in forming the basis of the Judge's verdict?

[2]Wright, *The Letter to the Romans*, 493. Emphasis added.

even one," Rom. 3:12), then to "reckon righteousness" to a defendant (Rom. 4:6) is more than giving him a status of "forgiven" or being a member of the covenant. With Wright's argument from Romans 4:6–8, there is a better way to understand the relationship between "reckoning righteousness" and "not reckoning sin." They do not have to be "equivalents" for the argument to work. In fact, the argument for "counting righteousness apart from works" is weakened by assuming Paul supported it merely by calling it equivalent to forgiveness. Paul wrote:

> *David also speaks of the blessing of the one to whom God counts righteousness apart from works: "Blessed are those whose lawless deeds are forgiven, and whose sins are covered; blessed is the man against whom the Lord will not count his sin."*

It is plausible that when Paul quotes Psalm 32 ("whose lawless deeds are forgiven") to support his claim that "God counts righteousness apart from works," he is making forgiveness and justification "equivalents." But I find it more plausible that in Paul's mind wherever sins are *not* counted, a positive righteousness *is* counted. In other words, the logic of Romans 4:6–8 may hang on Paul's understanding of Psalm 32 as implying that wherever there is divine forgiveness of lawless deeds—wherever sins are *not* counted—righteousness *is* counted. That is, the forgiven person is not considered by God merely as a *sinful* forgiven person, but as a righteous person—a person "to whom God counts righteousness apart from works."

Why might Paul see this implication in the psalm? One reason is that the psalm ends by calling the forgiven man "righteous."

> *Many are the sorrows of the wicked,*
> *but steadfast love surrounds the one who trusts in the LORD.*
> *Be glad in the LORD, and rejoice, O righteous,*
> *and shout for joy, all you upright in heart! (vv. 10–11)*

I am not saying that the psalmist has a full-blown doctrine of justification as imputed righteousness. I am simply observing that Paul may have meditated long and hard on the Psalms, including the often perplexing language of righteousness, sin, blamelessness, and forgiveness, and drew the inference that divine forgiveness never stands alone without God's counting the forgiven person as positively righteous.[3] That would account for the logic of Romans 4:6–8 better than assuming that *forgiveness* and *being counted righteous* are "equivalents."

JUSTIFICATION IS MORE THAN FORGIVENESS

With this in mind, we return to the law-court and the meaning of justification. If an *omniscient* and *just* judge found a person guilty as charged, the court would not say that clemency or forgiveness gives rise to the declaration of a *status of righteous*. Forgiveness and clemency can commute a sentence, but they cannot mean the judge *finds in the defendant's favor*. An omniscient and just judge never "finds in favor" of a *guilty* defendant. He always vindicates the claim that is *true*. If the defendant is guilty, the omniscient, just judge finds in favor of the plaintiff. The judge may show mercy. He has it in his power to bestow clemency, and to forgive, and not to condemn the guilty. But *not condemning the guilty* would never have been called "justification" or "finding in favor" or "bestowing the status of righteous."

Nevertheless, *justification* and *finding in favor* and *bestowing a status of righteous* are indeed what happen in the law-court of God when *guilty sinners* who believe in Jesus are on trial. God "justifies the *ungodly*" (Rom. 4:5). He declares them to be righteous, that is, to be not guilty of the charge. And the charge is: "None is righteous" (Rom. 3:10). So, if the discrepancy between being found "guilty as charged" and being given *the status of righteous* cannot be based on clemency alone, what is it based on?

This question is not driven by logic. It is driven by the way Paul

---

[3]Here is a flavor of what I mean by "the often perplexing language of righteousness, sin, blamelessness, and forgiveness." The Bible is willing to call us "righteous" even though "None is righteous, no, not one" (Rom. 3:10). And when it does so, it can at times mean that we not only have an imputed righteousness but also a life of lived-out but imperfect righteousness. You can see this paradoxical use of language clearly in several texts. For example, Ecclesiastes 7:20 says that "there is *not* a *righteous* man on earth who does good and never sins." But then he says to the Lord in verse 12, "You have upheld me because of [or in] my *integrity*." So there are non-righteous righteous. And there are sinners with integrity. The same thing can be shown from Paul's use of the word "blameless." Even though Paul speaks in Philippians 3:12 of his best efforts as imperfect, he still describes the believers as "blameless and innocent, children of God without blemish in the midst of a crooked and twisted generation" (Phil. 2:15). So there is an imperfect blamelessness just as there is a non-righteous righteousness and a sin-committing integrity. See Appendix 6 for more on how we fulfill the law.

speaks of justification in Romans. He describes the justification of the ungodly in the language of *imputation* when he refers to "the one to whom God counts [λογίζεται, *reckons, imputes*] righteousness apart from works" (Rom. 4:6). "Righteousness [is] counted [λογισθῆναι, *reckoned, imputed*] to them" (Rom. 4:11). Paul himself raises the question of an imputed righteousness that is not performed by the "ungodly" defendant in the courtroom.

THE PARADOXES THAT POINT TOWARD IMPUTATION

For virtually the entire history of the church, the answer has been, with various nuances, that God either imputes or imparts divine righteousness to the defendant because of his relationship with Christ. This was the central division between the Reformers and Roman Catholicism. One of the reasons for this is that the law-court that Wright has described seems to demand it, *if* the judge is omniscient and just—which he is. Exercising clemency toward, or forgiving, a guilty defendant does not provide a basis for justification. Commuting the sentence of the guilty person merely because of clemency or forgiveness is not what justification is. And an omniscient, just judge does not say that a defendant has moral righteousness when he is guilty of having no moral righteousness (Rom. 3:10)—unless there is a way that an alien moral righteousness can be counted as his.

Now why have I brought in *moral* righteousness? Doesn't that muddy the water? Isn't justification the bestowing of a *status* of "righteousness," not the declaration that one is *morally* righteous? I bring it in for two reasons. One reason is that in the context of Romans, the charge that has brought us into court is: "None is righteous, no, not one" (Rom. 3:10). Which means: "No one does good, not even one" (Rom. 3:12). This is a statement about our moral condition.

The other reason is that God is omniscient, and so his findings in court *always* accord with reality. The *status* bestowed will always accord with whether the *charge* sticks. When the charge itself is, "You have no moral righteousness before God" (cf. Rom. 3:10–18), the finding of an omniscient judge *in our favor* must be: "You do indeed have a moral righteousness before God and therefore a *status of acquittal* in this court."

Bringing *moral* righteousness into the law-court setting is not owing to Protestant and Roman Catholic tradition. It is owing to the context of Romans 1–3 and the demands of having an omniscient judge whose bestowal of a right standing in his court will always accord with what he knows to be true in the defendant's case.

A SUMMARY OF THE CRITIQUE SO FAR

Now let us gather up the various strands so far in my critique of Wright's law-court paradigm. We saw in chapter 3 that, as the Judge, God's righteousness is not simply his covenant faithfulness, or his acting impartially, or his dealing with sins properly. Those are some of what righteousness *does*, not what it *is*. God's righteousness is his unwavering allegiance to do what is right, that is, most ultimately, to uphold the infinite worth of his glory. The same holds true in principle for our moral righteousness. We were created to have this same unwavering allegiance to uphold the infinite worth of God's glory in all we do. That is what it would mean for a human being to be righteous.

The charge against us in God's law-court is that we do not have this righteousness. "None is *righteous*, no, not one . . . no one seeks *for God*" (Rom. 3:10–11). We are all guilty of "ungodliness and *unrighteousness* . . . [and have] exchanged the *glory of the immortal God* for images" (Rom. 1:18, 23; cf. 3:23). Nevertheless, God "justifies the ungodly" (Rom. 4:5)—the omniscient Judge does not merely show clemency or forgiveness and assign us a *status* of "righteous"; he finds *in our favor* precisely because he counts us as having the moral righteousness that we in fact do not have in ourselves. When the charge against us is read ("You do not have moral righteousness") and the verdict of the Judge is rendered ("I declare that you are not guilty as charged but *do* indeed have moral righteousness"), the righteousness in view in this declaration is real moral righteousness. I will argue later that this is the righteousness of Christ imputed to the guilty through faith alone. The declaration of justification in the law-court of God is not merely forgiveness; it is not merely the status of acquitted; it is counting the defendant as morally righteous though in himself he is not.

THE "NONSENSE" REALLY DOES HAPPEN

The third problem I see in Wright's way of setting up the law-court imagery is that he calls "nonsense" what in fact really does happen. Recall that he says,

> To imagine the defendant somehow receiving the judge's righteousness is simply a category mistake. That is not how the language works. . . . If and when God does act to vindicate his people, his people will then, metaphorically speaking, have the status of 'righteousness' . . . . *But the righteousness they have will not be God's own righteousness.* That makes no sense at all.[4]

We have seen that Wright's definitions of righteousness for the judge and the defendant do not account for Paul's understanding of how this law-court works. Now we add that, because of the work of Jesus Christ, it is not in fact nonsense to speak of the defendant in some sense sharing in the righteousness of the judge. It is not a category mistake to speak of the defendant "receiving the Judge's righteousness." This is, in fact, what the language of justification demands in a law-court where the Judge is omniscient and just and the charge is "none is [morally] righteous" (Rom. 3:10). Of course, it will jar the ordinary human categories. That is what the justification of the *ungodly* has always done—and is meant to do.

DOES IMPUTATION PROVIDE THE BASIS OF THE STATUS?

The crucial question is: Does Paul present the defendant as having, in some sense, the moral righteousness of the divine Judge because of Christ? What I mean by the "moral righteousness" of God is simply what I argued for above, namely, his unwavering allegiance to uphold the worth of his glory. That is the essence of his righteousness. And that is the moral righteousness he requires of us—that we unwaveringly love and uphold the glory of God in all we feel and think and do, that is, in the fulfillment of all his requirements.

But we have all failed. That is our unrighteousness (Rom. 1:18, 21, 23; 3:23). This is why we are on trial in God's law-court. We have not

---

[4]Wright, *What Saint Paul Really Said*, 99.

only exchanged the glory of God for images (Rom. 1:23) and failed to glorify and thank him (Rom. 1:21) but have dishonored him by breaking the law (Rom. 2:23) and caused his name to be blasphemed among the nations (Rom. 2:24). So none of us is righteous, not even one (Rom. 3:10). The question is: When the Judge finds in our favor, does he count us as having the required moral righteousness—not in ourselves, but because of the divine righteousness imputed to us in Christ?

My answer is yes, and I will return later (pp. 163–180) to give a fuller explanation and defense of this answer. Wright's answer is no. To review, he thinks that the whole discussion of imputing divine righteousness to humans is muddle-headed. It is simply not operating with proper biblical-historical categories. For the last fifteen hundred years, the discussions of this issue in the church have been misguided.[5] "If we use the language of the law-court, it makes no sense whatever to say that the judge imputes, imparts, bequeaths, conveys or otherwise transfers his righteousness to either the plaintiff or the defendant. Righteousness is not an object, a substance or a gas which can be passed across the courtroom."[6]

At this point, it may help to draw in more of Wright's related ideas to round out his picture of justification before we proceed to defend our understanding of imputation.

---

[5]"The discussions of justification in much of the history of the church, *certainly* [!] *since Augustine*, got off on the wrong foot—at least in terms of understanding Paul—and they have stayed there ever since." Ibid., 115. Emphasis added.
[6]Ibid., 98.

CHAPTER FIVE

JUSTIFICATION AND THE GOSPEL: WHEN IS THE LORDSHIP OF JESUS GOOD NEWS?

WHERE ARE THE PREACHERS OF THE GLORIOUS GOSPEL?

One of Wright's passions is to help us see more clearly the historical sweep and global scope of God's purposes in the gospel. This accounts for some of his reactions to the individualism and pietism that mark some preaching of the gospel. There simply aren't enough preachers who show the gospel to be what it is, the magnificent announcement of the lordship of Jesus, not only over my personal problems, but over all of history and all the nations and all the environment.

I rejoice in any effort to restore the supremacy of Christ over all things and to rescue the preaching of the gospel from myopic, individualistic limitations. But Wright's way of highlighting the global sweep of the gospel has the effect of marginalizing, and perhaps even negating, some aspects of the gospel that are precious, and without which all talk of rescuing the world from chaos is hollow.

THE MESSAGE OF JUSTIFICATION IS NOT THE GOSPEL?

For example, Wright is eager not to equate the gospel with the message of justification by faith alone or even with a message about how to "get saved." "Paul's gospel to the pagans was not a philosophy of life. Nor was it, even, a doctrine about how to get saved."[1] "The announcement of the gospel *results in* people being saved. . . . But 'the gospel' itself, strictly speaking, is the narrative proclamation of King Jesus. . . . When the herald makes a royal proclamation, he says 'Nero (or whoever) has become emperor.'"[2]

"'The gospel' itself refers to the proclamation that Jesus, the crucified and risen Messiah, is the one, true and only Lord of the world."[3] For Paul, this imperial announcement was "that the crucified Jesus of Nazareth had been raised from the dead; that he was thereby proved to be Israel's Messiah; that he was thereby installed as Lord of the world."[4]

The gospel has at its center the events of the cross and the resurrection. "For Paul, the reason why there is good news at all is that in and through the cross of King Jesus the one true God has dealt decisively with evil."[5] And Wright wants to emphasize *all* evil—my personal "sin, death, guilt and shame"[6] *and* the global evil that the prophets promised would be overcome when the Messiah ushers in the new age. This new age has come. That is the good news that Paul preaches. "He is announcing that the messianic promises of salvation have come true in Jesus."[7]

THE GOSPEL IS NOT AN ACCOUNT OF HOW PEOPLE GET SAVED?

I love faithful portrayals of the majesty of God and the greatness of Christ and the infinite reaches of the gospel. This accords perfectly with God's passion for his own glory. "For the earth will be filled with the knowledge of the glory of the LORD as the waters cover the sea" (Hab. 2:14). But I find it perplexing that Wright is so eager not to let the message of justification be part of the gospel. He says:

> I must stress again that the doctrine of justification by faith is not what Paul means by 'the gospel'. It is implied by the gospel; when the gospel is proclaimed, people come to faith and so are regarded by God

---

[1]Wright, *What Saint Paul Really Said*, 90. "[The gospel] is not, then, a system of how people get saved." Ibid., 45. "My proposal has been that 'the gospel' is not, for Paul, a message about 'how one gets saved', in an individual and ahistorical sense." Ibid., 60.
[2]Ibid., 45. Emphasis added.
[3]Wright, "Paul in Different Perspectives: Lecture 1."
[4]Wright, *What Saint Paul Really Said*, 46.
[5]Ibid., 52.
[6]Ibid., 157.
[7]Ibid., 53.

as members of his people. But 'the gospel' is not an account of how people get saved.[8]

If we come to Paul with these questions in mind—the questions about how human beings come into a living and saving relationship with the living and saving God—it is not justification that springs to [Paul's] lips or pen. The message about Jesus and his cross and resurrection—'the gospel' . . . —is announced to them; through this means, God works by his Spirit upon their hearts.[9]

There are significant problems with this claim. Exegetically the most obvious one is that the portrayal of Paul's preaching of the gospel in the book of Acts seems to contradict what Wright says. He says that the gospel "is not an account of how people get saved," and he says that "justification" does not spring to Paul's lips if we come to him with the question of how we can come into a saving relationship with God. In view of these claims, consider the way Acts presents Paul's preaching as it relates to justification, Jews, Gentiles, and eternal life.

Paul Proclaims Justification by Faith as Part of His Gospel

In Acts 13:14, Paul and Barnabas arrive in Pisidian Antioch. On the Sabbath day, they enter the synagogue and, after the reading of the law and the prophets, they are invited to speak "any word of encouragement for the people" (Acts 13:15). What follows is a radically God-centered narration of the history of Israel from Israel's election and stay in Egypt (v. 17) through the wilderness, the period of the judges, King Saul, and King David. From David, Paul makes the connection with Jesus. "Of this man's offspring God has brought to Israel a Savior, Jesus, as he promised" (v. 23). Then Paul refers to the words of John the Baptist and brings the story to a point with a reference to salvation: "Brothers, sons of the family of Abraham, and those among you who fear God, to us has been sent the message of *this salvation*" (v. 26).

---

[8]Ibid., 132–133.

[9]Ibid., 116. What Wright wants to stress is that when Paul walked into Thessalonica or Corinth his announcement was not, "You can be justified by faith." He announced Jesus as the Lord and his death and resurrection. But can we separate this announcement from justification in this way? Is the gospel only the first things we say, or is it also the explanation of why these things are good news? And in that explanation, from culture to culture, do we not have to help people understand their situation in terms that they may not at first understand? And when they trust in Jesus, do we not need to give them the truth of what they must trust him *for*? And is not God's not counting sins against them (2 Cor. 5:19) but rather reckoning righteousness to them apart from works (Rom. 4:6) part of what they trust Jesus for?

What is this salvation that Jesus has brought and Paul is announcing? Before telling them exactly what he is offering them as "good news," he tells them how God is bringing it about. He explains that Jesus was crucified, and that those who did it unwittingly fulfilled the word of the prophets (vv. 27–29). And he explains that God raised Jesus from the dead in accord with Psalm 2, Isaiah 55, and Psalm 16 (vv. 30–37). Paul says that all of this was the way "the gospel" was coming to them: "We bring you *the good news* [ἡμεῖς ὑμᾶς εὐαγγελιζόμεθα] that what God promised to the fathers, this he has fulfilled to us their children by raising Jesus" (vv. 32–33).

Then, when all the historical foundation has been laid, Paul announces the actual content of what makes this history, climaxing in Jesus' death and resurrection, "good news." The gospel, he says, has exactly to do with personal salvation, eternal life, and justification. "Let it be known to you therefore, brothers, that through this man forgiveness of sins is proclaimed to you, and by him everyone who believes is justified [δικαιωθῆναι] from everything from which you could not be justified [δικαιοῦται] by the law of Moses" (Acts 13:38–39, author's translation). When most of the Jewish people of the city spurned this message of justification, Paul said that in doing so they judged themselves "unworthy of eternal life." "Paul and Barnabas spoke out boldly, saying, 'It was necessary that the word of God be spoken first to you. Since you thrust it aside and judge yourselves unworthy of *eternal life*, behold, we are turning to the Gentiles'" (v. 46).

The next verse says that this very message of salvation—the one that offered forgiveness, justification, and eternal life to "everyone who believes"—would now be proclaimed to the Gentiles in accord with Isaiah 49:6. "We are turning to the Gentiles. For so the Lord has commanded us, saying, 'I have made you a light for the Gentiles, that you may bring *salvation* to the ends of the earth'" (Acts 13:46–47).

However one understands the *meaning* of "justification" in Acts 13:38–39, the *fact* of justification language is clear.[10] As far as I can

---

[10]Luke's use of δικαιόω (Luke 7:29, 35; 10:29; 16:15; 18:14; Acts 13:38–39) coheres naturally with Paul's use and suggests the meaning "consider or reckon someone to be just or righteous." My assistant David Mathis put this well: "Acts 13:38–39 falls in line with this usage. The parallel between 'in Jesus' and 'in Moses' law' is important to see. *In Jesus*, all those who believe are *considered* (or *counted*) to be righteous from all those demands by which *in Moses' law* they were not previously able to be considered righteous. In Moses' law, they were not able to be *considered* righteous because they were not righteous and Moses' law did not provide the righteousness for them. But in Jesus,

see, it is located precisely where Wright says it does not occur—as the climactic expression of the gospel to both Jews and then Gentiles, offering them forgiveness of sins, a right standing with God, and, in that way, eternal life. Even though there are different contextualization challenges in making "justification" understandable to Jews and Gentiles, what Acts makes plain is that the same "salvation" that Paul offers to the Jews is offered to the Gentiles.

For example, again, in Acts 28, Paul speaks to Jews from morning till evening "testifying to the kingdom of God and trying to convince them about Jesus both from the Law of Moses and from the Prophets" (v. 23). When they reject the message, Paul says, "Therefore let it be known to you that *this salvation of God* has been sent to the Gentiles; they will listen" (v. 28). There is good reason to believe that "this salvation" refers to the same "salvation" of Acts 13:23, 26, 47. It is the salvation of personal eternal life: "As many as were appointed to eternal life believed" (Acts 13:48). And this eternal life was promised through faith that embraced the forgiveness and justification that God offered through Jesus Christ.

Therefore, I find Wright's claim that "the doctrine of justification by faith is not what Paul means by 'the gospel'" to be misleading. And his claim that justification is not what comes to Paul's mind when he addresses the question of entering a "living and saving relationship with the living and saving God" does not square with Acts 13:38–48.

BELIEVE ON JESUS, NOT THE DOCTRINE OF JUSTIFICATION?

Perhaps Wright would clarify his meaning with the words, "We are not justified by faith by believing in justification by faith. We are justified by faith by believing in the gospel itself—in other words, that Jesus is Lord and that God raised him from the dead."[11] In *this sense*, he would say that the message of justification is not the gospel, and not a message about how we get saved.

But there is a misleading ambiguity in Wright's statement that we are saved not by believing in justification by faith but by believing in Jesus' death and resurrection. The ambiguity is that it leaves

---

while they are still unrighteous, they are able to be *considered* righteous because a righteousness has been provided for them, namely, Jesus' own righteousness."
[11]Wright, "New Perspectives on Paul," 261.

undefined what we believe in Jesus' death and resurrection *for*. It is
not saving faith to believe in Jesus merely for prosperity or health or a
better marriage. In Wright's passion to liberate the gospel from mere
individualism and to make it historical and global, he leaves it vague
for individual sinners.

The summons "Believe the gospel of Jesus' death and resurrection" has no content that is yet clearly *good news*. Not until the gospel
preacher tells the listener what Jesus offers him personally and freely
does this proclamation have the quality of good news. My point here
has simply been that from Acts 13:39 it is evident that one way Paul
preached the gospel was by saying, "By him [namely, Jesus] *everyone
who believes is justified* from everything from which you could not be
justified by the law of Moses." Of course, it is *Jesus* who saves, not the
doctrine. And so our faith rests decisively on Jesus. But the doctrine
tells us what sort of Jesus we are resting on and what we are resting
on him for. Without this, the word *Jesus* has no content that could be
good news.

THE LORDSHIP OF JESUS IS TERRIFYING, NOT GOOD NEWS

Coming at Wright's claims about the gospel from another angle, they
do not fit real life—neither Paul's nor ours. The announcement that
Jesus is the Messiah, the imperial Lord of the universe, is not good
news, but is an absolutely terrifying message to a sinner who has spent
all his life ignoring or blaspheming the God and Father of the Lord
Jesus Christ and is therefore guilty of treason and liable to execution.
Wright seems to overlook this when he deals with what happened in
the mind of Saul in his conversion on the Damascus road. He sums up
the change:

> Saul's vision on the road to Damascus thus equipped him with an
> entirely new perspective, though one which kept its roots firm and
> deep within his previous covenantal theology. Israel's destiny had been
> summed up and achieved in Jesus the Messiah. The Age to Come had
> been inaugurated. Saul himself was summoned to be its agent. He was
> to declare to the pagan world that YHWH, the God of Israel, was the
> one true God of the whole world, and that in Jesus of Nazareth he had

overcome evil and was creating a new world in which justice and peace should reign supreme.

Saul of Tarsus, in other words, had found a new vocation. It would demand all the energy, all the zeal, that he had devoted to his former way of life. He was now to be a herald of the king.[12]

This is not false, but by itself it is unrealistically intellectualistic. It is mainly conceptual and minimally experiential. No doubt Wright is aware of what Stephen Westerholm calls human beings' "massive, unremitting sense of answerability to their Maker."[13] But does he take it sufficiently into account? I do not think it would be wild speculation to suggest that when Saul, who had hated Jesus and his followers, fell to the ground under the absolute, sovereign authority of the irresistible brightness of the living Jesus, his first thoughts would not be about his concepts, but about his survival. His first thoughts would not be about a new worldview and a new vocation, but whether he would at that moment be destroyed. What astonished Saul to the end of his days was first and foremost that a persecutor of the church should receive *mercy* instead of being cast into outer darkness.

> *The saying is trustworthy and deserving of full acceptance, that Christ Jesus came into the world to save sinners, of whom I am the foremost. But I received mercy for this reason, that in me, as the foremost, Jesus Christ might display his perfect patience as an example to those who were to believe in him for eternal life. (1 Tim. 1:15–16; cf. 1 Cor. 15:9; Gal. 1:13; Phil. 3:6)*

ESCAPE FROM WRATH IS NOT A SUBPLOT OF THE GOSPEL

It is not sixteenth-century or twenty-first-century anachronistic psychologizing to say that *the good news* for Paul was, *first,* that a persecutor of Jesus could be given a right standing before God through faith. The good news was *not* that Jesus died and was raised—that was emphatically *bad* news at this moment! What turned that bad news of death and resurrection into good news was the teaching—the

---

[12]*What Saint Paul Really Said,* 37.
[13]Stephen Westerholm, "The 'New Perspective' at Twenty-Five," in *Justification and Variegated Nomism,* Vol. II: *The Paradoxes of Paul,* ed. D. A. Carson et al. (Grand Rapids, MI: Baker Academic, 2004), 38.

doctrine—that by faith alone this life and death of Jesus could be the ground of the justification of the ungodly, not condemnation. And this good news came *before* Paul ever thought through his new worldview with Jesus as the King and himself as his ambassador. That would come. But to treat the personal reality of Paul's own immediate and inescapable need under God's wrath as a secondary subplot to the global concerns of the gospel is to miss both the right ordering of Paul's message and what makes it relevant to every generation.

That God had not destined him for wrath but to obtain salvation through Jesus (1 Thess. 5:9) was the first and foundational wonder for Paul. It became increasingly real with every breath he took after the blazing glory, in his blindness, on the way to Damascus. The personal realities of knowing oneself loved, forgiven, and justified are not subordinate to the global wonders of the universal lordship of Jesus. Without these personal realities being known and received that lordship is terrifying.

NO GOOD NEWS TILL I HEAR THE TERMS OF THE AMNESTY

I rejoice with N. T. Wright in the cosmic scope of what the gospel has achieved. I am not eager to marginalize the hope "that the creation itself will be set free from its bondage to corruption and obtain the freedom of the glory of the children of God" (Rom. 8:21). That the material creation followed us into the Fall with chaos and corruption and futility and will follow us into redemption with glory is not a marginal truth. As I write these words, I have just delivered a message at the Gospel Coalition entitled "The Triumph of the Gospel in the New Heavens and the New Earth."[14] The renewal of creation to a glory far beyond the first paradise (1 Cor. 15:49–50), where believers in Jesus will magnify him in our new spiritual bodies forever, is the apex of our gospel hope.[15]

For the sake of these great realities, Wright wants to keep the

---

[14]You can read or listen to this message at http://www.desiringGod.org/ResourceLibrary/ ConferenceMessages/ByDate/2177_The_Triumph_of_the_Gospel_in_the_New_Heavens_and_the_ New_Earth/ (accessed 6–2–07).

[15]This is not a token concession on my part, but a deeply held conviction unfolded in my own preaching on repeated occasions. For my own exultation in the cosmic redemption of Christ and our part in it, see my sermons at www.desiringGod.org dated 8-17-80; 5-25-86; 8-8-93; 4-28-02; 5-5-02; 4-1-07; 4-8-07.

gospel from being a message for "how to get saved," and he wants to
keep the gospel distinct from the doctrine of justification by faith alone.
This is puzzling and seems to amount to keeping the gospel separate
from the very things that will make the lordship of Jesus good news
for sinners.

Why should a guilty sinner who has committed treason against
Jesus consider it good news when he hears the announcement that
this Jesus has been raised from the dead with absolute sovereign
rights over all human beings? If Wright answers, "Because the
narration of the events of the cross and resurrection are included
in the heralding of the King," the sinner will say, "What good is
that for me? How can that help me? Why does that provide hope
for me or any sinner?" If the gospel has no answer for this sinner,
the mere facts of the death and resurrection of Jesus are *not* good
news. But if the gospel has an answer, it would have to be a message
about how the rebel against God can *be saved*—indeed, how he can
be right with God and become part of the covenant people. I do
not think Wright needs to marginalize these essential and glorious
aspects of the gospel in order to strengthen his case that the gospel
has larger global implications.

The closest Paul comes to a definition of his gospel seems to be
1 Corinthians 15:1–3:

> Now I would remind you, brothers, of the gospel I preached to you,
> which you received, in which you stand, and by which you are being
> saved, if you hold fast to the word I preached to you—unless you
> believed in vain. For I delivered to you as of first importance what
> I also received: that Christ died for our sins in accordance with the
> Scriptures.

Here Paul explicitly says two things: We are "saved" through the
gospel (δι' οὗ καὶ σῴζεσθε), and the gospel is the message that Christ
died *"for our sins."* It is precisely the personal "for our sins" that
makes the heralding of the historic facts good news. And Paul is eager
to make explicit that this "for our sins" is good news because by it we
are "saved." This is at the heart of what makes the gospel *gospel*, and
not just an effect of the gospel.

JESUS' LORDSHIP IS GOOD NEWS WHEN
CONNECTED TO JUSTIFICATION

Wright wants to maintain that when Paul announces the gospel, the teaching on justification does not spring to Paul's lips or pen. When he approached people with "questions about how human beings come into a living and saving relationship with the living and saving God,"[16] he did not answer with the doctrine of justification. Without at all insisting that Paul always announced the truth of justification in every gospel message, I would still want to insist from Paul's own words that his announcement of the death and resurrection and lordship of Jesus became good news in Paul's preaching precisely because in some way he communicated that believing in this Christ brought about justification.

For example, notice how Romans 10:9 relates to Romans 10:10. It is true that "if you confess with your mouth that *Jesus is Lord* and believe in your heart that *God raised him from the dead*, you will be saved" (v. 9). Wright wants to stress the fact that when one believes the gospel, *this* is precisely what one believes—that Jesus is Lord and that God raised him from the dead. Yes. The announcement of Jesus' resurrection and lordship is good news. And we must believe it. But it can only be heard as good news if we give the guilty rebel the *promise* that believing this will save him and then give him some *reason* to hope that the risen King will not execute him for his treason. The end of verse 9 gives that promise: Believe this and "you will be saved." And the next verse gives the reason for this hope.

Verse 10 says, "For with the heart one believes and is justified [καρδίᾳ γὰρ πιστεύεται εἰς δικαιοσύνην], and with the mouth one confesses and is saved [στόματι δὲ ὁμολογεῖται εἰς σωτηρίαν]." Therefore, take heart, O rebel, "Everyone who calls on the name of the Lord will be saved" (v. 13). Does not the way verse 10 grounds verse 9 show that in Paul's mind the proclamation of the facts of Christ's death and resurrection and lordship become good news when some explanation is given about *how* they make us righteous before God rather than guilty? It is not just the *existence* of the truth of justification, but the *proclamation* of it that is a crucial part of the gospel. Therefore, it is confusing when Wright continues to say that the gospel, as Paul

---

[16]Wright, *What Saint Paul Really Said*, 116.

conceived it and announced it, is not a message about how to get saved and how to be justified.

In the next chapter we turn to wrestle with what happens in the initial divine act of justification and how it relates to the effectual call of God.

CHAPTER SIX

JUSTIFICATION AND THE GOSPEL: DOES JUSTIFICATION DETERMINE OUR STANDING WITH GOD?

A DEEPER REASON WHY JUSTIFICATION IS KEPT SEPARATE FROM THE GOSPEL

As we continue to wrestle with why Wright wants to emphasize that justification is not the gospel, it seems that something deeper is going on. Wright resists making justification part of the gospel for more reasons than simply his desire to highlight the global scope of the gospel.[1] What makes him say things like, "I must stress again that the doctrine of justification by faith is not what Paul means by 'the gospel'"?[2]

One answer seems to be that, in his understanding, justification is not part of God's work in conversion or the divine action whereby a person becomes a part of the covenant family. Rather, justification is a declaration that a person *has been* converted and is now, because of faith and God's effectual calling, in the covenant family. "'Justification' is not about 'how I get saved' but 'how I am declared to be a member of God's people.'"[3] The *gospel*—the announcement of Jesus' universal lordship to all people—is very much the means through which "God works by his Spirit upon their hearts"[4] to change them so that they become Christians. But justification is not part of that gospel or that

---

[1] Again, I rejoice with Wright in the cosmic proportions of God's redeeming work in Christ. That is not what I am criticizing. See footnotes 14 and 15 in chapter 5.
[2] Wright, *What Saint Paul Really Said*, 132.
[3] Wright, *Paul in Fresh Perspective*, 122.
[4] Wright, *What Saint Paul Really Said*, 116.

divine action by which a person becomes a Christian. For Wright, the nature of justification is such that it is not part of becoming a Christian. It is the declaration that one *has become* a Christian—a covenant member.

> Paul's conception of how people are drawn into salvation starts with the preaching of the gospel, continues with the work of the Spirit in and through that preaching, and the effect of the Spirit's work on the hearts of the hearers, and concludes with the coming to birth of faith, and entry into the family through baptism. 'No one can say "Jesus is Lord" except by the Holy Spirit' (1 Corinthians 12:3). But when that confession is made, God declares that this person, who perhaps to their own surprise believes the gospel, is thereby marked out as being within the true covenant family. *Justification is not how someone becomes a Christian. It is the declaration that they have become a Christian.*[5]

> [Justification] was not so much about 'getting in', or indeed about 'staying in', as about 'how you could tell who was in'. In standard Christian theological language, it wasn't so much about soteriology as about ecclesiology; not so much about salvation as about the church.[6]

The point is that the *word* 'justification' does not itself *denote* the process whereby, or the event in which, a person is brought by grace from unbelief, idolatry and sin into faith, true worship and renewal of life. Paul, clearly and unambiguously, uses a different word for that, the word 'call'. The word 'justification', despite centuries of Christian misuse, is used by Paul to denote that which happens immediately after the 'call':[7] 'those God called, he also justified' (Romans 8:30). In other words, those who hear the gospel and respond to it in faith are then declared by God to be his people, his elect, 'the circumcision', 'the Jews', 'the Israel of God'. They are given the status *dikaios*, 'righteous', 'within the covenant'.[8]

---

[5]Ibid., 125. Emphasis added.
[6]Ibid., 119.
[7]I am not aware of any teacher in the church who has reversed the order of *called* and *justified* in Romans 8:30. This part of Wright's analysis is not controversial. Of course, justification (immediately) follows God's effectual grace in his call, which awakens the faith through which we are justified. The misuse of justification that Wright opposes is an oversimplified equation of justification and conversion. Yes, these are not synonymous, and Wright's explanation of the "call" of God in awakening faith is essential to conversion (1 Cor. 1:24). But it does not follow that justification, as God's action in response to faith, is not also an essential part of conversion and an essential act of God in making someone part of his covenant family.
[8]Wright, *Paul in Fresh Perspective*, 121–122.

Keep in mind that the sequence Wright is describing here is made up of events that are so close together they are *temporally* indistinguishable. Wright calls this "Paul's own '*ordo salutis* [order of salvation].'"[9] God's "call" happens effectually; faith is *instantaneously* awakened because of that call. There is no lapse of time between God's call and our justifying faith. That's the nature of the call. When it exists, it has the immediate effect of awakening faith. Then, as Wright says, justification "happens *immediately* after the call." "God *at once* makes" this declaration.

This makes all the more remarkable Wright's zeal to remove justification from the event of becoming a Christian: "*Justification is not how someone becomes a Christian.*" What is driving this peculiar vigilance to make such a fine distinction between the temporally and causally inseparable events of divine calling/faith/justification? On many sweeping points, Wright is not so vigilant about making such fine distinctions. Something unusual seems to be at stake here.

DOES JUSTIFICATION ADD NOTHING TO THE CALL OF GOD?

The actual redeeming work of God in taking sinners from idolatry and sin into the position of fellowship with God and into membership in his covenant people is, first, the work of Christ on the cross, and then the work of the Spirit in giving birth to faith. This faith-awakening work, which is a kind of resurrection from the dead (Eph. 2:5), Paul designates as God's "call." It is not the *general* call that goes out from a pulpit or radio program and summons everyone to faith. Rather, it is the *effectual* call that accomplishes what it commands (1 Cor. 1:9, 24; 7:20, 24; Rom. 8:28, 30).

Hence, Paul writes to the Corinthians, "We preach Christ crucified, a stumbling block to Jews and folly to Gentiles, but to those who are *called*, both Jews and Greeks, Christ the power of God and the wisdom of God" (1 Cor. 1:23–24). God's call enables us to see and embrace the cross as the power and wisdom of God. That is, it awakens faith.

Wright's point is that when this call happens—when it awakens spiritual life and faith—we are, by that act, "in," that is, in the fam-

---

[9]Wright, "The Shape of Justification."

ily of God. Justification has nothing more to contribute to our being converted or becoming a Christian or being in the covenant family. God's act of justification is therefore what Wright calls a "second-order doctrine." Its design for this age is to give *assurance*, not salvation. "Justification by faith itself is a *second-order doctrine*: to believe it is both to have *assurance* (believing that one will be vindicated on the last day) and to know that one belongs in the single family of God."[10]

In other words, when the gospel is preached, it is not the doctrine of justification that is preached but the death and resurrection and lordship of Christ over the world. The Holy Spirit uses this news to awaken faith in the heart. This is God's divine call through the gospel. By this call and faith, we are made partakers of Christ's victory and become part of God's family. Then the doctrine of justification comes in and declares to us what has happened to us. It thus gives assurance—but does not save, or convert, or make us part of God's family.

> Justification, for Paul, is not (in Sanders's terminology) how one "gets in" to God's people but about God's declaration that someone *is* in. In other words, it is all about assurance—as we should have known from reading Romans. I have said it before: If we are thinking Paul's thoughts after him, we are not justified by faith by believing in justification by faith. We are justified by faith by believing in the gospel itself—in other words, that Jesus is Lord and that God raised him from the dead. If, in addition, we believe in justification by faith itself, we believe that—amazingly, considering what God knows about us—we are now and forever part of the family to whose every member God says what he said to Jesus at his baptism: you are my beloved child, with you I am well pleased.[11]

In other words, the divine act of justification is not part of what God does in putting us in right standing with himself but is the declaration that we are in that position. Thus, it is not part of the gospel proclamation nor of the event of conversion. I have argued above that justification is more than this.[12] I think that Simon Gathercole is correct on this point:

---

[10]Wright, "The Shape of Justification."
[11]Wright, "New Perspectives on Paul," 261.
[12]See chapter 2, 28-31 above.

Tom Wright's definition of justification as being "reckoned to be in the covenant with God" seems too minimal. To cite a longer definition [of justification by Wright]:

> Justification, to offer a fuller statement, is the recognition and declaration by God that those who are thus called and believing are in fact his people, the single family promised to Abraham, that as the new covenant people their sins are forgiven, and that since they have already died and been raised with the Messiah they are assured of final bodily resurrection at the last.[13]

This may not sound like a minimalistic definition of justification. We have seen above, however, that God's act of justification is not one of *recognition* but is, rather, closer to *creation*. It is God's *determination* of our new identity rather than a recognition of it.[14]

Wright rejects this view. In his insistence that the divine act of justification is not conversion and not part of the event by which we move from alienation to reconciliation and not part of the change from being foreigners to being part of God's forgiven people, he says, "The word *dikaioō* is, after all, a declarative word, declaring that something is the case, rather than a word for making something happen or changing the way something is."[15]

IN JUSTIFICATION GOD ACTUALLY PUTS US RIGHT WITH HIMSELF

If Wright only meant that justification is not part of conversion in the sense that the inner workings of the human heart are not what justification is, there would be no disagreement at this point. Agreed—justification does not consist in the changes of the human heart in conversion. But it *is* the change that takes place in the relationship between a sinner and God at the moment of faith. Wright agrees that "the *word* 'justification' . . . is used by Paul to denote that which happens immediately after the 'call,'"[16] but he denies that this "happening" effects our right standing with God. It only declares that this right standing has come about.

---

[13]N. T. Wright, "The Letter to the Galatians: Exegesis and Theology," in *Between Two Horizons: Spanning New Testament Studies and Systematic Theology*, ed. J. B. Green and M. Turner (Grand Rapids, MI: Eerdmans, 2000), 235.
[14]Simon Gathercole, "The Doctrine of Justification in Paul and Beyond," 229. See above, chapter 2, 28-31.
[15]Wright, "New Perspectives on Paul," 258.
[16]Wright, *Paul in Fresh Perspective*, 121-122.

However, in line with what Gathercole says above, Paul speaks of the *effect* of justification: "Therefore, since we have been justified by faith, we have peace with God" (Rom. 5:1). This most naturally means that what God did in the act of justifying us at the moment of faith was *effective* in giving us peace with God. God's act of justification does not merely *inform us* that we have peace with God; it *establishes* peace with God. The divine act of justification is constitutive of the event by which we obtain peace with God.[17]

Does Wright want us to think that because the call of God effectively awakens faith and unites us to Christ, there can be no other aspects to the work of God in conversion that are essential to the transition from alienated to reconciled? Nothing Paul says would require such a position. Therefore, we may conclude that justification should not be called a "second-order doctrine," only giving assurance but not part of the event by which we enter God's favor. Calling/faith/justification are parts of one event that brings us from God's enmity to his acceptance. There is a logical sequence, but to say that justification only comes *after* we are "in" would misrepresent Paul's treatment of justification as essential to the act of actually putting us in the right with God.

IS JUSTIFICATION CENTRAL POLEMICALLY BUT NOT EVANGELISTICALLY?

Wright can speak of the doctrine of justification in more *primary* terms than he does above. He has written, for example:

> I . . . discover that my call, my Reformational call, to be a faithful reader and interpreter of scripture impels me to take seriously the fact, to which many writers in the last two hundred years have called attention, that whenever Paul is talking about justification by faith he is also talking about the coming together of Jews and Gentiles into the single people of God. I did not make this up; it is there in the God-given texts. I do not draw from this observation the conclusion that some have done

---

[17] I confess I do not know how to put what Wright said above ("New Perspectives on Paul," 258) together with what he says in his commentary on *The Letter to the Romans*, 515: "Justification results in peace with God, in access to God's loving favor." On the one hand, it seemed that Wright was arguing that God's "call" is a clear act of God's "loving favor" and that therefore we were already "in" God's family of favor at the event of calling/faith, which was then followed by the assurance-giving declaration of acceptance called *justification*. But on the other hand, it sounds like "justification *results in* . . . access to God's loving favor" (emphasis added). The former sounds like justification does not make anything happen but only declares, and the latter sounds like justification makes something happen.

(I think particularly of Wrede and Schweitzer), namely that justification is itself a *mere secondary* doctrine, called upon for particular polemical purposes but not at the very centre of Paul's thought. On the contrary: since the creation, through the preaching of the gospel of Jesus Christ, of this single multi-ethnic family, the family God promised to Abraham, the family justified, declared to be in the right, declared to be God's people, on the basis of faith alone, the family whose sins have been forgiven through the death of the Messiah in their place and on their behalf, the family who constitute the first-fruits of the new creation that began with the bodily resurrection of Jesus—since the creation of this family was the aim and goal of all Paul's work, and since this work was by its very nature polemical, granted the deeply suspicious pagan world on the one hand and the deeply Law-based Jewish world on the other, it was natural and inevitable that Paul's apostolic work would itself involve polemical exposition of the results of the gospel, and that justification by faith, as itself *a key polemical doctrine*, would find itself *at the centre* when he did so.[18]

Thus, when Wright calls justification a "second-order doctrine," he does not mean a "mere secondary doctrine" or one that is not of *central* concern. It is a "key polemical doctrine"—which means, it seems, that the doctrine is key as a doctrine of *assurance* in a polemical situation, but still not part of the first-order gospel proclamation about how to be saved. Accordingly, Wright says:

The doctrine of "justification by faith" . . . was not the message [Paul] would announce on the street to the puzzled pagans (say) of Corinth; it was not the main thrust of his evangelistic message. It was the thing his converts most needed to know in order to be *assured* that they really were part of God's people.[19]

'Justification' is the declaration which God at once makes, that all who share this faith belong to Christ, to his sin-forgiven family . . . and *are assured* of final glorification.[20]

---

[18]Wright, "Paul in Different Perspectives: Lecture 1."
[19]Wright, *What Saint Paul Really Said*, 94. My guess is that Paul would not have drawn the line Wright does between what you say to a pagan to win him to faith and what you say to him afterwards to assure him that his faith has put him in a safe position. It is the hope of being in a safe position before God that a person needs to hear about in order to hear the gospel as good news. "If you believe, then such and such *will* be true of you" is the way the gospel speaks to unbelievers. See chapter 5 above (pp. 47–49) for an example of Paul's preaching that does not fit with Wright's statement here.
[20]Wright, "The Shape of Justification."

IS FUTURE JUSTIFICATION A SAVING ACT AND NOT JUST A DECLARATION?

This limitation of justification to the declaration of who is in the covenant is made harder to grasp when we recall that, for Wright, God's *present* act of justification is an "anticipation" of his *future* and final act of justification that is *more* than declarative.

It seems that, even though Wright says *dikaioō* is "a declarative word, declaring that something is the case, rather than a word for making something happen or changing the way something is,"[21] nevertheless, he wants to clarify that God's *future* act of justification is more than a declaration "that something is the case." It is an event that accomplishes final deliverance. For example, he says:

> This declaration, this vindication, occurs twice. It occurs in the future, as we have seen, on the basis of the entire life a person has led in the power of the Spirit—that is, it occurs on the basis of "works" in Paul's redefined sense. And near the heart of Paul's theology, it occurs in the present as *an anticipation of that future verdict*, when someone, responding in believing obedience to the call of the gospel, believes that Jesus is Lord and that God raised him from the dead. . . . And . . . *the final declaration will consist not in words so much as in an event, namely, the resurrection of the person concerned into a glorious body like that of the risen Jesus*. . . .[22]

This last sentence emphasizes the fact that the final eschatological justification is *not* only a declaration of what is the case but is an event that completes the salvation of the believer.[23] Without this event, there would be no final salvation.

> Evildoers (i.e. the Gentiles, and renegade Jews) would finally be judged and punished; God's faithful people (i.e. Israel, or at least the true Israelites) would be vindicated. Their redemption, which would take the physical and concrete form of political liberation . . . and ultimately of resurrection itself, would be *seen as* the

---

[21]Wright, "New Perspectives on Paul," 258.

[22]Ibid., 260. Last emphasis added.

[23]Technically, Wright wants to preserve the parallel declaratory nature of first and final acts of justification. But when he says that the second declaration is a declaration by means of an event, especially the resurrection, he introduces a dimension of justification that is not merely declaratory but profoundly—what shall we say—metaphysical, bodily, saving, consummative.

great law-court showdown, the great victory before the great judge.[24]

Thus, according to Wright, justification in that day will not be an act of public confirmation of a past, once-for-all, imputed righteousness received in this life at the first act of faith (as I will maintain below). Rather, the final justification will be something more than confirmation. "Justification in the *present* . . . anticipates the future verdict."[25] But that future verdict is *effective*. It is an *act* of salvation, not just an *announcement* or confirmation.

THE GREAT SHOWDOWN

Final justification, he says, is a great showdown between God and evil. Our eternal destiny is at stake. If God finds in our favor, we are not condemned. If he does not, we are. This decision of God's final law-court is what the present declaration of justification was pointing to. Justification in the *present* is not an act that puts us into the covenant people. It declares that we *are* in. "Justification, for Paul, is not . . . how one 'gets in' to God's people but about God's declaration that someone *is* in."[26] But justification *in the future* is God's great showdown with evil and a great *act* of salvation. It does determine who, finally, is in. And the crucial question for the final meaning of justification is: *What will be the final ground of our acceptance in the presence of God?* That is what we turn to in the next chapter.

The upshot of the last two chapters is that Wright's claim that "the doctrine of justification by faith is not what Paul means by 'the gospel'"[27] and his claim that "justification is not how someone becomes a Christian"[28] are misleading. The kind of gospel preaching that will flow from Wright's spring will probably have global scope to it but will not deal personally with the human heart of sin with clear declarations of *how* Christ dealt with sin and *how* the fearful heart can find rest in the gospel of grace—the active grace that, while not exhausted by God's act of justification, does include it.

---

[24]Wright, *What Saint Paul Really Says*, 33–34.
[25]Wright, "The Shape of Justification."
[26]Wright, "New Perspectives on Paul," 261.
[27]Wright, *What Saint Paul Really Said*, 132.
[28]Ibid., 125.

CHAPTER SEVEN

THE PLACE OF OUR WORKS
IN JUSTIFICATION

WITH THE UNDERSTANDING OF Wright's view of justification that we have seen so far, we may now ask: What is the *basis* or *ground* of justification—in the present and at the end? We should be alert immediately that the word *basis* is going to be a problem. Wright's use of it is not precise, as we will see. We will come to that difficulty directly. But we may venture a preliminary answer to the question and then bring in the needed nuances as we go along. Wright's answer would be something like this: In the future at the final court scene, God the Judge will find in our favor *on the basis of the works* we have done—the life we have lived—and in the present he anticipates that verdict and declares it to be already true *on the basis of our faith*[1] *in Jesus.*

> The first mention of justification in Romans is a mention of justification by *works*—apparently with Paul's approval (2:13: 'It is not the hearers of the law who will be righteous before God, but the doers of the law who will be justified'). The right way to understand this, I believe, is to see that Paul is talking about the *final* justification. . . . The point is: who will be vindicated, resurrected, shown to be the covenant people, on that last day? Paul's answer, with which many non-Christian Jews would have agreed, is that those who will be vindicated on the last day are those in whose hearts and lives God will have written his law, his Torah. As Paul will make clear later on in the letter, this process can-

---

[1] In his work Wright makes affirmations of justification *in the present* by faith alone. But I do not find them to be perspicuous. The reason is that Wright sometimes speaks of faith as "faithfulness" or sometimes as "obedience." The result is that one feels unsure that Wright means by "faith alone" what is ordinarily meant. We will deal with this below. See chapter 8, 130–131.

not be done by the Torah alone; God has now done in Christ and by the Spirit what the Torah wanted to do but could not do [alluding to Rom. 8:3–4].[2]

In other words, Paul believes that all men will face a final judgment (law-court) in which people will "be vindicated, resurrected, shown to be the covenant people"—that is, justified, *by works*. When he says "by works," he does not mean by legalism or by merit or by earning, but by the obedience of our lives that is produced by the Holy Spirit through faith. Wright sees Romans 8:3–4 as an explanation of Romans 2:13: It is "the doers of the law who will be justified." "The doers of the law" refer to Christians described in Romans 8:3–4.

For God has done what the law, weakened by the flesh, could not do. By sending his own Son in the likeness of sinful flesh and for sin, he condemned sin in the flesh, in order that the righteous requirement of the law might be fulfilled in us, who walk not according to the flesh but according to the Spirit.

ARE "THE DOERS OF THE LAW" CHRISTIANS?

According to Wright, "the doers of the law" are those who "walk by the Spirit" and thus fulfill the "righteous requirement of the law," which is possible because God condemned sin in the flesh of Jesus.[3] This means that justification, which happens with final and complete salvation in the future, and by way of anticipation in the present, will be based on the life of obedience that we live in the power of the Spirit.

The Spirit is the path by which Paul traces the route from *justification by faith in the present to justification, by the complete life lived, in the future.* You cannot understand justification by faith in Romans 3 and 4 unless you see it flanked by the long statement of judgment according to works in Romans 2.1–16 and the spectacular scene in Romans 8 which explains why there is indeed 'no condemnation for those who are in the Messiah, Jesus'.[4]

[2]Wright, *What Saint Paul Really Said*, 126–127.
[3]Wright takes "the righteous requirement of the law" (τὸ δικαίωμα τοῦ νόμου) in Romans 8:4 to refer to God's righteous decree, "Do this and you will live." "The main sentence with which Paul then explains how God has done what the law could not do must then be understood as follows: God condemned sin in the flesh of Jesus, so that the life the law offered could rightly be given to those led by the Spirit." Wright, *The Letter to the Romans*, 577–578.
[4]Wright, *Paul in Fresh Perspective*, 148. Emphasis added.

Obviously Romans 2:13 is enormously significant for Wright's understanding of justification. He returns to it again and again as a programmatically decisive word from Paul. We will do well then to pay close attention to the context and what Paul is saying.

THE CONTEXT OF ROMANS 2:13

In Romans 2:1–5, Paul pointed out that the people in his day with high moral standards, especially many of his own kinsmen (the Jews), were guilty of hypocrisy. They point the finger at the immoral Gentiles (mentioned in Rom. 1:18ff.), but in doing so, Paul says, they indict themselves, because they do the same kind of things.

Then he explains in verses 6–10 that the judgment on Jew and Gentile is going to be "according to . . . works" (κατὰ τὰ ἔργα αὐτου), not according to their ethnic or religious advantages. Jews and Gentiles will receive or not receive eternal life on the same terms. Paul does not spell out how the deeds actually function in the final judgment. Theoretically, (1) the deeds could be the basis in a meritorious way; or (2) they could be the basis as Spirit-wrought fruits of faith; or (3) they might be, not the basis, but the evidence and confirmation of faith in Christ who cancels the debt of all sin; or, (4) extending that last possibility, they could also be the evidence and confirmation of faith in Christ as the one in whom we are counted righteous with his righteousness. In this text Paul does not settle which of these four possibilities is true. His point here is: Jews and Gentiles are equally subject to eternal life or wrath without respect to their ethnic distinctives.

In verse 11, Paul states the principle or the truth about God underlying this train of argument: "For there is no partiality with God" (NASB). This is why God will judge the Jews and the Gentiles not according to their appearance or their circumstances or their cultural or religious advantages, but according to something more intrinsic. This is something fundamental about God. He is impartial.

But there is an objection that has to be answered. So Paul takes another step in his argument. The objection goes like this: You say, Paul, that God is going to judge all people according to their deeds, and therefore impartially; but, in fact, God gave the law of Moses only to the Jews, and so they have access to what deeds are required of them, and the rest of the world doesn't. So how can you say that God is

impartial to judge according to deeds when he has told only one group
of people what deeds they must do?

The first part of Paul's answer is in verse 12: The reason we know
God is impartial is because "all who have sinned without the law [that
is, nations who don't have the Old Testament law of Moses] will also
perish without the law, and all who have sinned under the law [Jews
who have the law of Moses] will be judged by the law." We can see that
this is a direct response to an objection: They don't have equal access
to what they will be held accountable for! The point is that the law of
Moses will not be brought in to condemn those who sinned with no
access to the law of Moses. It will be used only to judge those who had
access to it.

When someone perishes who never heard of the law of Moses, it is
not because they never heard that law. Not hearing the law of Moses
will not condemn anyone. And hearing it will not save anyone. That's
what Paul says next in verse 13: "It is not the hearers of the law who are
righteous before God, but the doers of the law who will be justified." In
other words, having access to the moral law of Moses and hearing it is
not an advantage at the final judgment. At the judgment, the question
will not be: How much of the law did you *hear*? The question will be:
Did you *do* it?

THE GENTILES HAVE THE WORK OF
THE LAW WRITTEN ON THEIR HEARTS

Before I comment on the meaning of "it is . . . the doers of the law
who will be justified," let me finish tracing Paul's argument in this
paragraph. A new objection emerges immediately after what Paul said
in verse 13. Somebody is going to say, "How can anyone *do* what the
law requires if they don't have a copy of the law to read and follow?
Paul, you say that *doing* and not *hearing* is what counts, but still those
who have the law are at an advantage, because they know what they
have to do."

Verses 14–15 are Paul's answer to this objection. "When Gentiles,
who do not have the law, by nature do what the law requires, they are
a law to themselves, even though they do not have the law. They show
that the work of the law is written on their hearts, while their conscience also bears witness, and their conflicting thoughts accuse or even

excuse them." This is Paul's answer to the question: "How can God be impartial in judging according to our *deeds* if the Jews have a written record of the required deeds and the Gentiles don't?" His answer is that the Gentiles *do* have the law. The deeds required in the moral law of God ("work of the law," v. 15) are written on their hearts. Or, as verse 14 says, "They are a law to themselves." Then he says in verse 15b that the evidence for this is that the moral behavior of all kinds of people all over the world shows that they have a sense of many true, God-given, moral obligations, and their conscience confirms this with the conflicting self-defenses and self-accusations that it constantly brings up.

WHO ARE THE GENTILES WITH THE WORK OF THE LAW ON THEIR HEARTS?

Many today, including N. T. Wright,[5] understand the Gentiles in verses 14–15 who have the "work of the law . . . written on their hearts" to be Christian Gentiles who are experiencing the fulfillment of the new-covenant promise of Jeremiah 31:33. I find Tom Schreiner's careful analysis of the arguments on both sides of this issue compelling. He points out that the thought flows most naturally if the Gentiles in view are not Christians but pagans who are distant from any special revelation. That is why the main statement in verse 14, "They are a law to themselves," is so crucial here, and yet so out of place if the Gentiles are Christians. It would be very strange to say that believers are "a law to themselves."

Moreover, Paul does *not* say, with Jeremiah 31:33, that these Gentiles have "*the law*" written on their hearts." He says that "*the work* of the law [τὸ ἔργον τοῦ νόμου] is written on their hearts" (v. 15). This is not the wording of Jeremiah 31, but it fits well with the point that what the Gentile pagans have on their hearts is not the very law of Moses but rather an impulse to do the kind of "work" that the law requires.

Finally, Schreiner points out that the function of the conscience in verse 15 is described in a way that would seem strange if it referred to a believer who is a "doer of the law." "Their conscience also bears witness, and their conflicting thoughts accuse or even excuse them." Schreiner comments, "Any notion that this is saving obedience is ruled

[5]Wright, *The Letter to the Romans*, 441-442.

out by this clause, for the text emphasizes that 'accusing' thoughts
predominate. . . . Indeed, the words ἤ καὶ ("or even") that precede
ἀπολογουμένων ("defending") intimate that the defending thoughts are
relatively rare, or at least the exception rather than the rule. Therefore,
the doing of the law described in verse 14 should not be understood as
a consistent and regular observance of the law."[6]

PUTTING THE PIECES TOGETHER

So we may now put the whole train of thought before us, from verse
11 on. First, Paul says that "there is no partiality with God" (v. 11,
NASB). Then, he defends this in verse 12 by saying that God's judgment
will come to the world according to how they respond to the measure
of truth to which they have access. Then he explains (v. 13) that mere
hearing of the law is no advantage to the Jew at the judgment day, and
not hearing it is no disadvantage to the Gentile, because *doing* rather
than *hearing* is the issue. Then, he explains (vv. 14–15) that the law
really is available to those who have no access to the law of Moses,
because God has written what the law requires on the heart and given
all of us a conscience to awaken us to this moral knowledge in our
hearts.

Paul expressed these points earlier in Romans 1:32 ("They *know*
the ordinance of God, that those who practice such things are worthy
of death," NASB) and Romans 1:26 ("Women exchanged the natural
function for that which is unnatural," NASB) and Romans 1:21 ("They
knew God"). And the point of it all is to stress that every human being
is truly and justly guilty before God because everyone has access to the
truth but suppresses it (Rom. 1:18). None lives up to this truth, nor
even up to the demands of his own conscience. Nevertheless, all are
accountable to God and will be without excuse at the judgment day.
All Jews and all Gentiles are accountable to God and guilty before him
under the power of sin.

JUSTIFICATION BY WORKS?

Now we are in a better position to comment on Romans 2:13 where
Paul says, "It is not the hearers of the law who are righteous before

---

[6]Thomas Schreiner, *Romans*, Baker Exegetical Commentary on the New Testament (Grand
Rapids, MI: Baker, 1998), 124. The entire section dealing with the arguments pro and con is on
pp. 119–125.

God, but the doers of the law who will be justified." Again, as we saw
with verses 6–11, Paul does not say *how* being a "doer of the law"
functions in relation to being justified at the last day. At least the same
four possibilities that I mentioned above exist, plus one more: Doing
the law could be (1) the basis of justification in a meritorious way; or
(2) it could be the basis as Spirit-wrought fruits of faith; or (3) it could
be, not the basis, but the evidence and confirmation of faith in *another*
basis, namely, Christ who cancels the debt of all sin; or, extending that
last possibility beyond forgiveness, (4) it could also be the evidence and
confirmation of faith in Christ as the one in whom not only forgiveness
but also divine righteousness is counted as ours. Or (5) Paul could be
stating a principle that he affirms but that he believes never comes to
pass for sinful people. Thus, John Stott says, "This is a theoretical or
hypothetical statement, of course, since no human being has ever fully
obeyed the law (cf. 3:20)."[7]

What is *not* said in verse 13 is that people are justified "*by* works."
Paul does not use the phrase ἐξ ἔργων ("from works"), which I take to
be roughly what is usually meant by the English phrase "on the basis of
works," as opposed to the phrase "according to works" (κατὰ τὰ ἔργα
αὐτοῦ).[8] Paul is clear that "*by works of the law* no human being will

[7]John Stott, *Romans: God's Good News for the World* (Downers Grove, IL: InterVarsity Press,
1994), 86. Douglas Moo writes:
> The question arises here again (as in vv. 7 and 10): Who are those whom Paul views as
> vindicated in the judgment by their doing of the law? . . . As in vv. 7 and 10, therefore, we
> think it more likely that Paul is here simply setting forth the standard by which God's jus-
> tifying verdict will be rendered. This verse confirms and explains the reason for the Jews'
> condemnation in v. 12b; and this suggests that its purpose is not to show how people can
> be justified but to set forth the standard that must be met if a person is to be justified.
> As he does throughout this chapter, Paul presses typical Jewish teaching into the service
> of his "preparation for the gospel." Jews believed that "doing" the law, or perhaps the
> intent to do the law, would lead, for the Jew already in covenant relationship with God,
> to final salvation. Paul affirms the principle that doing the law can lead to salvation;
> but he denies (1) that anyone can so "do" the law; and (2) that Jews can depend on
> their covenant relationship to shield them from the consequences of this failure. (Moo,
> *Romans,* NICNT [Grand Rapids, MI: Eerdmans, 1996], 147-148.)

[8]Wherever the phrase ἐξ ἔργων is connected to justification in Paul, the point is that justification
does not happen this way. Rom. 3:20; 9:11, 32; 11:6; Gal. 2:16; 3:2, 5, 19; Eph. 2:9; Titus 3:5. In
Matthew 12:37 and James 2:21, 24–25, justification is said to happen "by your words" (ἐκ . . .
τῶν λόγων σου) or "by works" (ἐξ ἔργων). Other contextual factors incline me to take Jesus and
James to mean not that justification is "based on" our deeds the way our justification is "based on"
Christ as our righteousness, but rather that our deeds *confirm* our faith in Jesus so that he remains
the sole basis of our acceptance with God, in the sense that his death alone covers our sins and his
righteousness alone provides all the obedience that God requires of us *for God to be totally for
us*—the perfect righteousness implicitly required in the phrase, "God counts righteousness apart
from works" (Rom. 4:6). It is likely that Matthew and James are using the word δικαιόω differently
than Paul is (just as Matthew and Paul use καλέω differently, Matt. 22:14; Rom. 8:30). So, James
and Matthew may also be appropriating the phrase "from works" differently than Paul. While Paul
chooses to never employ that phrase in reference either to present justification or future judgment,

be justified in his sight, since through the law comes knowledge of sin" (Rom. 3:20).[9] Rather, he says, "We hold that one is justified *by faith apart from works of the law*" (Rom. 3:28). Does this mean that the statement "It is . . . the doers of the law who will be justified" (v. 13) *only* expresses a principle of *doing* over against *hearing* so as to remove the objection that the Gentiles don't have access to "hearing"?

Given the demands of the flow of the argument in Romans 2:6–16 which we saw above, I doubt that we can press this statement very far for the defense of justification by works. Paul makes a statement that *in this context* functions as a *principle* (*doing*, not *hearing*, will matter at the judgment), rather than a declaration about *how* that doing relates to justification—let alone whether the doing of Christ may supply what our doing lacks. The verse was not written to carry that much freight. However, the verse does raise the question that must be answered: How does the obedience of the Christian relate to his justification?

HOW I SEE WORKS RELATING TO JUSTIFICATION

Let me declare myself clearly here: I believe in the *necessity* of a transformed life of obedience to Jesus by the power of the Spirit through faith as a public evidence and confirmation of faith at the Last Day for all who will finally be saved. In other words, I believe it is *actually* true, not just hypothetically true, that God "will render to each one according to his works [τὰ ἔργα αὐτοῦ]: to those who by patience in well-doing seek for glory and honor and immortality, he will give eternal life" (Rom. 2:6–7). I take the phrase "according to" (κατὰ) in a sense different from "based on." I think the best way to bring together the various threads of Paul's teaching on justification by faith apart from works (Rom. 3:28; 4:4–6; 11:6; Eph. 2:8) is to treat the necessity of obedience not as any part of the basis of our justification, but strictly as the evidence and confirmation of our faith in Christ whose blood and righteousness is the sole basis of our justification. How this is the

---

James and Matthew, without differing from Paul conceptually, employ a phrase that Paul wouldn't to say something (conceptually) that Paul would. I am not saying that there are distinct and uniform usages of the two phrases ἐξ ἔργων and κατὰ τὰ ἔργα. The latter can carry the sense of "on the basis of" at times, though not always. Therefore, we must draw our conclusions concerning Paul's understanding of the function of works in relation to justification not merely from the phrases themselves, but from the wider teaching of the apostle as well.

[9] I think Douglas Moo is right that "'doers of the law' are no more and no less than those who 'do the works of the law'; and 'works of the law,' Paul claims, cannot justify (cf. 3:20, 28)." Moo, *Romans*, 147.

case, while justification is by faith alone apart from any basis in that very obedience, has been one of the main themes of my preaching and writing for the last thirty years.[10]

A CONSPIRACY OF SILENCE?

Wright thinks Reformed pastors and scholars do not pay enough attention to the relationship between justification and works. When he spoke at the 2003 Edinburgh Dogmatics Conference, he said that there seemed to be

> a massive conspiracy of silence about something that was quite clear for Paul (as indeed for Jesus). Paul, in company with mainstream second-Temple Judaism affirms that God's final judgment will be in accordance with the entirety of a life led—in accordance, in other words, with works. He says this clearly and unambiguously in Romans 14.10–12 and 2 Corinthians 5.10. He affirms it in that terrifying passage about church-builders in 1 Corinthians 3. But the main passage in question is of course Romans 2.1–16.[11]

Whether there was a conspiracy of silence in Edinburgh, there surely has not been one in the history of Reformed reflection on Scripture, or in the Reformed confessions. The thinking on this issue has been sustained, detailed, meticulously careful, and often profound. The fruit of that thinking and exegesis is found in the confessions.

The Augsburg Confession
The historic Lutheran Augsburg Confession was written by Philipp Melanchthon (1497–1560), sanctioned by Martin Luther, and presented by the German Protestants to Charles V in 1530. It describes the relationship between justifying faith and the subsequent life of obedience in the following terms:

---

[10]See most fully my extended treatment of this issue in *The Purifying Power of Living by Faith in Future Grace* (Sisters, OR: Multnomah, 1995). See also "The Pleasure of God in Personal Obedience and Public Justice," in John Piper, *The Pleasures of God* (Sisters, OR: Multnomah, 2000, orig. 1991), 233–257; "Fighting for Joy Like a Justified Sinner," in *When I Don't Desire God: How to Fight for Joy* (Wheaton, IL: Crossway Books, 2004), 71–94; *What Jesus Demands from the World* (Wheaton, IL: Crossway Books, 2006), especially 174–180, 242–248; "Letter to a Friend Concerning the So-Called Lordship Salvation," http://www.desiringgod.org/ResourceLibrary/Articles/ByDate/1990/1496_Letter_to_a_Friend_Concerning_the_SoCalled_Lordship_Salvation/.
[11]Wright, "New Perspectives on Paul," 253.

(IV) [The churches with common consent among us] teach that men cannot be justified before God by their own powers, merits, or works; but are justified freely for Christ's sake through faith, when they believe . . . (VI) Also they teach that this faith should bring forth good fruits, and that men ought to do the good works commanded of God, because it is God's will, and not on any confidence of meriting justification before God by their works.

Thus far, the Augsburg Confession simply says that justifying faith "*should* bring forth good fruits." But in Article XX it goes deeper in explaining this connection:

Because the Holy Spirit is received by faith, our hearts are now renewed, and so put on new affections, so that they are able to bring forth good works. For thus saith Ambrose: "Faith is the begetter of a good will and of good actions." . . . Hereby every man may see that this doctrine [of justification by faith alone] is not to be accused, as forbidding good works; but rather is much to be commended, because it showeth after what sort we must do good works. For without faith the nature of man can by no means perform the works of the First or Second Table. Without faith, it cannot call upon God, hope in God, bear the cross; but seeketh help from man, and trusteth in man's help. So it cometh to pass that all lusts and human counsels bear sway in the heart so long as faith and trust in God are absent.[12]

The doctrine of justification by faith "showeth after what sort [i.e., way] we must do good works." I take this to mean that the Augsburg Confession is not content to say that good works merely exist alongside justifying faith, but also arise from that faith. "Faith is the begetter of . . . good actions." The power of "lusts and human counsels" is broken where this faith is present.

A Swiss Confession

The First Helvetic Confession was composed by Swiss theologians (Heinrich Bullinger, Simon Grynaeus, Oswald Myconius, etc.) at Basel, Switzerland, in 1536. It represented the faith of all the cantons of Switzerland at that period of the Reformation. Article XIII is entitled "How the grace of Christ and his merit are imparted to us and what

---

[12]Quoted from Philip Schaff, ed., *The Creeds of Christendom* (Grand Rapids, MI: Baker, 1977, orig. 1877), 3:10–11, 24–25.

fruit comes from them." It reads, "We come to the great and high deeds of divine grace and the true sanctifying of the Holy Spirit not through our merit or powers, but through faith, which is a pure gift and favor of God." Then Article XIV explains the connection between this faith and works:

> This same faith is a certain, firm, yes, undoubting ground, and a grasping of all things that one hopes from God. From it love grows as a fruit, and, by this love, come all kinds of virtues and good works. And, although the pious and believing practice such fruit of faith, we do not ascribe their piety or their attained salvation to such works, but to the grace of God. This faith comforts itself with the mercy of God, and not its works, even though it performs innumerable good works. This faith is the true service which pleases God.[13]

Thus the Helvetic Confession affirms that love grows from faith and produces all virtues. Faith does not simply exist alongside the fruit of obedience, but itself "performs innumerable good works."

The Thirty-Nine Articles of the Church of England
The Thirty-Nine Articles of Religion of the Church of England was published as an expression of Anglican Reformed faith in 1571. Its teaching on justification and good works is refreshingly straightforward and clear:

> We are accounted righteous before God, only for the merit of our Lord and Saviour Jesus Christ by Faith, and not for our own works or deservings. Wherefore, that we are justified by Faith only, is a most wholesome Doctrine, and very full of comfort. . . . Albeit that Good Works, which are the fruits of Faith, and follow after Justification, cannot put away our sins, and endure the severity of God's judgment; yet are they pleasing and acceptable to God in Christ, and do spring out necessarily of a true and lively Faith; insomuch that by them a lively Faith may be as evidently known as a tree discerned by the fruit.[14]

A life of obedience "springs out necessarily" from a true and lively faith. Good works "are the fruits of Faith." Justifying faith is

---

[13]Quoted from ibid., 218, my own translation from the original German.
[14]Quoted from ibid., 494.

not merely alongside good works, but is also the agency employed by the grace of God to give rise to good works. Thus good works are the evidence of authentic faith.

The Westminster Confession of Faith

Perhaps the best known Confession of the Reformed faith is the Westminster Confession of Faith, published in England in 1647. Chapter XI of the Confession says:

> (1) Those whom God effectually calleth he also freely justifieth; not by infusing righteousness into them, but by pardoning their sins, and by accounting and accepting their persons as righteous: not for anything wrought in them, or done by them, but for Christ's sake alone . . . (2) Faith, thus receiving and resting on Christ and his righteousness, is the alone instrument of justification; *yet is it not alone in the person justified, but is ever accompanied with all other saving graces, and is not dead faith, but worketh by love.*[15]

Thus the Confession boldly declares that the faith that is the "alone instrument of justification" also "work[s] by love." It affirms, therefore, that justifying faith is also sanctifying faith. It "work[s] by love." The Confession makes explicit (by its footnotes) that the words "work[s] by love" are a reference to Galatians 5:6 ("For in Christ Jesus neither circumcision nor uncircumcision counts for anything, but only faith working through love"). It thus establishes a *necessary* connection between the faith that justifies and the obedient life of love. It says that justifying faith *"is ever accompanied with all other saving graces, and is not dead faith, but worketh by love."* The word *ever* implies that there can be no sustained life of the justified saint without also the outworking of grace in a life of love.[16]

This is why the Reformed tradition has been able to affirm those texts of Jesus and Paul and James and the writer to the Hebrews and Peter and John that make moral transformation (especially the fruit of

---

[15]Quoted from ibid., 626. Emphasis added.
[16]Robert L. Dabney puts it this way: "Since the same faith, if vital enough to embrace Christ, is also vital enough to 'work by love,' 'to purify our hearts.' This, then is the virtue of the free gospel, as a ministry of sanctification, that the very faith which embraces the gift becomes an *inevitable* and a divinely powerful principle of obedience" (emphasis added). Robert L. Dabney, "The Moral Effects of a Free Justification," in *Discussions: Evangelical and Theological* (London: Banner of Truth, 1967, orig. 1890), 1:96.

love) *necessary* for final salvation.[17] And yet, unlike N. T. Wright, they have been jealous to clearly distinguish works, on the one hand, as a *necessary evidence* of the faith that alone unites to Christ for justification from works, on the other hand, as *the basis* of justification.[18]

I do not mean to treat the Reformed confessions as having authority on a par with Scripture. What has been taught in the past does not settle what should be taught in the future. Scripture, rightly understood, remains the sole infallible authority in these matters. But I do want to affirm that when Wright gives the impression that the biblical texts that connect justification with works have not been rigorously handled both exegetically and theologically, it is misleading. In fact, in my view, his own references to justification "by the whole life lived" or "by works" seem unreflective compared to the history of Reformed exegesis.

GAFFIN ON FUTURE JUSTIFICATION AND WORKS

In January 2005, Wright joined Richard Gaffin and others at a Pastors Conference in Monroe, Louisiana, to deal with issues relating to justification. In this conference Gaffin offered good exegesis that moved in a different direction than Wright on this matter of the basis of future

---

[17]Matthew 6:15: "If you do not forgive others their trespasses, neither will your Father forgive your trespasses." John 5:28–29: "Do not marvel at this; for an hour is coming when all who are in the tombs shall hear his voice and come out, those who have done good to the resurrection of life, and those who have done evil to the resurrection of judgment." Romans 8:13: "If you live according to the flesh you will die, but if by the Spirit you put to death the deeds of the body, you will live." Galatians 6:8–9: "The one who sows to his own flesh will from the flesh reap corruption, but the one who sows to the Spirit will from the Spirit reap eternal life. And let us not grow weary of doing good, for in due season we will reap, if we do not give up." Hebrews 12:14: "Strive for peace with everyone, and for the holiness without which no one will see the Lord." James 2:17: "Faith by itself, if it does not have works, is dead." First Peter 3:9: "Do not repay evil for evil or reviling for reviling, but on the contrary, bless, for to this you were called, that you may obtain a blessing." First John 1:7: "If we walk in the light, as he is in the light, we have fellowship with one another, and the blood of Jesus his Son cleanses us from all sin." First John 2:4: "Whoever says 'I know him' but does not keep his commandments is a liar, and the truth is not in him." First John 3:14: "We know that we have passed out of death into life, because we love the brothers. Whoever does not love abides in death."

[18]Thus, in a classic restatement of the doctrine of justification, James Buchanan invites us to consider how Good Works stand related to Faith, and to Justification, respectively. They are the effects of faith, and, as such, the evidences both of faith, and of justification. That they are the effects of faith is clear; for "whatsoever is not of faith is sin" [Rom. 14:23]; and "without faith it is impossible to please God" [Heb. 11:6]; and "the end of the commandment is charity, out of a pure heart, and of a good conscience, and faith unfeigned" [1 Tim. 1:5]. It is equally clear that, being the effects, they are also the evidences, of a true and living faith; for "a man may say, Thou hast faith, and I have works: show me thy faith without thy works, and I will show thee my faith by my works" [James 2:18]; and all the good works, which are ascribed to believers under the Old Testament, are traced to the operation of faith [Heb. 11:4, 7, 8, 23, 32]. James Buchanan, *The Doctrine of Justification* (Edinburgh: Banner of Truth, 1961, orig. 1867), 357.

justification. Gaffin subsequently published his lectures under the title
By Faith, Not by Sight: Paul and the Order of Salvation. Interacting
with Wright along the way, he came to the following conclusion:

> For Christians, future judgment according to works does not oper-
> ate according to a different principle than their already having been
> justified by faith. The difference is that the final judgment will be the
> open manifestation of that present justification. . . . And in that future
> judgment their obedience, their works, are not the ground or basis.
> Nor are they (co-)instrumental, a coordinate instrument for appropri-
> ating divine approbation as they supplement faith. Rather, they are the
> essential and manifest criterion of that faith, the integral "fruits and
> evidences of a true and lively faith."[19]

Gaffin's exegetical efforts in *By Faith, Not by Sight* and the careful work of many other scholars, and my own efforts to understand
Scripture persuade me that this is the true biblical understanding of the
function of works in the final judgment.

There is a good deal of overlap between Wright and Gaffin (and
me) in that we all want to put full and proper stress on the importance
of real, ethical obedience in accordance with the mind of the apostle
Paul (as well as the rest of the New Testament writers). I have no hesi-
tancy in agreeing with Wright when he says, "The attempt to shore
up justification by faith by saying that the life we now live will be
irrelevant at the final judgment is unPauline, unpastoral and ultimately
dishonouring to God himself."[20] On that we agree. But how far does
this agreement extend when we press carefully into Wright's meaning
of "basis" when describing the function of works in final justification?
To that we now turn.

---

[19]Richard B. Gaffin, *By Faith, Not By Sight: Paul and the Order of Salvation* (Waynesboro, GA:
Paternoster, 2006), 98.
[20]Wright, "Paul in Different Perspectives: Lecture 1."

CHAPTER EIGHT

DOES WRIGHT SAY WITH DIFFERENT WORDS WHAT THE REFORMED TRADITION MEANS BY "IMPUTED RIGHTEOUSNESS"?

I MENTIONED AT THE beginning of chapter 7 that when Wright speaks of final justification "on the *basis* of the entire life a person has led in the power of the Spirit—that is . . . on the *basis* of 'works,'"[1] we should be aware that he does not use the word *basis* with nuanced theological precision. I promised we would come to that directly and try to honor the variety of expressions Wright uses. I do not want to expose Wright to the flame of criticism just because there are incendiary words (like *basis*) that seem to imply, but may not, that he is vulnerable to such criticism. Taken as a whole, his position concerning the final basis of justification is ambiguous.

Unlike Gaffin,[2] Wright repeatedly refers to works—the entirety of our lives—as the "basis" of justification in the last day.[3] However, Wright also uses the language of judgment and justification "according to works" in a way that inclines one to think that the terms "according to" and "on the basis of" may be interchangeable for him. For example, he refers to Romans 2:13 and says, "Here is the first state-

---

[1]Wright, "New Perspectives on Paul," 260. Emphasis added.
[2]See chapter 7, note 19.
[3]"Present justification declares, on the basis of faith, what future justification will affirm publicly (according to 2:14–16 and 8:9–11) on the basis of the entire life." Wright, *What Saint Paul Really Said*, 129.

ment about justification in Romans, and lo and behold it affirms justification *according to works.*[4] "Paul, in company with mainstream second Temple Judaism, affirms that God's final judgment will be *in accordance with* the entirety of a life led—in accordance, in other words, with works."[5]

But in these contexts where he is discussing justification *on the basis of works* or *according to works,* he does not discuss the finer distinctions between "based on" and "according to." I suspect his view of how works really function in relation to final justification would become a good bit clearer if Wright discussed this difference. But when we turn to Wright's commentary for help with understanding the basis of the coming judgment in the text that he repeatedly refers to, namely, Romans 14:10–12 ("we will all stand before the judgment seat of God"), what we read is this:

> There is no tension in Paul's mind between this and 8:1, where there is no condemnation for those who are in Christ. He has already indicated in 2:1–16 that there will be a coming day when all will be judged; the fact that the Christian believer is assured of a favorable verdict on that day does not make it any less serious as 1 Cor 3:10–17 indicates well enough.[6]

Huge and important questions go unaddressed here. The allusion to 1 Corinthians 3:10–17 ("he himself will be saved, but only as through fire," v. 15) as confirming the seriousness of the final judgment does not work. At the place where it cries out for reflection, Wright does not come to terms with the fact that Paul threatens baptized professing Christians not just with *barely* being saved, but with *not* being saved at all at the last judgment (Gal. 5:21; 6:7–9; 1 Cor. 6:9). The whole question of how Paul can speak this way and how our works actually function at the last day are passed over. This is a silence where we very much need to hear Wright speak with detail and precision, since the issues are so controversial and so important for the central doctrine of justification. There is, as far as I can see, emphatically more to be learned from the history of exegesis, referred to in the last chapter,

---

[4]Wright, "New Perspectives on Paul," 253. Emphasis added.
[5]Ibid. Emphasis added.
[6]Wright, *Letter to the Romans,* 738.

than there is from Wright on the complexities of *how* our works function in the final judgment.

BASIS? SIGNS? EVIDENCE?

But let us probe as carefully as we can into the varied terminology that Wright uses to describe how works function in our final justification. There are a few places where he speaks in a way that sounds like the more traditional Protestant view of works *confirming* the authenticity of faith and union with Christ. For example, referring again to Romans 2:13 ("the doers of the law . . . will be justified") he says:

> The "works" *in accordance with which* the Christian will be vindicated on the last day are not the unaided works of the self-help moralist. Nor are they the performance of the ethnically distinctive Jewish boundary-markers (Sabbath, food-laws and circumcision). *They are the things which show, rather, that one is in Christ*; the things which are produced in one's life as a result of the Spirit's indwelling and operation. In this way, Romans 8:1–17 provides the real answer to Romans 2:1–16.[7]

This is very similar to the way Gaffin or I or the Protestant tradition would talk. Our Spirit-wrought fruits of obedience are "things that *show* . . . that one is in Christ.*" In accord with this use of the word *show*, he also uses the word *signs* in the following section:

> [Paul] is not as concerned as we are about the danger of speaking of the things he himself has done—though sometimes, to be sure, he adds a rider, which proves my point, that it is not his own energy but that which God gives and inspires within him (1 Cor. 15.10; Col. 1.29). But he is still clear that the things he does in the present, by moral and physical effort, *will count to his credit on the last day, precisely because they are the effective signs that the Spirit of the living Christ has been at work in him.*[8]

And in another place he uses the word *evidence*: "On the last day the final judgment will be made *on the evidence* of the complete life

---

[7]Wright, "New Perspectives on Paul," 254. Emphasis added.
[8]Ibid. Emphasis added. Surely Wright knows that he is using misleading language when he says that Paul's works will "*count to his credit* on the last day." Does he mean this strictly in the sense that there will be a credit column and a debit column in our lives, and that our good works will cause the credit column to be larger? It sounds like it. But I doubt it. But this kind of loose use of biblically and historically loaded language is not making his position clearer.

that someone has led."[9] Thus, it could appear that Wright is falling right in line with the historic Protestant view that the role of our works at the last judgment will be to *show* that we are in Christ, and thus function as *evidences* and *signs* that "the Spirit of the living Christ has been at work in" us, so that justification is *not*, in the traditionally negative sense, "based on" our works, but rather is "in accordance with" our works.

WHAT OUR WORKS SIGNIFY AT THE FINAL JUDGMENT

One key difference in Wright's view from the historic Protestant understanding of how our works relate to our final judgment is that the reality that they signify is not precisely the same. In other words, it may be that we do agree that our works at the last day are essential as "signs" or as "evidences" or as "showing" something that has gone before; but do we agree what this "something" is? Wright has mentioned two things. One is that our works "show . . . that one is in Christ." The other is that our works are "signs that the Spirit of the living Christ has been at work in [us]." Our works must give evidence of these two realities because, Wright says, these are the two bases of our final justification:

> Why is there now "no condemnation"? Because, on the one hand, [1] God has condemned sin in the flesh of Christ . . . and, on the other hand, [2] because the Spirit is at work to do, within believers, what the Law could not do—ultimately, to give life, but a life that begins in the present with the putting to death of the deeds of the body and the obedient submission to the leading of the Spirit.[10]

[9]Wright, "Paul in Different Perspectives: Lecture 1." Emphasis added. Similarly, in a debate with Paul Barnett, Wright said, "My view of the place of good works in justification at the last judgment is I hope, exactly that of Paul in Romans 2:1–6, and in Romans 14 and in 2 Corinthians 5, where it is quite clear that the things that Christians do in the power of the Spirit in obedience to Christ in the present will be part of *the evidence submitted on the last day*. That has nothing to do with works-righteousness in the usually fashionable sense—nothing to contribute to justification by faith in the present, as the thing which constitutes the Christian in the present as *dikaios* (righteous)." Quoted by Tony Payne, "The Wright Stuff," *The Briefing*, Issue 334 (July 2006): 6. The reason this is not clear is (1) he doesn't say "evidence" of *what*. He does not say that our works are evidence of a union with Christ *by which the obedience of Christ is imputed to us*. The precision that the history of thinking on this issue has produced in many writers is missing in Wright at this point. (2) He says our works do not "contribute to justification by faith *in the present*." This seems to imply that he wants to say that they *do* "contribute" in some way in the future differently than in the present. And his frequent use of the word *basis* seems to suggest that "justification by faith" would be a fitting description of our final justification in the same way it is for our present experience of justification.
[10]Wright, "New Perspectives on Paul," 254.

Here are the two foundations for our final justification: Christ's bearing our condemnation in his own flesh (Rom. 8:3), and the Spirit working in us an obedient submission to God (Rom. 8:4). Both are the reason there is no "no condemnation" (Rom. 8:1). These two bases correspond to the two realities to which our works are evidence: We are in Christ and so have died with him in his penal death for us, and his Spirit is in us bearing the fruit of obedience.

But at this point it is unclear how these two realities are related to each other in securing our final justification. When Wright says that our works—our entire life lived—will be the basis of our justification *in the sense of showing that we are "in Christ"* (if my understanding is correct), what is it about being *in Christ* that will provide the foundation for our justification at the last day? And how is this reality of being in Christ such a surety of our justification that our works themselves are only *evidence* or *signs* of the surety, but not part of it? I am not sure Wright would want to say it that way, but I am trying to give him the benefit of the doubt at this point—at least from my standpoint.

COMMON GROUND ON IMPUTATION?

To help us wrestle with this question (if not answer it with total confidence), we may quote at length one of the most important sections of his work that I have read. It is important because in it he addresses people (like me) who cherish the traditional view of the imputed righteousness of Christ and tries to find as much common ground as possible, suggesting that we may be saying the same thing in different ways.

> The covenant plan of God has what may loosely be called a 'participationist' aspect, and this, too, is part of the glorification of God, as I have already shown from Romans 15. Abraham's true family, the single 'seed' which God promised him, is summed up in the Messiah, whose role precisely *as* Messiah is not least to draw together the identity of the whole of God's people so that what is true of him is true of them and vice versa. Here we arrive at one of the great truths of the gospel, which is that the accomplishment of Jesus Christ is *reckoned* to all those who are 'in him'. This is the truth which has been expressed within the Reformed tradition in terms of 'imputed righteousness', often stated in terms of Jesus Christ having fulfilled the moral law and thus hav-

ing accumulated a 'righteous' status which can be shared with all his people. As with some other theological problems, I regard this as saying a substantially right thing in a substantially wrong way, and the trouble when you do that is that things on both sides of the equation, and the passages which are invoked to support them, become distorted.

The central passage is in fact Romans 6, and I think it is because much post-reformation theology has tended to fight shy of taking seriously Paul's realistic theology of baptism that it has sought to achieve what Paul describes in that chapter and elsewhere by another route. It is very significant that the Messiah died to sin; we are in the Messiah through baptism and faith; therefore we have died to sin. The Messiah rose again and is now 'alive to God'; we are in the Messiah through baptism and faith; therefore we have risen again and are now 'alive to God'. This is what Paul means in Galatians 3 when he says that as many as have been baptized into the Messiah have put on the Messiah, and that if we thus belong to the Messiah we are Abraham's seed, heirs according to the promise. There is indeed a *status* which is *reckoned* to all God's people, all those in Christ; and this status is that of *dikaiosune*, 'righteousness', 'covenant membership'; and this covenant membership, in order to *be* covenant membership, must be a covenant membership in which the members have died and been raised, because until that has happened they would still be in their sins. 'I through the law died to the law, that I might live to God; I have been crucified with the Messiah; nevertheless I live; and the life I now live in the flesh I live by the faith of the Son of God who loved me and gave himself for me' [Gal. 2:19–20]. If this is what you are trying to get at by the phrase 'imputed righteousness', then I not only have no quarrel with the substance of it but rather insist on it as a central and vital part of Paul's theology. What I do object to is calling this truth by a name which, within the world of thought where it is common coin, is bound to be heard to say that Jesus has himself earned something called 'righteousness', and that he then reckons this to be true of his people (as in the phrase 'the merits of Christ'), whereas on my reading of Paul the 'righteousness' of Jesus is that which results from God's *vindication* of him as Messiah in the resurrection; and, particularly, that this is what Paul means when he speaks of 'God's righteousness', as though that phrase denoted the righteous status which God's people have in virtue of justification, whereas in fact the phrase, always and everywhere else from the Psalms and Isaiah onwards, refers to God's *own* righteousness as the creator and covenant God; and, underneath all of this, I object to the misreading of several key Pauline texts that results, and the marginalization in consequence of themes which have major importance for Paul but which this theology manages to ignore. The mistake, as I see it, arises from the combination of the Reformers' proper sense of something being accomplished in Christ Jesus which is then reckoned to us, allied with their overemphasis on the category of *iustitia* as the catch-all, their consequent underemphasis on Paul's frequently repeated theology of our *participation in* the Messiah's death and resurrection, and their failure to locate Paul's soteriology itself on the larger map of God's plan for the whole creation. A proper re-emphasis on 'God's righteousness' as God's *own* righteousness should set all this straight.[11]

WRIGHT'S EXPRESSION OF IMPUTED RIGHTEOUSNESS?

In answering the question why union with Christ is so crucial at the last day, Wright's key sentence is this one:

> [Christ's] role precisely *as* Messiah is not least to draw together the identity of the whole of God's people so that what is true of him is true of them and vice versa. Here we arrive at one of the great truths of the gospel, which is that the accomplishment of Jesus Christ is *reckoned* to all those who are 'in him'.

Here he says at least two key things. One is that when believers are identified with Christ, *"what is true of him is true of them and vice versa."* The other is that *"the accomplishment of Jesus Christ is* reckoned *to all those who are 'in him.'"* Here is where Wright believes he is expressing "the truth which has been expressed within the Reformed tradition in terms of 'imputed righteousness.'"

This is true as long as one speaks only of the *general structure* of union with Christ: *All Jesus accomplished is reckoned to us.* Or: *What is true of him is true of us.* If we took the analysis no further, we would say: Yes, that is certainly what the traditional view says. But if one asks what Wright believes is *in fact* reckoned to us, or what *in fact* it is about Christ that is true of us, the ways divide. He himself makes this plain as he explains the difference between his view and the traditional view of the imputation of Christ's righteousness.

[11]Wright, "Paul in Different Perspectives: Lecture 1."

His understanding of the traditional view is that "Jesus Christ . . . fulfilled the moral law and thus . . . accumulated a 'righteous' status[12] which can be shared with all his people." Thus being *in Christ* is crucial, in the traditional view, because Jesus has a righteousness that we need, now and at the last judgment, and it is imputed to us when we are united to him by faith alone.

But Wright thinks this is a misunderstanding of Paul, for it misses the point of what Christ's righteousness is. Wright says, "On my reading of Paul the 'righteousness' of Jesus is that which results from God's *vindication* of him as Messiah in the resurrection." In other words, when we think of imputation, we should not think of Christ's obedience—his moral righteousness, or his fulfillment of the law—but rather his position of being vindicated into a glorious resurrection life after his atoning death. So it is not *the "status" of a fulfilled moral law* that is reckoned to us in union with Christ, but *the status of vindication*, that is, covenant membership.

> There is indeed a *status* which is *reckoned* to all God's people [this would be the meaning of *imputation* in Wright's system], all those in Christ; and this status is that of *dikaiosune*, 'righteousness', 'covenant membership'; and this covenant membership, in order to *be* covenant membership, must be a covenant membership in which the members have died and been raised, because until that has happened they would still be in their sins.

THE DIFFERENCES ON IMPUTATION BEGIN TO APPEAR

The difference between the understanding of imputation in Reformed exegesis and Wright's exegesis begins to appear. In historic Reformed exegesis, (1) a person is in union with Christ by faith alone. In this union, (2) the believer is identified with Christ in his (a) wrath-absorbing death, (b) his perfect obedience to the Father, and (c) his vindication-securing resurrection. All of these are reckoned—that is, imputed—to the believer in Christ. On this basis, (3) the "dead," "righ-

---

[12]I assume Wright is speaking loosely here rather than precisely, since the traditional view would want to stress that what Jesus "accumulated" was not just a "status" but a real life of perfect obedience—righteousness in that sense. This is what is imputed to us, not just a status or a position. This, of course, is not what Wright means by righteousness, and that is one of the main differences between the two views.

teous," "raised" believer is accepted and assured of final vindication and eternal fellowship with God.

In Wright's exegesis, the middle element in step 2 is missing (2b), because he does not believe that the New Testament teaches that Christ's perfect obedience is imputed to us. Thus the pattern is: (1) A person is in union with Christ by faith alone (expressed in baptism). (2) The believer is identified with Christ in his wrath-absorbing death (there is no identification with or imputation of Christ's perfect obedience) and his vindication-securing resurrection. Both of these are reckoned—that is, imputed—to the believer in Christ. On this basis, (3) the "dead" and "raised" believer is accepted and assured of final vindication and eternal fellowship with God.

Summarized, the two admittedly oversimplified patterns would be:

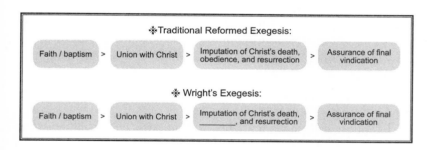

Neither of us intends to say that there are any temporal gaps in this sequence. Both of us know that there are elements of the *ordo salutis* missing from this sketch. The aim is to sort out fairly how close we are, and yet, perhaps, how different.

UNION WITH CHRIST: IMPARTED NEWNESS AS IMPUTED NEWNESS?

The question at this point is: Does the missing element—the imputation of Christ's perfect obedience as part of what is reckoned to us in union with Christ—have any significant reverberations in Wright's system? To answer this question, it is relevant to observe from the extended quotation above (from "Paul in Different Perspectives: Lecture 1") that when Wright wants to explain his understanding of imputation, he reaches not for Romans 4:1–6 or Romans 5:12–19, but for Romans 6:1–6. Let me quote it again:

> The central passage is in fact Romans 6, and I think it is because much post-reformation theology has tended to fight shy of taking seriously Paul's realistic theology of baptism that it has sought to achieve what Paul describes in that chapter and elsewhere by another route. The Messiah died to sin; we are in the Messiah through baptism and faith; therefore we have died to sin. The Messiah rose again and is now 'alive to God'; we are in the Messiah through baptism and faith; therefore we have risen again and are now 'alive to God'.

What is less than clear in Wright's effort to find common ground with the historic Protestant understanding of "imputed righteousness" is whether his view of union with Christ tends to merge the *imputation* of a new position with the *impartation* of a new nature. That is, when he says that union with Christ means *All Jesus accomplished is reckoned to us* and *What is true of him is true of us*, does he include in "all Jesus accomplished" and "what is true of him" not just the imputation of his legal status as vindicated, but also his real nature by the Spirit so that our moral transformation is included in what Wright thinks we should mean by "imputed righteousness"?

In choosing Romans 6 as the "central passage" for illuminating "the truth which has been expressed within the Reformed tradition in terms of 'imputed righteousness,'" Wright seems to suggest that in his mind the really new moral nature that "walk[s] in newness of life" (Rom. 6:4) is part of what Reformed folk should mean by "imputed righteousness" in union with Christ. I am not sure of this. But the following sentences seem to point in this direction. This time he clarifies his understanding of what "imputed righteousness" could rightly mean using Galatians 2:19–20:

> 'I through the law died to the law, that I might live to God; I have been crucified with the Messiah; nevertheless I live; and the life I now live in the flesh I live by the faith of the Son of God who loved me and gave himself for me'. *If this is what you are trying to get at by the phrase 'imputed righteousness',* then I not only have no quarrel with the substance of it but rather insist on it as a central and vital part of Paul's theology.[13]

---

[13]Wright, "Paul in Different Perspectives: Lecture 1." Emphasis added.

It is not clear what "this" refers to when he says, "If *this* is what you are trying to get at by the phrase 'imputed righteousness' . . . ," but it appears to refer to the main thing that is happening in Galatians 2:20, namely, that Paul's new life in Christ is being lived by faith in the Son of God. It is unclear whether Wright is merging our *imputed* position in Christ as vindicated before God with an *imparted* newness of nature that lives by faith. I don't think Wright would even like this distinction, since both are totally gracious gifts of God; but this is what has to be spelled out if he wants to make clear the degree of common ground with those whose exegesis has led them to the view of imputed righteousness that he thinks is poorly expressed in traditional categories.

SAME WORDS, DIFFERENT MEANING

The upshot of all this is that when Wright describes our works in relation to final judgment as "the things which *show* . . . that one is in Christ," he does not mean what most Reformed exegetes have meant when they speak like that. *They* mean that the necessary works—the imperfect but real life of love—at the last day *show* that there has been authentic faith and union with Christ whose atoning death and imputed obedience are the sole ground of acceptance and vindication, apart from any grounding in our Spirit-enabled, imperfect deeds. Wright, we have seen, does not believe Paul taught such an imputation of Christ's obedience.

Therefore, even though Wright describes our works at the last judgment as "signs" and "evidence" "according to which" (or sometimes "on the basis of which") we are justified, nevertheless, he does not use that language to preserve the truth of "imputed righteousness" in the more traditional sense. What, then, in Wright's system, does this description of works as "signs" point to? Clearly, it points to the fact that union with Christ by faith secures a status of vindication for us that we have only because of union with Christ, not because of our merit or "self-help moralism." But what is less clear is whether it points also to a Spirit-wrought transformation "in Christ" that also functions coordinately with the death and resurrection of Christ as the ground or basis of our final vindication.

He does say that these works in the end are *"signs that the Spirit of the living Christ has been at work in him,*" and he does make "no condemnation" (Rom. 8:1) depend (without distinction as to how it depends) both on the death of Christ *and* on our transformation. "Why is there now 'no condemnation'? Because, on the one hand, [1] God has condemned sin in the flesh of Christ . . . and, on the other hand, [2] because the Spirit is at work to do, within believers what the law could not do—ultimately, to give life."[14]

WHERE DOES SAYING NO TO IMPUTED OBEDIENCE LEAD?

We asked above: Does the missing element—the imputation of Christ's perfect obedience as part of what is reckoned to us in union with Christ—have any significant reverberations in Wright's system? My answer is that it seems to have these effects:

1. It leaves the gift of the status of vindication without foundation in real perfect imputed obedience.[15] We have no perfect obedience to offer, and, Wright would say, Christ's obedience is not imputed to me, nor does it need to be. He does not believe that this is a biblical category. So we have no perfect obedience as the foundation of our status of vindication (i.e., justification).

2. This absence of a foundation for our vindication, in real perfect obedience, results in a vacuum that *our own Spirit-enabled, but imperfect, obedience* seems to fill as part of the foundation or ground or basis alongside the atoning death of Jesus. I say "seems to," since I

---

[14]Wright, "New Perspectives on Paul," 254.
[15]The demand for perfection is implicit in the holiness of God who is "of purer eyes than to see evil and cannot look at wrong" (Hab. 1:13) and is made explicit throughout the Bible. For example, James 2:10: "Whoever keeps the whole law but fails in one point has become accountable for all of it." Hebrews 2:2: "Since the message declared by angels proved to be reliable, and every transgression or disobedience received a just retribution . . ." Hebrews 10:1–4: "Since the law has but a shadow of the good things to come instead of the true form of these realities, it can never, by the same sacrifices that are continually offered every year, make perfect those who draw near. Otherwise, would they not have ceased to be offered, since the worshipers, having once been cleansed, would no longer have any consciousness of sins? But in these sacrifices there is a reminder of sins every year. For it is impossible for the blood of bulls and goats to take away sins." Leviticus 26:14–16: "If you will not listen to me and will not do all these commandments, if you spurn my statutes, and if your soul abhors my rules, so that you will not do all my commandments, but break my covenant, then I will do this to you: I will visit you with panic." Galatians 3:10: "All who rely on works of the law are under a curse; for it is written, 'Cursed be everyone who does not abide by all things written in the Book of the Law, and do them.'" On this crucial Pauline text, see the lengthy treatment by Tom Schreiner defending its use in this sense, as demanding obedience to all that the law requires. *The Law and Its Fulfillment: A Pauline Theology of Law* (Grand Rapids, MI: Baker, 1993), 44–59. Of course, both the Old and New Testaments made provision for those who fail (all humans), but the very nature of the provision made (substitution of a sacrifice) proved our falling short of the demand for the perfect obedience of faith.

would be happy for Wright to clarify for his reading public that this, in fact, is *not* what he believes.[16]

3. The ambiguity about how works function in "future justification" leaves us unsure how they function in present justification. Wright is emphatic about present justification being by "faith alone."

> What is 'justification by faith' all about? Paul's answer is that it is *the anticipation, in the present time, of the verdict which will be issued on the last day.* . . . They are then, because of God's declaration, 'righteous' in the *covenantal* sense that they are members of the single family God promised to Abraham, in the *forensic* sense that the divine lawcourt has already announced its verdict in their case, and in the *eschatological* sense that this verdict properly anticipates the one which will be issued, in confirmation, on the last day.[17]

But calling the present justification an anticipation of the "final justification" while being ambiguous about the way our works function in the "final justification" is not a strong way to assure us that present justification is not grounded in Spirit-enabled transformation.[18] Sentences like the following one perplex: "Justification by faith, the verdict issued in the present time over gospel faith which anticipates the verdict issued in the future over the entire life, thus produces the solid assurance of membership, now and in the future, in the single family promised to Abraham."[19] Surely, Wright can see that correlating the "verdict . . . over gospel faith" in the present with the "verdict . . . over the entire life" in the future seems to undermine present justification as justification *by faith alone*.

Similarly, in his comments on Romans 8:3–4, he says, "This in no way compromises present [only present?] justification by faith. What is spoken of here is the future verdict, that of the last day, the 'day' Paul

---

[16]Wright would probably protest: "Does this mean, after all, some kind of semi-Pelagianism in which God first infuses 'righteousness' into me and then declares that he likes what he sees? Have we abandoned the *extra nos* of the gospel? By no means. That is simply to take what I have said and filter it back through the old misunderstandings of the word 'righteousness' which I have been careful to rule out." Wright, "Paul in Different Perspectives: Lecture 1." I wish I could vouch for how "careful" Wright has been to rule out misunderstandings. But it seems to me that there is enough ambiguity still that a protest like this does not settle the matter in view of the rest of what he says.

[17]Wright, "Paul in Different Perspectives: Lecture 1." Emphasis in original.

[18]Nor does it help our clarity about the role of Spirit-wrought works in justification to read, "The Spirit is the path by which Paul traces the route from *justification by faith in the present to justification, by the complete life lived, in the future.*" Wright, *Paul in Fresh Perspective*, 148. Emphasis added.

[19]Ibid.

described in [Rom.] 2:1–16. That verdict will correspond to the present
one, and will *follow from* (though not, in that sense, be earned or merited by), the Spirit-led life of which Paul now speaks."[20] How can one
read this without hearing the implication that we should treat the present justification but *not* the "future justification" as being "by faith"?
Whatever Wright means by saying the future justification "follows
from" our Spirit-led life, he apparently intends for us to distinguish
this from justification by faith alone. So again I ask: Does not the effort
to call the present justification an anticipation of the final one tend to
undermine the truth that present justification is by "faith alone"?

He calls this present justification an "anticipation" of future justification, and yet they seem to have two different foundations.[21] Again,
I use the word *seem* as an invitation to Wright to express himself with
more precision if he wants us to understand clearly where he stands.

STILL MORE AMBIGUITY ON FAITH ALONE

Adding to the ambiguity of how our works function in justification is
Wright's apparent conflation of "faith," on the one hand, and "faithfulness" (or faithful obedience), on the other hand. On the one hand,
he says, "All who believe in the gospel belong [to the family of God],
and that is the only way you can tell—not by who their parents were,
or how well they have obeyed the Torah (or any other moral code)."[22]
This sounds like Wright believes that no obedience of any kind can be
a part of faith. No "moral code" is part of "believing the gospel." But
on the other hand, Wright says:

> One of Paul's key phrases is 'the obedience of faith'. Faith and obedi-
> ence are not antithetical. They belong exactly together. Indeed, very
> often the word 'faith' itself could properly be translated as 'faithful-
> ness', *which makes the point just as well*. Nor, of course, does this
> then compromise the gospel or justification, smuggling in 'works' by

---

[20]Wright, *The Letter to the Romans*, 580. Emphasis added.
[21]He says of present justifying faith, "This faith looks backwards to what God has done in Christ,
by means of his own obedient faithfulness to God's purpose (Rom. 5.19; Phil. 2.6), relying on that
rather than on anything that is true of oneself." Wright, "The Shape of Justification." But would
this be true of us as we walk into the law-court of the last day? Would one not rely "on anything
that is true of oneself"? Does he not direct us to the way we have lived? And if so, how is the present
justification a mere "anticipation" of the final justification? Does justification by faith anticipate
justification by works? How then is justification now not really a reliance on "anything true of
oneself"?
[22]Wright, *Paul in Fresh Perspective*, 121.

the back door. That would only be the case if the realignment I have been arguing for throughout were not grasped. Faith, *even in this active sense,* is never and in no way a qualification, *provided from the human side,* either for getting into God's family or for staying there once in. It is the *God-given* badge of membership, neither more nor less.[23]

This is not clear. But I think he is saying: The reason that defining *faith* as *faithful obedience* is not a smuggling in of "works" is because the faithful obedience is "God-given," not "provided from the human side." But that is not the issue—whether it is produced by us semi-Pelagian-like or given by God in sovereign grace. The issue is whether justification by faith really means justification by works *of any kind,* whether provided by God or man. *That* is the issue, and Wright again leaves us with the impression that human transformation and Spirit-wrought acts of obedience are included in the term "faith" when he speaks of present justification being by faith alone.

WHAT IS THE UPSHOT OF THIS CHAPTER?

As much as I try to see Wright's construction of Pauline theology as saying the same thing as the Reformed tradition, I don't think he is. Here again is his hopeful affirmation of common ground:

Here we arrive at one of the great truths of the gospel, which is that the accomplishment of Jesus Christ is *reckoned* to all those who are 'in him'. This is the truth which has been expressed within the Reformed tradition in terms of 'imputed righteousness', often stated in terms of Jesus Christ having fulfilled the moral law and thus having accumulated a 'righteous' status which can be shared with all his people. As with some other theological problems, I regard this as saying a substantially right thing in a substantially wrong way, and the trouble when you do that is that things on both sides of the equation, and the passages which are invoked to support them, become distorted.

My conclusion is that Wright's position on the *meaning*[24] and the *basis* of justification are not "substantially" the same as what has been affirmed in the Reformation tradition by "imputed righteousness"

---

[23]Wright, *What Saint Paul Really Said*, 160. Emphasis added.
[24]See especially chapter 6 (above).

on the basis of "faith alone" through the blood and righteousness of
Christ alone. That, of course, he would remind us, is no proof that he
is mistaken. Scripture, not tradition, is decisive. I agree with that. My
hope is that, in the limits of this book, the exegesis offered, and the
exegesis of others referred to, will prove to be compelling.

CHAPTER NINE

PAUL'S STRUCTURAL CONTINUITY WITH
SECOND-TEMPLE JUDAISM?

ONE IMPORTANT WAY TO pursue greater clarity about Wright's understanding of justification and how works function in relation to justification is to probe his understanding of the "agitators" (as he calls them) behind the letter to the Galatians and his understanding of Paul's Jewish background in general. According to Wright, the term "works of the law" (ἔργα νόμου, Gal. 2:16; 3:2, 5, 10) referred not to law-keeping in general, but to the acts of circumcision, Sabbath-keeping, and dietary regulations.[1] These, he explains, were pursued, not for the purpose of earning a right standing with God, or getting saved, or entering the covenant people, but rather as a "badge" to show that those who did these "works of law" would be found on the last day to belong, by grace, to God's people. Paul's problem with this was not that these Jewish people were trying to earn God's favor by their own self-wrought righteousness, but rather that they failed to see their calling to reach the nations and instead used their "badge" to exclude Gentiles from the covenant. They did not see that now, in Jesus, Gentiles are to be included in the covenant in such a way that Jews and Gentiles would be marked out by only one badge, namely, faith in Jesus.

MAINTAINING A STRUCTURAL CONTINUITY
WITH JUDAISM

In other words, by seeing only ethnocentrism and not "legalism" in the agitators, Wright is able to see more structural unity between Paul and

---

[1]N. T. Wright, *Paul for Everyone: Galatians and Thessalonians* (Louisville: Westminster John Knox, 2004), 32.

his Jewish background. That is, Paul does not present his new Christian
faith as one free from legalism and his old Jewish faith as one fraught
with legalism. Both are rooted in grace. Thus, Wright sees a basic *structural* continuity between first-century Judaism and Christianity. "Paul,
in company with mainstream Second Temple Judaism,[2] affirms that
God's final judgment will be in accordance with the entirety of a life
led—in accordance, in other words, with works."[3] This continuity with Second-Temple Judaism is built on the conviction that this
Judaism did not attempt to obtain or maintain the saving favor of God
by law-keeping, as is often assumed, but rather assumed divine favor
because of unconditional election and kept the law in dependence on
grace. Thus, Wright agrees with E. P. Sanders that "the Jew keeps the
law out of gratitude, as the proper response to grace."[4]

The structural continuity, therefore, between Judaism and
Christianity means that both Paul and Judaism understood salvation
in *formally* similar ways. One way to describe the structure would be
as follows:

> Free and gracious entrance into the covenant
>
> ∨
>
> a life of obedience to God out of gratitude for this grace
>
> ∨
>
> final justification on the basis of the entire life lived.

This is, of course, oversimplified and purely *structural* without any distinctions in content. But it is significant for understanding how Wright
sees Paul in the wider context of Second-Temple Judaism.

---

[2]The term "Second Temple Judaism" refers to the Jewish religion during the period of the Second
Temple (515 B.C. to A.D. 70).
[3]Wright, "New Perspectives on Paul," 253. Emphasis added. In his study of justification in the
Qumran community (especially in his study of 4QMMT), Wright says that their documents "reveal
nothing of the self-righteous and boastful 'legalism' which used to be thought characteristic of Jews
in Paul's day." "4QMMT and Paul: Justification, 'Works,' and Eschatology," 106. Note: The usual
abbreviation for 4QMMT is MMT.
[4]Wright, *What Saint Paul Really Said*, 19.

Paul Against the Backdrop of Qumran: A Structural Similarity

In spite of this formal similarity, the differences between Paul and his non-Christian Jewish contemporaries were significant. Wright illumines both the similarities and differences in an extended comparison and contrast between Paul and Qumran in his essay "4QMMT and Paul: Justification, 'Works,' and Eschatology."[5]

The key passage from this Qumran document reads as follows:

> [26]Now, we have written to you [27]some of the works of the Law, those which we determined would be beneficial for you and your people, because we have seen that [28]you possess insight and knowledge of the Law. Understand all these things and beseech Him to set [29]your counsel straight and so keep you away from evil thoughts and the counsel of Belial. [30]Then you shall rejoice at the end time when you find the essence of our words to be true. [31]And *it will be reckoned to you as righteousness*, in that you have done what is right and good before Him, to your own benefit [32]and to that of Israel.[6]

Wright sums up his argument in relation to this text in six points:

(1) The context within which the key line C31 [referring to section 31 in the preceding quote] may best be understood is explicitly *covenantal* and *eschatological*.

(2) The halakhic[7] precepts offered in the text are intended to function as indicators, boundary-markers, of God's eschatological people; this is the meaning of "justification by works" in the *present* time, anticipating "the end of time".

(3) Paul, arguably, held a version of the same covenantal and eschatological scheme of thought; but in his scheme the place MMT gave to "works of Torah" was taken by "faith".

(4) Paul's doctrine, like that of MMT, was not about "getting in" but about *community definition*.

(5) The Pauline halakhah, if that is what it is, plays a quite different role within his community definition to that which halakhah plays in MMT.

---

[5]Cited in footnote 3 above. This document (4QMMT) is from fragmentary manuscripts found in a cave at Qumran, which was officially published in 1994 and that scholars date in the first or second century B.C.

[6]4QMMT C26–32.

[7]The *halakhah* was a body of written practical applications of canonical Hebrew laws.

(6) MMT is written neither by nor for Pharisees. Just as the 'works' it prescribes are not those of the Pharisees, so we cannot assume that the form and structure of its doctrine of justification are identical, or even similar, to that of the Pharisees, or of the Galatian 'agitators', or of Peter in Galatians 2.[8]

Thus, there is one kind of *structural* similarity, Wright maintains, between Paul and Qumran: Both think of justification in terms of covenant membership and in terms of the end times. Moreover, the last judgment will bring the final verdict of covenant membership, and this verdict can be known *now* by certain boundary-markers or badges of the covenant community. For Qumran, the boundary-markers are "halakhic precepts"—that is, ethical teachings based on the law. What is the meaning of "boundary-markers"?

The point is not that by keeping these precepts the readers will show that they are morally or ethically superior to other Jews,[9] or that they have gained more merit by moral effort. Rather, it is because *these works of Torah will mark them out in the present time as the true, returned-from-exile, covenant people of Israel.* These "works" will not *earn* them membership in God's eschatological people; they will *demonstrate* that they are God's people. The key line here is C30, in the context of C28–29:

28 . . . Consider all these things and ask Him that He strengthen 29 your will and remove from you the plans of evil and the device of Belial 30 so that you may rejoice at the end of time, finding that this selection of our practices is correct.

In other words, if through prayer and the moral strength which God supplies (C28–29) you keep these precepts, you will rejoice at the end of time, in finding that the advice given herein, this selection of commands, was on the right track. That is when (C31) "it will be reckoned to you as righteousness when you perform what is right and good before him". "Righteousness", in context here as in the biblical passages quoted, must mean more than simply "a moral or virtuous deed." The whole point of MMT is that those who keep the precepts it urges are thereby marked out as God's covenant people, part of the true, returned-from-exile, eschatological community. The practice of

---

[8]Wright, "4QMMT and Paul: Justification, 'Works,' and Eschatology," 112.
[9]That is a difficult statement to embrace. Perhaps he means for the word "superior" to have negative connotations of pride, for surely the point of teaching someone how to live is that they avoid *inferior* ways of life.

Torah according to this interpretation, will signify, in the present time, that the practitioners are "righteous" in this sense: they are the people with whom Israel's God is in covenant, the people who, like David, have their sins forgiven. This is what MMT has to say on the subject of "justification".[10]

Wright would say that *structurally* (not in terms of the content of the boundary-markers) Paul's understanding of the eschatological context of justification is similar. At this point, Wright would see himself *structurally* more in line with Qumran than with "mainstream Christian tradition":

> In using the term "justification" in this context we have seen that it refers to something other than its normal referent in mainstream Christian theological discussion, not least since the Reformation.
>
> In that tradition, "justification" refers to the event or process by which people come to be Christians, sometimes conceived in a narrower sense, sometimes in a broader. But the "reckoning of righteousness" in this text is not about how someone comes to be a member of the sect. It is the recognition, the indication, that one is already a member. It is what marks someone out as having already made the transition from outsider to insider, from (in the sect's eyes) renegade Jew to member of the eschatological people.[11]

Another similarity between Paul and Qumran, according to Wright, is that the term "works of the law" is understood not as describing efforts to be accepted by God, but rather as the markers that set off God's graciously chosen people in the present.

> "Works of the law" function here, in other words, *within* the broader covenantal and eschatological scheme which has been set out. They cannot be abstracted from it either into a more generalized system of timeless halakhah or into a wider "legalism" to which Paul's doctrine of justification, in its traditional Reformation sense, could then be opposed. . . .

---

[10]Wright, "4QMMT and Paul: Justification, 'Works,' and Eschatology," 116. For my criticism see below, but here it should at least be noted that Wright sees more in these few sentences than they can easily bear. The actual words, "It will be reckoned to you as righteousness, *in that you have done what is right*," would seem, on an ordinary reading, to just as easily lead one to see "righteousness" here as "having done what is right," rather than signifying "they are the people with whom Israel's God is in covenant."

[11]Ibid., 117.

The "works" commended in MMT, then, are designed to mark out God's true people *in the present time*, the time when the final fulfillment of Deuteronomy has begun but is not yet concluded. They are designed (C30) "so that you may rejoice *at the end of time*, finding these words of ours to be true". I.e. so that you may be "justified." Proven to have been in the covenant. These extrabiblical commands will thus enable the sect to *anticipate* the verdict of the last day.[12]

JUSTIFICATION BY WORKS IN QUMRAN AND PAUL

Wright argues that all of this is structurally similar to Paul, and that the key difference is that Paul does not affirm "justification by works" in the present. That is, in Qumran (and in the antagonists of Galatia), the "works of the law" are the boundary-markers or badges by which one shows himself to be part of the true covenant people *now*. But that is emphatically, Wright says, what Paul opposes. This is the point of his rejection of "justification by works of the law." The Messiah has come and died and risen and reigns, and all such boundary-markers, especially any that would separate Jew from Gentile, have been done away with *as boundary-markers* and have been replaced by one thing: faith in Jesus. That is the one and only boundary-marker or badge of the Christian community.

> This brings us to the key comparison between MMT and Paul. Paul, arguably, held a version of the same covenantal and eschatological scheme of thought as MMT; but, in his scheme, the place taken by "works of Torah" in MMT was taken by "faith."[13]

In other words, Wright claims:

> The shape of the scheme is the same, the content different. We may set this out in the diagram on the following page.
>   Paul's doctrine has exactly the same *shape* as that of MMT. Justification (to use the shorthand term which MMT does not employ, and which Paul uses only rarely) is God's verdict, the verdict of the last day. This verdict can be brought forward into the present, and thus known ahead of time, when certain identity markers are present. In

---

[12]Ibid., 117–118.
[13]Ibid., 118.

other words, with this evidence you can tell in the *present* who will be justified in the *future*. For MMT, that evidence is the adoption of a particular halakhah. For Paul, it is faith in Jesus Christ. . . .[14] Paul's theology, like that of MMT, is covenantal and eschatological in form. But within the form there is radically different content.[15]

The point Paul is driving at is the polar opposite of the central concern of MMT. Instead of highlighting legal precepts which define Israel over against the Gentile world, or which mark out one group of sectarian Jews over against another, he claims to have found the way in which the biblical promises themselves marked out the family of Abraham, making room as they did so for that family to include believing Jews and believing Gentiles side by side (e.g. Romans 4.9).[16]

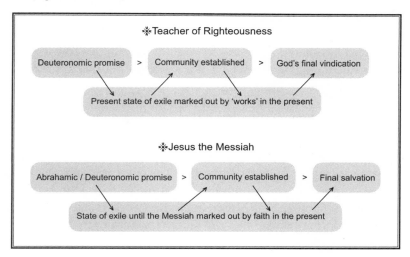

Of course, what Paul found was that Jesus is Messiah and Lord. Therefore, faith in Jesus replaces all "legal precepts" as the badge of the true covenant people of God. That is, faith alone replaces all "works of the law" as the markers that define the Christian church. Thus, Paul did not oppose "works of the law" (ἔργα νόμου, Rom. 3:20, 28; Gal. 2:16; 3:2, 5, 10) in the way in which mainstream Christian tradition thought he did. He did not oppose them as Old Testament commands per se, or as legalistic efforts to earn God's

---

[14]Ibid., 120–121.
[15]Ibid., 122.
[16]Ibid., 123–124.

favor. Rather, he opposed them as being too narrow and exclusive.[17] They excluded Gentiles, and they did not flow from a confession as Jesus as Lord.

Similarly, Paul did not oppose "justification by works" in the way in which mainstream Christian interpretation thought he did. "Both [MMT and the Pharisees] would have believed in something Paul would have recognized (and rejected) as *justification by works*, *namely the definition of the eschatological people of God in terms of particular halakhah*; but they would have disagreed with each other on what precisely those works were to be."[18]

Notice the definition of "justification by works." It refers, in Paul's thinking, not to the effort to get right with God, or to gain God's favor by doing works; rather, it refers to the effort to "[define] the eschatological people of God in terms of particular halakhah." The problem Paul faced in Galatia, for example, was not that the adversaries were trying to merit anything from God, nor was the problem that they were trying to "get in" to the covenant. The problem was one of failure to recognize Jesus as the reality that defines the covenant people and the failure to embrace a "marker" or "badge" of the covenant that could include Gentiles, namely, faith in Jesus.[19]

In this way, Wright sees in 4QMMT an eschatological *structure* of justification that is similar to Paul's. "The point of contact between Paul and MMT is to be found in *the form and structure* of their respective eschatological schemes, not in the 'works' that the one was urging and in the 'works' that the other was resisting."[20] This *structure* includes a kind of "inaugurated eschatology" for both. However, Wright does not suggest that either the pre-Christian Paul or the "agitators in Galatia" shared this added feature in the common Jewish eschatological structure of justification. But, omitting this element, the eschatological *structure* of justification in Paul and Qumran was the common view of Judaism.[21]

---

[17]"What, then, is Paul attacking under the label 'works of the law'? Not, we must insist, what one might call proto-Pelagianism, the belief that one must earn one's justification and salvation by unaided good works." Ibid., 124.
[18]Ibid., 128.
[19]"Faith is not, in other words, the thing one 'does' in order to earn acceptance with God. It is the gift of God, and it forms the badge—the one and only legitimate badge—of membership in the true family of Abraham." Ibid., 123.
[20]Ibid., 125–126. Emphasis added.
[21]"Although MMT is written neither by nor for Pharisees, the shape of its doctrine of justification (covenantal and eschatological) may well have been similar to that of the Pharisees, since, as we have

That common view, as we saw earlier, looks roughly like this:

> **Free and gracious entrance into the covenant**
>
> ∨
>
> **a life of obedience to God out of gratitude for this grace**
>
> ∨
>
> **final justification on the basis of the entire life lived.**

IMPLICATIONS OF THIS STRUCTURAL SIMILARITY WITH QUMRAN

This understanding of first-century Judaism is an integral part of Wright's system. If it were to prove inaccurate, there would need to be a pervasive rethinking of many things because of how many aspects of the system are tied to this one. We may sum up some of these aspects from what we have seen so far.

1. Judaism is a religion of grace, not legalism. Being in a saving relationship with God is not merited by doing works but received as a gift and responded to with gratitude.

> [Sanders's] major point, to which all else is subservient, can be quite simply stated. Judaism in Paul's day was not, as has regularly been supposed, a religion of legalistic works-righteousness. If we imagine that it was, and that Paul was attacking it as if it was, we will do great violence to it and to him. . . . The Jew keeps the law out of gratitude, as the proper response to grace—not, in other words, in order to *get* into the covenant people, but to *stay* in. Being 'in' in the first place was God's gift. This scheme Sanders famously labeled as "covenantal nomism" (from the Greek *nomos*, law).[22]

2. The "works" that the agitators in Galatia were demanding from

---

seen, it corresponds closely at a structural level to that which Paul expounds, and Paul may well have retained the shape of Pharisaic thinking while filling it with new content. . . . The pre-Christian Saul of Tarsus certainly believed that God's true people would be vindicated at the last day, and that the way in which this true Israel was to be known in the present time was by keeping the whole biblical Torah (Gal 5.3)." Ibid., 128–129.
[22]Wright, *What Saint Paul Really Said*, 18–19.

the Christians did not stir up self-exalting dependence on one's own
deeds for God's favor, but defined the covenant people in an ethnically
limited way through Jewish customs. Yet they were still a response of
gratitude to grace. "Galatians 3, being about circumcision, makes the
point, because Paul did not see circumcision at all as a 'good work'
which one might do as part of a self-help moralism, but always an
ethnic badge."[23]

3. The term "works of the law" does not refer, in Judaism or in
Paul, to moral efforts to earn or gain God's favor, but to gratitude-
awakened markers of who the covenant people are and who will prove
to be vindicated as such at the final judgment.

> Circumcision is not a 'moral' issue; it does not have to do with moral
> effort, or earning salvation by good deeds.[24]

> Can one tell in the present who precisely will be vindicated when God
> finally acts in fulfillment of his righteousness, of his covenant obliga-
> tions? Yes, reply many Jews of Paul's day. The present sign [that is,
> "badge" or "marker"] of our future vindication consists in our pres-
> ent loyalty to the covenant obligations laid upon us by our God. Our
> 'works of the law' [circumcision, etc.] demonstrate in the present that,
> when God acts, we will be seen to be his people. Thus there arises that
> theology of 'justification by works' which Paul was at such pains to
> demolish.[25]

4. "Justification by works" is thus opposed by Paul not because
it is thought to be an act of God that grants his favor to those who
do sufficient works, but rather because it was mistakenly taken to be
God's declaration that his people were those who wear the badge of
works—works such as circumcision, dietary laws, and Sabbath-keeping. Paul opposes this and puts another badge in the place of works,
namely, faith in Jesus.

5. "Justification by faith," accordingly, is not an act of God which
grants his favor to those who put their faith in Jesus. One does not get
into God's favor through justification. Rather, "justification by faith"
is the declaration by God of who is already in God's favor—in the cov-

[23]Wright, *Paul in Fresh Perspective*, 148.
[24]Wright, *What Saint Paul Really Said*, 120.
[25]Ibid., 99.

enant. It is "*the anticipation, in the present time, of the verdict which will be issued on the last day.*"[26] "Present justification declares, on the basis of faith, what future justification will affirm publicly (according to 2:14–16 and 8:9–11) *on the basis of* the entire life."[27]

6. The gospel is the announcement that Christ has become the expression and ground of God's grace so that the forgiveness that Jews were expecting from God, through their grace-based works, now comes through Jesus.[28] His resurrection and lordship over all things makes all ethnic limitations of the Christian "badge" inappropriate. Faith in him is now the only badge that defines who the covenant people are. This badge, therefore, opens the door to all ethnic groups.

IS WRIGHT'S UNDERSTANDING TRUE?

These six aspects of Wright's understanding of Paul in his first-century context are interwoven in such a way that one of the most integral threads holding the system together is Wright's assessment of first-century Jewish experience as a life built on God's grace, and his assessment of Paul's antagonists in Galatia as representatives of that general experience. We turn now to assess this particular construction of Paul's relationship to Judaism.

---

[26]Wright, "Paul in Different Perspectives: Lecture 1."
[27]Wright, *What Saint Paul Really Said*, 129.
[28]Wright notes that "forgiveness is mentioned in MMT C24–26 in connection with righteous kings in general and with David in particular. They were forgiven, says the writer, because of their works. No, says Paul; despite their lack of works." Wright, "4QMMT and Paul: Justification, 'Works,' and Eschatology," 123.

CHAPTER TEN

THE IMPLICATIONS FOR JUSTIFICATION OF THE SINGLE SELF-RIGHTEOUS ROOT OF "ETHNIC BADGES" AND "SELF-HELP MORALISM"

DOES WRIGHT SUCCEED IN portraying first-century Judaism, and Paul's pre-Christian life as a Pharisee, and the experience of the Jewish agitators in Galatia as a life of "gratitude, as the proper response to grace"? I don't think so. I will try to give some reasons for this in what follows, and then show what effect it has on his understanding of justification in Paul.[1]

ARE "WORKS OF THE LAW" ONLY ETHNIC BADGES?

Wright's understanding of the term "works of the law" is not based only, or even mainly, he would say, on external sources like Qumran, but on his exegesis of Paul's letters. He sees them as *an ethnic badge worn to show that a person is in the covenant* rather than *deeds done*

---

[1] My conclusions are not unlike those of others. One summary of the critics is supplied by James M. Hamilton Jr., "N. T. Wright and Saul's Moral Bootstraps: Newer Light on 'The New Perspective,'" in *Trinity Journal*, 25NS (2004), where he concludes "that the portion of Wright's magnificent edifice that rests on E. P. Sanders's reconstruction of Palestinian Judaism is sagging. We have seen that the foundation stone that Wright got from Sanders is out of shape when compared to the writings from the period. Avemarie has shown that Sanders's description does not match the Tannaitic materials. Elliott demonstrates that his work does not fit the Qumran and Pseudepigraphical literature. Gundry, Schreiner, Das, Kim, Gathercole, and many others (including Sanders himself) argue that the Pauline literature does not match the description of Judaism that Sanders offers, and my brief examination of Galatians 3 agrees with their work. To the extent, then, that N. T. Wright's conclusions regarding the nature of Paul's conversion and his conception of justification depend on Sanders's Judaism, the picture is distorted."

to show that they deserve God's favor. One of his key exegetical arguments for this view is from Romans 3:27–30.

Then what becomes of our boasting? It is excluded. By what kind of law? By a law of works? No, but by the law of faith. For we hold that one is justified by faith apart from works of the law. Or is God the God of Jews only? Is he not the God of Gentiles also? Yes, of Gentiles also, since God is one—who will justify the circumcised by faith and the uncircumcised through faith.

Wright argues as follows from this text:

'Where then is boasting?' asks Paul in 3:27. 'It is excluded!' This 'boasting' which is excluded is not the boasting of the successful moralist; it is the racial boast of the Jew, as in 2:17–24. If this is not so, 3:29 ('Or is God the God of the Jews only? Is he not of Gentiles also?') is a *non sequitur*. Paul has no thought in this passage of warding off a proto-Pelagianism, of which in any case his contemporaries were not guilty. He is here, as in Galatians and Philippians, declaring that there is no road into covenant membership on the grounds of Jewish racial privilege.[2]

Paul has just said that God is the justifier of the one who has faith in Jesus (Rom. 3:26). Then he makes the point that this justification by faith excludes boasting. He repeats this ground in verse 28: "For we hold that one is justified by faith apart from *works of the law*." In other words, what excludes boasting is justification by faith *apart from works of the law*.

Here is the controversial phrase "works of the law." Wright contends that the words "apart from works of the law" are not aimed at "the successful moralist." That is, Paul is not addressing the problem of doing deeds as the ground of getting or keeping God's favor. Rather, he is addressing the problem of ethnic boasting. Something like: "We have the badge of membership and you don't." Wright's argument is that verse 29 would be a *non sequitur* if this were not what Paul means by "works of the law."

On the contrary, I would argue that there are contextually sensitive, compelling interpretations of the logic of these verses that are not

---

[2]Wright, *What Saint Paul Really Said*, 129.

dependent on seeing "works of the law" as ethnic badges. For example, moving backward, consider the following. The statement "God is one" leads to the inference that he "will justify the circumcised by faith and uncircumcised through faith" (v. 30). In other words, the oneness of God implies oneness in the way he justifies Jew and Gentile, namely, by faith (not by works of the law). This unit then—the singular God implying a singular way of justification for all peoples (v. 30)—is the explanatory ground (εἴπερ, *since*) of verse 29 ("Or is God the God of Jews only? Is he not the God of Gentiles also? Yes, of Gentiles also.") In other words, we know that God is not a tribal deity limiting his saving grace and rights to one people (v. 29), *because,* being one, God has one way to save all the peoples (v. 30).

The rhetorical question beginning with "or" ("*Or* is God the God of the Jews only?") is then a ground[3] of verse 28, supporting the claim that justification is by faith apart from works of the law. God's unity implies a unity of how one is justified among all peoples (v. 30). This in turn supports God's universal and single-method justifying intention for all peoples (v. 29). This in turn supports the statement that this single-method way of justifying is by faith and not by works (v. 28) as he clarifies in verse 30 (" . . . who will justify the circumcised *by faith* and the uncircumcised *through faith*").

This single method of justifying cuts the nerve of all boasting—both Jewish and Gentile—since the very nature of faith is to look away from itself to Jesus (v. 26) rather than to one's works. The focus in the argument is not mainly on "works of the law" but on faith as the universally accessible and universally humbling way of justification. Of course, the boasting of ethnocentrism is excluded, but Paul is also condemning the use of the law (or any moral code) to commend oneself for justification by law-keeping. It is very likely, contrary to Wright's conclusion, that Paul has in view the "boasting of the successful moralist." It is likely that this kind of pride is virtually inseparable from ethnocentrism (as we will see below).[4]

---

[3]This is the usual way Paul uses the word *or* in rhetorical questions: Rom. 2:4; 7:1; 1 Cor. 6:2, 9, 16, 19; 11:22; 2 Cor. 13:5.
[4]Very briefly I should perhaps mention one other argument in favor of treating "works of the law" as the deeds of law-keeping in general rather than as ethnic badges like circumcision, dietary laws, etc. Romans 4:6 says, "David also speaks of the blessing of the one to whom God counts righteousness *apart from works* [χωρὶς ἔργων]." This refers, in the context of Psalm 32 where Paul is quoting, to what David has done as "sins" and "lawless deeds." So the "works" that he is without are the *moral* works that he has transgressed. His failure is not ceremonial. Therefore, since Romans 4:1–6 comes

IS LEGALISM RULED OUT BY BELIEVING IN GRACE?

Wright is aware that his reading of 4QMMT is not the only one. He claims that the teachings of 4QMMT "reveal nothing of the self-righteous and boastful 'legalism' which used to be thought characteristic of Jews in Paul's day."[5] However, we will see in what follows that this is doubtful. Wright bases this claim on the fact that the author of MMT instructs his followers to pray for God's enablement in keeping the works of the law: "Understand all these things and beseech Him to set your counsel straight and so keep you away from evil thoughts and the counsel of Belial" (sections 28–29). But we will see later on that such a prayer does not warrant the conclusion that belief in grace-wrought righteousness rules out legalism. Paul may well have considered reliance on works of the law for final justification to be hopeless and dishonoring to Christ *even if* a person prayed for divine enablement to perform them. Appealing to Qumran's reliance on God's help in answer to prayer to perform "works of the law" does not in itself demonstrate the absence of "legalism" and "self-righteousness."[6]

---

in to support and explain the statements made about "works of the law" in 3:20, 28, we should not assume that the term "works of the law" is more narrowly conceived than "works" in Rom. 4:6. See, for example, Simon Gathercole, *Where Is Boasting?*, 247. "*It is crucial to recognize that the New Perspective interpretation of 4:1–8 falls to the ground on this point: that David although circumcised, sabbatarian, and kosher, is described as without works because of his disobedience*" (his emphasis). For the wider defense of the term "works of the law" as simply a reference to law-keeping, I must lean here on the work of others. See especially Douglas Moo's summary and defense in *The Epistle to the Romans*, 206–210, and the excursus which follows, 211–217 ("Excursus: Paul, 'Works of the Law,' and First-Century Judaism"), as well as his articles "'Law,' 'Works of the Law,' and Legalism in Paul," *Westminster Theological Journal* 45 [1983]: 73–100, and "Review of D. P. Fuller. Gospel and Law: Contrast or Continuum? The Hermeneutic of Dispensationalism and Covenant Theology," *Trinity Journal* 3 [1982], 99–102. See also T. R. Schreiner, "'Works of the Law' in Paul," *Novum Testamentum* 33 [1991]: 217–244, and *The Law and Its Fulfillment*, 179–204; Stephen Westerholm, *Perspectives Old and New: The "Lutheran" Paul and His Critics* (Grand Rapids, MI: Eerdmans, 2004), 300–321; and Moisés Silva, "The Law and Christianity: Dunn's New Synthesis," *Westminster Theological Journal* 53 [1991]: 339–53, and "Faith Versus Works of Law in Galatians," in *Justification and Variegated Nomism*, ed. Carson et al., Vol. 2 (Grand Rapids, MI: Baker, 2004), 217–248.

[5]Wright, "4QMMT and Paul: Justification, 'Works,' and Eschatology," 106.

[6]Tom Schreiner makes the helpful distinction between formal statements implying grace over against the way people may truly live: "Legalism may also exist in practice, even if grace is trumpeted in theory. Religionists may easily proclaim the primacy of grace and actually live as if the determining factor was human effort. The history of the Christian church amply demonstrates that a theology of grace does not preclude legalism in practice. It would be surprising if Judaism did not suffer from the same problem. Legalism threatens even those who hold to a theology of grace since pride and self-boasting are deeply rooted in human nature. . . ." "Theology . . . is not measured only by formal statements but also by what it stresses. Any theology that claims to stress God's grace but rarely mentions it and that elaborates human responsibility in detail inevitably becomes legalistic in practice, if not theory." Schreiner, *Law and Its Fulfillment*, 115–116. Schreiner points to Wright's statement in *The New Testament and the People of God* (222) where he says, "The Pharisees believed that their brand of fidelity to the traditions of the fathers was the divinely appointed programme of Torah intensification, and thus *the means of Israel's rescue*" (emphasis added).

The most crucial lines in 4QMMT for Wright are: "And it will be reckoned to you as righteousness, in that you have done what is right and good before Him, to your own benefit, and to that of Israel" (C31–32). However, these lines are not transparently supportive of his understanding of justification. A more natural reading would seem to be that the words "in that you have done what is right" signify the meaning of the righteousness that will be reckoned to the obedient sectarian, namely, simple obedience to what the law requires. Wright's effort to place these words in the service of his understanding of justification as the declaration of who are members of the covenant people does not seem compelling to me. The person who stands before God at the last day with the assumption that he will be justified "in that [he has] done what is right and good" is more likely a candidate for Jesus' indictment: They "trusted in themselves that they were righteous"—even though they say, "God, I *thank you* that I am not like other men" (Luke 18:9, 11).

Wright seems to operate with the assumption that there can be no legalism and no self-righteousness where a person depends on God's grace to do the works that he expects to be the basis of his justification at the last day. But that has not been shown. It may, in fact, be the case that looking to *any* works (with or without grace as the enabling power) put forward as the basis of justification is hopeless and dishonors what Christ can achieve and provide.

We have seen in the previous chapter that simply appealing to Romans 2:13 and the terminology of "the doers of the law . . . will be justified" does not account for the complexity of how, in Paul's theology, good works relate to justification in the end. I have argued that these works will demonstrate the authenticity of faith that looks away from all self-wrought *or Spirit-wrought* obedience in us to the blood and obedience of Jesus as the punishment and perfection that God requires. It seems to me that Wright has not strengthened his case by his arguments from 4QMMT.

Not Legalistic, Only Ethnocentric?

Another problem with Wright's reconstruction of the first-century setting that illumines the position of the "agitators" in Galatia and in turn sheds light on Paul's understanding of justification is that this reconstruction seems to miss some of the implications of ethnocentricity. Insisting, as Paul's Jewish opponents did, that Gentiles wear the Jewish badge of circumcision, dietary restrictions, and Sabbath-keeping is not, Wright would say, legalistic; it is ethnocentric. The problem with these antagonists was not that they were relying on the badge in order to be God's people (which happened by a gracious election); the problem was that they wanted to keep that relationship for themselves.

Among the historical and exegetical objections that scholars have raised against this reconstruction of the background of Paul's thought,[7] one that has not been expressed as frequently is that Wright, and other representatives of the New Perspective on Paul, offer an inadequate analysis of the roots of ethnocentrism. Can one, for example, draw a line between the evil of legalism and the evil of lovelessness?

What did Paul's opponents believe as grace-dependent people? Wright answers: They believed *not* that their "works of law" made them members of the covenant, but rather that the works showed that they were members already by God's grace.

> Our 'works of the law' [circumcision, etc.] demonstrate in the present that, when God acts, we will be seen to be his people. Thus there arises that theology of 'justification by works' which Paul was at such pains to demolish.[8]

But, Wright insists, Paul aimed to demolish "justification by works" *not* because it was legalistic, that is, *not* because the "works of law" were viewed as the basis of membership in the covenant, but rather because these "works of the law" (circumcision, dietary laws, etc.) were the wrong sign of the grace-based life. They were ethno-

---

[7]See footnote 5. For example, after extensive analysis of the Jewish sources, Simon Gathercole concludes,
> The Jewish expository tradition, summarized by Paul in Romans 4:2 ["If Abraham was justified by works, he has something to boast about, but not before God"], asserts that works were the means whereby Abraham (and thus Israel) was justified and declared to be a friend of God: obedience was not just an indication of covenant membership. In 1 Maccabees 2:52 (cf. Damascus Document), it is Abraham's 'being-found-faithful-in-testing' that is the subject of the verb phrase 'was reckoned as righteousness.' In the phrases 'by works' and 'by faith," the preposition (ἐκ, ἐξ) in both cases denotes the means to, or basis of, justification. The exegesis of the Jewish texts in chapters 1–4 [of Gathercole's book] . . . entirely validates an understanding of Romans 4:2 and 4:4 in terms of commutative justice. The antithesis that [Richard] Hays, [James] Dunn, and Wright construct, between obeying the Torah as a means to righteousness and elements of the Torah marking out the righteous, is false. A distinction between commutative justice and covenantal markers would be entirely foreign to Paul. (*Where Is Boasting?*, 248–249)

[8]Wright, *What Saint Paul Really Said*, 99.

centric. Now that the Messiah had come, faith in Christ was the only proper badge for a grace-dependent covenant member. Israel's mistake was not in the way she related to God (grace vs. works), but in the way she related to the Gentiles. "In seeking to establish a status of righteousness, of covenant membership, which will be for Jews and Jews only, she [Israel] has not submitted to God's righteousness."[9]

For Wright, exclusivism is the antagonists' key problem. But *structurally* they share with Paul an understanding of grace and obedience and final justification by works. These opponents were, presumably, what Paul himself had been as a non-legalistic, grace-rooted Shammaite Pharisee before the Damascus road, for Wright says, "His zeal for Torah was not . . . a Pelagian religion of self-help moralism."[10]

Following E. P. Sanders[11] (on this but certainly not every point), Wright agrees that first-century Pharisaism was a grace-based religion that has been much misunderstood and falsely maligned.

> Saul, I used to believe, was a proto-Pelagian, who thought he could pull himself up by his moral bootstraps. What mattered for him was understanding, believing and operating a system of salvation that could be described as 'moralism' or 'legalism': a timeless system into which one plugged oneself in order to receive the promised benefits, especially 'salvation' and 'eternal life', understood as the post-mortem bliss of heaven.
>
> I now believe that this is both radically anachronistic (this view was not invented in Saul's day) and culturally out of line (it is not the Jewish way of thinking). To this extent, I am convinced, Ed Sanders is right: we have misjudged early Judaism, *especially Pharisaism*, if we have thought of it as an early version of Pelagianism.[12]

One of the problems with this is that you do not have to articulate full-blown Pelagianism to be guilty of self-righteousness in relating to God.[13] We need to let Paul and Jesus help us go deeper in our

---

[9]Ibid., 108. For my understanding of "seeking to establish their own righteousness" and "not submitting to God's righteousness" in Romans 10:3–4, see Appendix 1 on Romans 9:30–10:4.
[10]Ibid., 35.
[11]The seminal book was E. P. Sanders, *Paul and Palestinian Judaism: A Comparison of Patterns of Religion* (Minneapolis: Fortress, 1977).
[12]Ibid., 32. Emphasis added.
[13]Tom Schreiner alerts us with the help of Robert Stein that legalism is endemic to the human heart, not just a few religions: "My colleague, Robert H. Stein, has remarked that, if Judaism were not legalistic at all, it would be the only religion in history that escaped the human propensity for works-righteousness." *The Law and Its Fulfillment*, 115.

understanding of the Pharisees, the pre-Christian Pharisee Paul, and the opponents of Paul. There are kinds of self-righteousness and subtle forms of legalism[14] that do not take the form of full-blown Pelagianism.

WAS PAUL'S PRE-CHRISTIAN VISION SHAPED BY GRATITUDE FOR GRACE?

To the degree that the pre-Christian Paul was typical[15] of the Pharisees of his day, the picture is not as grace-based as the newer view implies. By his own testimony, Saul the Pharisee (Phil. 3:5) was *not* living a life of dependence on grace walking in favor with God. He said that he and all others who rejected Christ were "dead in . . . trespasses" (Eph. 2:5). He explicitly included himself in the indictment: "We all once lived [among the sons of disobedience] in the passions of our flesh, carrying out the desires of the body and the mind, and were by nature children of wrath, like the rest of mankind" (Eph. 2:3).

Paul's own description of himself before his conversion to Jesus was that he was not a humble supplicant of grace (even if his theology claimed this) but an arrogant blasphemer in his very service of God. "Formerly I was a blasphemer, persecutor, and insolent

---

[14]I found the following quote from Matt Perman in a personal e-mail on 10-12-06 so illuminating I want to include it here: "When I read E. P. Sanders, what stood out to me was that legalism was in almost every quote that he gave from Judaism in his attempt to prove that it was not legalistic. It became clear to me that Sanders doesn't seem to know what legalism is. In fact, it appears that this is the case with most of the New Perspective. They appear to be thinking only in terms of hard legalism, which is the notion that either your works bribe God or that they are self-produced by our own effort. But, as you flesh it out, hard legalism does not exhaust the definition of legalism. There is also soft legalism, which is the belief that your God-empowered obedience justifies you before God, or that you 'become saved' by faith but 'remain saved' by God-produced works (which includes the idea that final justification is based on obedience). In fact, Sanders acknowledged that the first-century Jews believed that they got into the covenant by grace but 'stayed in' by works. But he failed to realize that this is legalism. The New Perspective—and those taking their initial cues from it—typically conflate legalism and Pelagianism, seeming to think that because they (or the first-century Jews) are not Pelagians, they therefore cannot be legalists. It needs to be made crystal-clear that these are distinct issues. You can utterly reject Pelagianism and yet be a legalist. You can be a Calvinist legalist, an Augustinian legalist, a believing-in-grace-empowered-works legalist. . . . This is perhaps the central issue of the debate and is probably a big part of the reason that they are going wrong. The essence of legalism is the belief that our right standing with God is based on, comes by means of, or is sustained by our works—regardless of whether those works are self-produced (hard legalism) *or* whether they are completely produced by God's grace in us (soft legalism). . . . Related to this, some have seemed to think that the Reformation was primarily about Pelagianism, as though Luther's and Calvin's issue with Rome was over self-produced works. But the Reformation was first about legalism, whether the works we do justify us, regardless of whether they are grace-empowered or not. The distinction between Pelagianism and legalism is so crucial. . . . Even though they overlap, Pelagianism and legalism are distinct issues." See also footnote 24 below.

[15]He was, by his own testimony, an exceedingly zealous Pharisee, but this means he was on the same wavelength with the rest, only better at it. "If anyone else thinks he has reason for confidence in the flesh, I have more" (Phil. 3:4).

opponent [βλάσφημον καὶ διώκτην καὶ ὑβριστήν]" (1 Tim. 1:13). Paul's pre-Christian religion positioned him squarely under the wrath of God ("children of wrath, like the rest of mankind").[16] He was not God's friend or follower. He was not loyal to the God of the covenant. Of course, he *thought* he was, and would no doubt have spoken of the election *of grace*. But Jesus (in line with Paul's own testimony of Eph. 2:2–3) said that many Pharisees did not have God as their father, but the devil:

> *Jesus said to them, "If God were your Father, you would love me, for I came from God and I am here. I came not of my own accord, but he sent me. . . . You are of your father the devil, and your will is to do your father's desires. He was a murderer from the beginning [as Acts 9:1 describes Paul prior to his conversion], and has nothing to do with the truth, because there is no truth in him." (John 8:42, 44)*

This fits with Paul's own testimony that as a Pharisee before his conversion he was "following the prince of the power of the air," that is, the devil (Eph. 2:2). Wright does not, as far as I can see, express any amazement that Paul looked back on his pre-Christian devotion to pharisaic Torah-keeping as demonic. In Paul's very service to God he was blaspheming. He saw his religion as the consummate expression of hubris (ὑβριστήν, 1 Tim. 1:13).

---

[16]Of course, there were Jews in Jesus' and Paul's day who were humbly trusting the promises and seeking the kingdom and ready to recognize the Messiah when he came—like Anna and Simeon and Zechariah and Elizabeth (Luke 1:5–6; 2:25–38). But Paul did not see himself as one of these, and Jesus did not see most of the Pharisees in this category. There was a profound difference between the "blamelessness" (ἄμεμπτό) of the pre-Christian Paul (Phil. 3:6) and the "blamelessness" (ἄμεμπτοι) of Zechariah and Elizabeth (Luke 1:6). Douglas Wilson has expressed this difference pointedly:

> Now I grant that Zechariah was a sinner, needing forgiveness. Yet I take Luke's record of his blamelessness straight on, taking it to mean that Zecharias was a faithful covenant member, honestly availing himself of the means provided for sins within the covenant arrangement. But in my view, Saul was in a different realm entirely. Saul was a flaming hypocrite before his conversion, and not like Zecharias at all. Before Christ came, had Zecharias and Saul been hit by the same truck, Zecharias would have been saved and Saul lost. This would have happened on the same principles that lead us to believe that David was saved and Korah was lost. This is not an obscure point. Saul tells us this in a number of places, including in this passage of Philippians under discussion. He is clearly mocking himself, because right before he tells us of his so-called "blamelessness," he identifies the people who *currently* think just like he *used* to think as dogs, as evil workers, as mutilators of the flesh (Phil. 3:2). Is he wanting us to believe that he was a blameless dog, a blameless evil worker, a blameless mutilator of the Abrahamic sign? (http://www.dougwils.com/Print.asp?Action=Anchor& –CategoryID=1&BlogID=1617)

JESUS' ASSESSMENT OF THE PHARISEES AND PAUL'S CONFESSION

There is no reason to reject the teaching of Jesus concerning most of the Pharisees in his experience, of which Paul, by his own testimony, was a classic example.[17] "They do all their deeds to be seen by others. For they make their phylacteries broad and their fringes long, and they love the place of honor at feasts and the best seats in the synagogues and greetings in the marketplaces and being called rabbi by others" (Matt. 23:5–7). In other words, their pursuit of Torah was not out of gratitude to God, but out of craving for human glory. This is why they could not believe on Jesus: "How can you believe, when you receive glory from one another and do not seek the glory that comes from the only God?" (John 5:44). Jesus made a distinction between what they *said* they believed and the true condition of their hearts.

The Pharisees were committed to establishing their own righteousness, even if they claimed to believe that it was by God's gracious enabling. And the most natural understanding of the meaning of that "righteousness" is simply obedience to the law with a view to glorifying God. But Jesus said it was only external and therefore hypocritical: "You clean the outside of the cup and the plate, but inside they are full of greed and self-indulgence . . . you are like whitewashed tombs, which outwardly appear beautiful, but within are full of dead people's bones and all uncleanness. So you also outwardly appear *righteous* to others, but within you are full of hypocrisy and lawlessness" (Matt. 23:25, 27–28). They were lovers of money (Luke 16:14) and, by this and other means, were an "adulterous" generation (Matt. 12:39; 16:4).

Their zeal for righteousness included proselytizing: "Woe to you, scribes and Pharisees, hypocrites! For you travel across sea and land to make a single proselyte, and when he becomes a proselyte, you make him twice as much a child of hell as yourselves" (Matt. 23:15). Therefore, in spite of all their self-understanding to the contrary, Jesus says *these* Jewish leaders (not all Jewish people!) are *not* going to be justified at the final judgment: "You serpents, you brood of vipers, how are you to escape being sentenced to hell?" (Matt. 23:33).

---

[17]The fact that Nicodemus was a Pharisee and seemed to have a different spirit showed that there were exceptions to the general indictment (John 3:1; 7:50; 19:39).

Both Jesus and Paul would have said that before his conversion Paul hated God and hated people. Of course, this was *not* Paul's self-understanding at the time. But Jesus said that a person's attitude toward Jesus himself revealed the truth: "Whoever hates me hates my Father also" (John 15:23). And Paul confessed from his Christian vantage point that he actually hated others: "We ourselves were once foolish, disobedient, led astray, slaves to various passions and pleasures, passing our days in malice and envy, hated by others and *hating one another*" (Titus 3:3).

In view of Jesus' penetrating and devastating indictment of the Pharisees, and in view of Paul's testimony that he was one from that group (Gal. 1:13; Phil. 3:6; Eph. 2:2–3; 1 Tim. 1:13–14; Titus 3:3), it seems to be a historical fantasy to portray the pre-Christian Saul or his later opponents in Galatia as true lovers of God who had drunk from the fountain of divine grace and who therefore genuinely followed the Torah out of heartfelt gratitude to God. No doubt there were such grace-dependent, gratitude-driven Jewish people, but it is doubtful that Paul and the Pharisees whom Jesus knew and Paul's opponents in Galatia were among them. My aim here is not to say that Wright has a rosy picture of Paul's antagonists in Galatia, but to make clear that the picture was not rosy and that saying "legalism" was not the problem may overlook the deeper connections between other sins and depths of legalism that are not as obvious.[18]

THE DEPTH OF EVIL IN ETHNOCENTRISM

Turning from the Qumran community and first-century Pharisaism, we focus on what appears to be an insufficient analysis of the problem of ethnocentrism. Wright talks as though there is a significant difference between the evil of legalistic boasting in works, on the one hand, and the evil of loveless boasting in ethnic distinctives, on the other hand. He identifies the underlying reason that Paul and other Jews rejected Jesus

---

[18]If some of the New Perspective defenders (not N. T. Wright) choose to attribute this portrait of the Pharisees not to Jesus but to later Christian communities, then not only must they assume that they know more than those communities *about Jesus*, but also that they know more than those communities *about the Pharisees in or near those very communities*. If I have to choose which testimony to believe about the nature of the Pharisees, I choose to believe the testimony of the early Christians, not the reconstruction of twenty-first-century scholars whose biases are no less dangerous than those of early Christians.

as Jesus' threat to their ethnocentrism, not his threat to their so-called "self-help moralism."

> When Paul's fellow Jews rejected Jesus (as Paul did himself to begin with), and when they continue to reject the message about Jesus which Paul proclaims, he sees the underlying reason: they recognize, as he has had to recognize, that it will mean abandoning the idea of a covenant membership which will be inalienably hers and hers alone.[19]

Yes. But that is only the tip of an iceberg of evil that Jesus exposes and Paul confesses. Jesus said, "Woe to you, scribes and Pharisees, hypocrites! For you shut the kingdom of heaven in people's faces. For you neither enter yourselves nor allow those who would enter to go in" (Matt. 23:13). It does not matter that the immediate reference here is the exclusion of other *Jewish* people by the legal demands the Pharisees were making. The principle holds. Exclusivism rooted in religious pride remains the same. Jesus identifies the ethnic exclusiveness of the Pharisees as deeply rooted in morally reprehensible pride—that is, self-righteousness. "You are those who justify yourselves before men, but God knows your hearts. For what is exalted among men is an abomination in the sight of God" (Luke 16:15). For Jesus, the line between ethnic pride and moral pride vanishes. Ethnocentrism and self-righteousness are morally inseparable.

In such hearts, the use of the law will inevitably be self-justifying, whatever the theology one professes. In Paul's battle with those who seek to establish their own righteousness, he was not dealing merely with ethnocentrism but the kind of heart that uses whatever it takes up as part self-commendation to God and man.

TWO ADDITIONAL PROBLEMS

Wright's general orientation toward Second-Temple Judaism—that "the Jew keeps the law out of gratitude, as the proper response to grace"[20]—encounters at least two additional problems. First, it seems to fly in the face of what Jesus says about how the Pharisees in general experienced and shared mercy. And second, it seems to overlook the reality that the root of ethnic pride is the same root as legalism, namely,

---

[19]Wright, *What Saint Paul Really Said*, 108.
[20]Ibid., 19.

self-righteousness, and that this root can produce branches that boast in God's grace.

"I Desire Mercy, Not Sacrifice"

In regard to the first problem, Jesus' basic statement about the hermeneutic that guided the Pharisees' pursuit of Torah was: "Go and learn what this means, 'I desire mercy, and not sacrifice'" (Matt. 9:13; 12:7). In other words, they do not handle the Torah faithfully because they do *not* have a "proper response to grace." They do not grasp—or, more crucially, are not grasped by—the precious reality of the *mercy* of God and its implications for how to read the Bible and treat people. They may *say* that they are depending on grace. But Jesus said they are not.

Jesus made it plain in the parable of the unforgiving servant (Matt. 18:23–35) that a person who is demanding and unforgiving has not truly experienced God's grace. The evidence that this was generally true of the Pharisees is that "they tie up heavy burdens, hard to bear, and lay them on people's shoulders, but they themselves are not willing to move them with their finger" (Matt. 23:4). This is not the work of "gratitude as a proper response to grace." "He who is forgiven little, loves little" (Luke 7:47).

Legalism and Ethnocentrism Have the Same Root: Self-righteousness

In regard to the second objection to the general view that "the Jew keeps the law out of gratitude, as the proper response to grace,"[21] it is important to see that, from Jesus' standpoint, relational exclusivism (ethnic or otherwise) is rooted in self-righteousness, which means that ethnocentrism and legalism have the same root. This connection between self-righteousness and exclusivism is one of the points of Jesus' parable that begins, "He also told this parable to some who trusted in themselves that they were righteous [δίκαιοι],[22] and treated others with contempt" (Luke 18:9). A deep root of "treating others with contempt" (whether the others are ethnically similar publicans or ethnically different Gentiles) is: "[They] trusted in themselves that they

---

[21]Ibid.

[22]The meaning of "righteousness" here is simply morally right behavior in obedience to what God requires for his glory. It is found, for example, in Matthew 6:1, "Beware of practicing your *righteousness* before other people in order to be seen by them."

were righteous [τοὺς πεποιθότας ἐφ' ἑαυτοῖς ὅτι εἰσὶν δίκαιοι]." In other words, the exclusivistic treatment of others is one manifestation of the self-righteousness that trusts in its own law-keeping. Legalism and ethnocentrism have the same root. They are not separate conditions of the soul.

Jesus' parable of the Pharisee and the tax collector also shows that the branches of this root of exclusivistic self-righteousness can, amazingly, make protests and prayers to the effect that *all is of grace.* Thus, the Pharisee prays, "*God, I thank you* that I am not like other men, extortioners, unjust, adulterers, or even like this tax collector" (Luke 18:11). Is this not a clear warning to us that finding grace-dependent statements in Second-Temple Judaism does not demonstrate that the hearts of those who made those statements were not at root self-righteous?

This is why we said above that Wright's view of possible legalism in Qumran was inadequate. He claimed that the teachings of 4QMMT "reveal nothing of the self-righteous and boastful 'legalism' which used to be thought characteristic of Jews in Paul's day."[23] But now we have seen that this cannot be successfully defended by saying that the author instructs his followers to *pray* for God's gracious help in keeping the works of the law ("Understand all these things and *beseech Him to set your counsel straight and so keep you away from evil* thoughts and the counsel of Belial," sections 28–29 of MMT). Jesus makes plain in Luke 18:11 that such prayers do not prove the absence of self-righteousness, which is the root of legalism, even when protests of depending on grace are present.[24]

---

[23]Wright, "4QMMT and Paul: Justification, 'Works,' and Eschatology," 106.

[24]Stephen Westerholm, in partial dependence on Heikki Räisänen, draws our attention to a crucial distinction that we saw once already (footnote 14 above), namely, the difference between hard and soft legalism:

> [Räisänen] notes that, while legalism involves the view that 'salvation consists of the observance of precepts,' boasting and self-righteousness may, but do not always, accompany this notion. When they do not, we may speak of a 'soft' or 'torah-centric' form of legalism; when they do, we have a 'hard' or 'anthropocentric' legalism. To this we may add that 'soft' legalists, who try to obey God's law because they believe God has commanded them to do so, may not believe that they are thereby 'earning' their salvation, still less that they are 'establishing a claim' on God based on their own 'merit.' Surely love for God, or even fear of his judgment, are adequate motives for obedience to his commands. No such explanation as hypocrisy, self-seeking, merit-mongering, and outright rebellion against God need be invoked to explain why religious people would attempt to do what they believe God has commanded them. To think otherwise is to insist, for example, that Psalm 119 expresses the religion of a sham, and that Deut. 30:16 commands it.

THE FUTILE DIFFERENTIATION

I would suggest, therefore, that Wright's effort to distinguish the "racial boast" of the Jew from the boast of the "successful moralist" is both futile and, in the end, pointless because the racial boast is rooted in self-righteousness that is the fundamental problem with the legalist. Wright says, "This 'boasting' which is excluded [in Rom. 3:27] is not the boasting of the successful moralist; it is the racial boast of the Jew."[25] But Jesus has shown us that boasting in one's human distinctives—whether racial, cultural, or moral—is rooted in trusting in oneself as righteous (Luke 18:9). This is true even if the human distinctives are thought of as gifts of God (Luke 18:11). Both the racial boast and the moral boast show that, no matter what one *believes* about grace, the heart is not properly resting in the *God* of grace—that is, in the obedience he provides *outside* of us and *for* us—but is trusting in *self* (even, perhaps, the self one may believe God has graciously created).

Unfortunately, in most definitions of legalism by New Testament scholars, the possibility of 'soft' legalism is not even considered. The 'legalist,' for Cranfield, is the one who tries to use the law 'as a means to the establishment of a claim upon God, and so to the defense of his self-centeredness and the assertion of a measure of independence over against God. He imagines that he can put God under an obligation to himself, that he will be able so adequately to fulfill the law's demands that he will earn for himself a righteous status before God.' For Moule, legalism is 'the intention to claim God's favour by establishing one's own rightness.' For Hübner, those who see righteousness as based on works define their existence in terms of their own activities, leave God out of consideration, and, in effect, 'see themselves as their own creator.' For [Daniel] Fuller, legalism 'presumes that the Lord, who is not 'served by human hands, as though he needed anything' (Acts 17:25), can nevertheless be bribed and obligated to bestow blessing by the way men distinguish themselves.'

Such definitions would be innocent enough if they were accompanied by an awareness that 'legalists' of this kind represent only some of those who interpreted Deut. 30:16 as saying that obedience to God's law was the way to life. But all too frequently there is no such awareness. The alternative to faith is not (as it is in Paul) simply 'works,' whether they are 'good or bad'—a statement which embraces both 'soft' and 'hard' legalism—but rather the sinful, self-seeking, merit-claiming works of the (necessarily 'hard') legalist. Whereas Paul can contrast faith in Christ with 'the works of the law,' and mean by the latter no more than the deeds commanded by the law, the very notion of 'works' is so inextricably linked in the minds of some scholars with self-righteousness and pride that (as we have seen) the 'works of the law' can only be conceived as sinful. It is not surprising that for such scholars, the 'law' whose works are viewed as sinful cannot be seen as divine, but inevitably becomes the legalistically distorted form of God's law which prevailed (we are confidently told) among the Jews of Paul's day. But—it must be emphasized—in Paul's argument it is human deeds of any kind which cannot justify, not simply deeds done 'in a spirit of legalism.' *Paul's very point is lost to view when his statements excluding the law and its works from justification are applied only to the law's perversion.* (Stephen Westerholm, *Israel's Law and the Church's Faith: Paul and His Recent Interpreters* [Grand Rapids, MI: Eerdmans, 1988], 132–134)

[25]Wright, *What Saint Paul Really Said*, 129.

WHEN A BADGE OF GRACE BECOMES A
BOAST IN SELF

Both Jesus and Paul saw this deeper problem in the Pharisees and, by implication, in Paul's opponents in Galatia. The issue was not whether one should wear a *Jewish* badge to signify one's reliance on grace or a *Christian* badge to signify one's reliance on grace. The issue was that the Jewish badge itself (circumcision, diet laws, etc.) had become the trust of many Jews (like the Pharisee in the parable of Jesus) and was thus a means of exalting self, not God (even, for some perhaps, while thanking the grace of God), and had therefore led to contempt for others, and was therefore a morally unrighteous form of legalism.

Wright is correct to say, "The Jewish longing for a great law-court scene, a great assize, in which they would be on one side and the Gentiles on the other, seems to have gone *horribly* wrong."[26] Yes. And we learn from Jesus and Paul *how* horribly wrong it had gone. It was not merely the "wrong" of a mistaken badge of God's gracious activity. It was the wrong of turning gracious national election into racial *and moral* superiority to the exclusion of the nations—all of which was rooted in the exaltation of self—including the God-elected, Torah-keeping, supposedly Spirit-assisted, righteous self. The effort to disassociate this mind-set from legalism is not successful or helpful. On the contrary, this mind-set is itself a form of legalism.

THE UNITY OF RACIAL BOASTING AND
SELF-HELP MORALISM

Wright's repeated claim that Paul was confronting "Jewish racial privilege,"[27] not "self-help moralism,"[28] is an unhelpful and misleading differentiation. Something had gone "horribly wrong." Racial privilege, with all its badges, had become the ethical twin sister of "self-help moralism." Both nullified grace. Both were expressions of confidence

---
[26]Ibid., 127. Emphasis added.
[27]"Paul has no thought in this passage [Rom. 3:27–29] of warding off a proto-Pelagianism, of which in any case his contemporaries were not guilty. He is here, as in Galatians and Philippians, declaring that there is no road into covenant membership on the grounds of *Jewish racial privilege*." Ibid., 129. Emphasis added.
[28]"Paul did not see circumcision at all as a 'good work' which one might do as part of a self-help moralism, but always an ethnic badge." *Paul in Fresh Perspective*, 148. "[Saul's] zeal for Torah was not, however, a Pelagian religion of self-help moralism." *What Saint Paul Really Said*, 35. "[Rom. 1:16–17] does not, therefore, mean 'the gospel reveals justification by faith as the true scheme of salvation, as opposed to Jewish self-help moralism.'" Ibid., 126.

in self that it was upright because of human distinctives (one claiming that these were from God, both acting as though they were not). Both exalted self and boasted before God, and neither expressed the spirit of Jesus' words, "We are unworthy servants; we have only done what was our duty" (Luke 17:10). It is morally irrelevant whether the self-exaltation comes from thinking they have achieved a superiority by *moral* performances (like the Ten Commandments) or by *religious* performances (like circumcision) or by *being born by God's grace* into a certain group.

SELF-RIGHTEOUSNESS AS THE HOPE OF SALVATION IS WHAT JUSTIFICATION DEALS WITH

Therefore, it is not misleading to say that Paul was confronting a deep legalism when he articulated his doctrine of justification. The root of this legalism was self-righteousness, in whatever ethnic or moral dress. Inevitably, self-righteousness implies that one's own moral condition is the basis of self-exalting *exclusion* in relation to men and hoped-for *inclusion* in relation to God. Being Jewish by birth—and therefore by grace—was not a saving category for Paul (Rom. 9:3, 6–8). Perishing or being saved hung on whether one trusted in one's own moral condition (self-righteousness) or the moral condition of a Substitute (Christ-righteousness). Which would be the basis of being counted just and therefore included in everlasting joy with God (1 Pet. 3:18)? This is what justification dealt with.

We turn, finally, to give biblical foundation to the doctrine of the imputation of God's righteousness in Christ through faith alone, now and for eternity.

CHAPTER ELEVEN

"THAT IN HIM WE MIGHT BECOME THE RIGHTEOUSNESS OF GOD"

THERE ARE WAYS TO DEFINE the righteousness of God so that it becomes nonsense to speak of the imputation of that righteousness to us. N. T. Wright's treatment of the righteousness of God is certainly not eccentric. Thinking of God's righteousness mainly as God's covenant faithfulness has become the scholar's new tradition in the past forty years or so. This was not compelling to me thirty-five years ago when I was immersed in the academic literature, and it is less so today after thirty years of trying to make sense out of texts for the sake of preaching. The confusion introduced into the understanding of justification in recent decades stems significantly from this new and sometimes unquestioned watchword of the scholarly world.

Wright's understanding of the righteousness of God is not simplistic. He moves thoughtfully back and forth between covenantal and law-court portrayals of the righteousness of God. The reason for this is that "the covenant was there in the first place to deal with the sin of the world, and (to the Hebrew mind) you dealt with sin through the law-court, condemning the sinner and 'justifying', i.e. acquitting or vindicating, the righteous."[1] But whether covenantal language or law-court language is used, Wright regards the conception of God's righteousness as something that can be imputed to us or counted as ours as at best a category mistake. This is plainest in his statement about imputation in the sphere of the law-court:

---

[1] Wright, *What Saint Paul Really Said*, 33.

If we use the language of the law-court, it makes no sense whatever to say that the judge imputes, imparts, bequeaths, conveys or otherwise transfers his righteousness to either the plaintiff or the defendant. Righteousness is not an object, a substance or a gas which can be passed across the courtroom.[2]

THE DIVINE RIGHTEOUSNESS THAT WE NEED

I have tried to show that Wright's understanding of the righteousness of God is an unrealistic limitation of how Paul understands the righteousness of God.[3] Paul's vision of God's righteousness is not synonymous with God's covenant faithfulness or his impartiality in court. It is deeper than both of these. They are *some* of what righteousness *does*, not what righteousness *is*. God's righteousness is no more *defined by* covenant-keeping than a man's integrity is *defined by* his contract-keeping. There are a hundred other things integrity prompts a person to do besides keep contracts. And there are a hundred other things God's righteousness prompts him to do besides keep covenant. The unifying root of righteousness giving rise to all these things was there before the covenant and is not limited to or defined by it.

God's righteousness, we have argued,[4] is his commitment to do what is right. Or, pressing beneath the surface to discern the standard by which God defines what is "right," righteousness consists most deeply in God's unwavering allegiance to himself. "He cannot deny himself" (2 Tim. 2:13). His righteousness is his unswerving commitment to uphold the worth of his glory. That is the essence of his righteousness.

Thus the moral righteousness he requires of us is the same—that we unwaveringly love and uphold the glory of God. He does not demand that we glorify him part of the time or that we glorify him with pretty good zeal. His demand is unwavering and complete allegiance of heart, soul, mind, and strength.[5] But we have all failed. That is our unrighteousness. "The wrath of God is revealed from heaven against all ungodliness and *unrighteousness* of men . . . they did *not* glorify him as God . . . and [they] *exchanged the glory* of the immortal God" (Rom. 1:18, 21, 23, author's translation). This is why we are

---

[2] Ibid., 98.
[3] See chapter 3.
[4] See chapter 3, pp. 37-43.
[5] On God's demand for perfection, see above chapter 8, footnote 15.

on trial in God's law-court. We have exchanged the glory of God for images and failed to glorify and thank him but have dishonored God by breaking the law (Rom. 2:23) and caused his name to be blasphemed among the nations (Rom. 2:24). So none of us is *righteous*, not even one (Rom. 3:10). That is the charge against every member of the human race.

The question, then, that we posed earlier is: When the Judge finds in our favor, does he count us as having the required God-glorifying moral righteousness—an unwavering allegiance in heart and mind and behavior? And does this counting us as righteous happen because we meet this requirement for perfect God-glorifying allegiance in our own heart and mind and behavior, or because God's righteousness is counted as ours in Christ? I said I would return to give my answer.

Yes, the latter is what I believe happens in justification. God counts us as having his righteousness in Christ because we are united to Christ by faith alone. That is, we are counted as perfectly honoring and displaying the glory of God, which is the essence of God's righteousness, and which is also a perfect fulfilling of the law. This is what God imputes to us and counts us as having because we are in Christ who perfectly honored God in his sinless life. It is not nonsense. It is true and precious beyond words.

WHERE WILL PREACHING GO IN WRIGHT'S WAKE?

Before interacting with Wright on one of the most important texts on the imputation of divine righteousness, I think we should take note of what is at stake. Following N. T. Wright in his understanding of justification will result in a kind of preaching that will at best be confusing to the church. This preaching, as we have seen, will speak of final justification "by the complete life lived" or "on the basis of the whole life."[6] And then, while defending this way of speaking from Romans 8:1–11, this preaching will say, "This is why, when Paul looks ahead to the future and asks, as well one might, what God will say on the last day, he holds up as his joy and crown, *not the merits*

---

[6]"The Spirit is the path by which Paul traces the route from *justification by faith in the present* to *justification, by the complete life lived, in the future.*" Wright, *Paul in Fresh Perspective*, 148. Emphasis added. "Paul has . . . spoken in Romans 2 about the final justification of God's people on the basis of their whole life." Ibid., 121.

and death of Jesus, but the churches he has planted who remain faithful to the gospel."[7]

This is where preaching will go in the wake of Wright's influence. That Wright would use this language really is astonishing. He construes and preaches 1 Thessalonians 2:19 in a way that makes it support his understanding of future justification on the basis of our behavior. There is no basis for this in the text. And he even goes so far as to underline his point by expressing the negation that what Paul appeals to in the last day is "not the merits and death of Jesus." The text says:

> We wanted to come to you—I, Paul, again and again—but Satan hindered us. For what is our hope or joy or crown of boasting before our Lord Jesus at his coming? Is it not you? For you are our glory and joy. (1 Thess. 2:18–20)

It is remarkable that Wright says, "When Paul looks ahead to the future and asks, as well one might, what God will say on the last day, he holds up as his joy and crown, *not the merits and death of Jesus.* . . ." This negation—"not the merits and death of Jesus"—is seriously misleading. Leave aside the loaded and notoriously ambiguous word "merits" and just focus on the negation, "not . . . the death of Jesus." Is this true—that when Paul ponders what God might ask in the last day, he does not hold up the death of Jesus?

No, it is not. When Paul contemplates the basis of his escape from wrath in his first letter to the Thessalonians, it is precisely to the death of Christ that he looks. In 1 Thessalonians 5:9–10 he says, "God has not destined us for wrath, but to obtain salvation through our Lord Jesus Christ, *who died for us* so that whether we are awake or asleep we might live with him." In other words, when Paul explicitly contemplates the basis of his escape from wrath in the final day, he does not mention the church planting that God has enabled him to achieve. He mentions the death of Christ.

An illuminating analogy to 1 Thessalonians 2:19 is 1 Corinthians 3:6–8: "I planted, Apollos watered, but God gave the growth. So neither he who plants nor he who waters is anything, but only God who gives the growth. He who plants and he who waters are one, and each will receive his wages according to his labor." This last phrase

---

[7]Wright, *Paul in Fresh Perspective*, 148. Emphasis added.

suggests that variable rewards come to different Christians. If so, then Paul's exultation over his converts in 1 Thessalonians is likely because they signify the same grace of God referred to in 1 Corinthians 3:6 ("God gave the growth . . . each will receive his wages according to his labor"). This is not a reference to final justification, but to rewards of those who are justified (1 Cor. 3:14–15).

In 1 Thessalonians 2:19 Paul calls the church his "crown of boasting [καυχήσεως] before our Lord Jesus at his coming." Since Paul said in Galatians 6:14 that he should have no other boast (καυχᾶσθαι) than the cross, I take this "boast" in 1 Thessalonians 2:19 as something that reflects and highlights the value of the cross. Probably this happens because these saints in Thessalonica came into being by the power of the cross (1 Cor. 1:17–18, 24; 2:4–5). There is nothing in 1 Thessalonians 2:19–20 that suggests that the fruit of Paul's ministry in the saints would lead us to understand or speak of justification the way Wright does. The fruit of Paul's work in the churches he has planted may be (1) evidence of his faithfulness in ministry, and of God's grace, and thus the reason he will receive rewards; or (2) it may be the visible evidence of Paul's faith in Christ, and so the reason his faith is viewed as authentic. His exultation in his converts is not connected by Paul to his justification or to his escape from wrath the way the death of Christ is in 1 Thessalonians 5:9. Since I think Wright's way of handling 1 Thessalonians 2:19 is symptomatic of where preaching will go under his influence, I have written this book and turn now to one last effort to point in another direction.

IN SUPPORT OF THE IMPUTATION OF GOD'S RIGHTEOUSNESS IN CHRIST

The key question is: Does Paul believe and teach the imputation of Christ's obedience for those who are in Christ by faith alone? Since I have already written a small book in defense of imputation, and posted online over 200 expositions of Romans,[8] I will only point toward the key texts in Paul and refer to the more detailed exegetical defense in that book. Mainly I would like to engage N. T. Wright on one of the

---

[8]John Piper, *Counted Righteous in Christ: Should We Abandon the Imputation of Christ's Righteousness?* (Wheaton, IL: Crossway Books, 2002). For the sermons, see, http://www.desiring God.org/ResourceLibrary/Sermons/ByScripture/10/.

most important verses in Paul concerning the imputation of divine righteousness, namely, 2 Corinthians 5:21.

ROMANS 4:3–8

The biblical language of imputation is found most strikingly perhaps in Romans 4:3–8, where Paul picks up the language for imputing from Genesis 15:6 and gives his interpretation. The Greek word λογίζομαι can be translated "count" or "reckon" or "impute." It occurs five times in the following verses:

> *3For what does the Scripture say?* "Abraham believed God, and it was counted [imputed, reckoned, ἐλογίσθη] to him as righteousness." *4Now to the one who works, his wages are not counted [λογίζεται] as a gift but as his due. 5And to the one who does not work but trusts in him who justifies [δικαιοῦντα] the ungodly, his faith is counted [λογίζεται] as righteousness, 6just as David also speaks of the blessing of the one to whom God counts righteousness [λογίζεται δικαιοσύ-'νην] apart from works: 7"Blessed are those whose lawless deeds are forgiven, and whose sins are covered; 8blessed is the man against whom the Lord will not count [λογίσηται] his sin." (Rom. 4:3–8)*

Here the term *justifies* (δικαιόω) in verse 5a is explained in terms of the "imputing of righteousness" (v. 5b). "To the one who does not work but believes in him who *justifies* [δικαιοῦντα] the ungodly, his faith is *counted* [or imputed, λογίζεται] as righteousness." So justification is conceived in terms of "counting (or imputing) as righteous." Unlike Wright's emphasis that justification must call to mind the image of the final law-court, Paul sees rather, in *this* case, the picture of a ledger—a book in which are "counted" a person's "wages." The key statement is that not working but trusting results in righteousness being reckoned to our account.

GATHERCOLE ON THE POSITIVE RECKONING OF RIGHTEOUSNESS

Simon Gathercole has written one of the most thorough critiques of E. P. Sanders, James Dunn, and N. T. Wright. His summary comments on the positive imputation described in Romans 4:1–8 will be useful to include here.

It is crucial to recognize that the New Perspective interpretation of 4:1–8 falls to the ground on this point: that David although circumcised, sabbatarian, and kosher, is described as without works because of his disobedience.[9]

We should go further, however, and point out the positive contribution these verses make to Paul's doctrine of justification. It is striking that . . . forgiveness is seen as a vital component of justification. This can, again, be seen within the wider context of justification as God's declarative, creative action that brings about his will out of its opposite. God's justification of David "apart from works" has two components that are two sides of the same coin. Both echo the "heavenly books" imagery, such as we saw above in *Jubilees* 30 where justification and the heavenly books were integrally related. We can imagine a ledger for each person that records both sins and righteousness. In the case of the first, Paul follows David in recognizing that blessedness consists in the "sin" side of the ledger being wiped clean. David is the paradigmatic sinner whose sins need, in the threefold assertion of 4:7–8, forgiveness, covering, and "nonreckoning." God's declarative act of justification of the sinner (4:5) requires his act of the "nonreckoning" of sin (4:8). However, this is simultaneous with God's *positive* reckoning of righteousness on the other side of the ledger [that is, positive imputation!]. Again, where there was no righteousness, where David was "without works," God creatively "counts" righteousness. This is Paul's God: "the one who justifies the ungodly."[10]

ROMANS 5:18–19

Romans 5:18–19 points in the same direction. Only here Paul is explicit that the righteousness counted as ours is Christ's obedience.

[18]*Therefore, as one trespass led to condemnation for all men, so one act of righteousness leads to justification and life for all men.* [19]*For as by the one man's disobedience the many were made sinners, so by the one man's obedience the many will be made righteous.*

My conclusion on this text from *Counted Righteous in Christ* is as follows:

---

[9]Gathercole, *Where Is Boasting?*, 247. His emphasis. The point is that many New Perspective advocates emphasize that the "works of the law" are precisely circumcision, Sabbath-keeping, and kosher eating, so that if you do them, you *do* have "works." But David had them and was "without works" (v. 6, χωρὶς ἔργων) because of his *moral* failures. For my treatment of Romans 4:1–8 in context, see John Piper, *Counted Righteous in Christ*, 54–68.
[10]Gathercole, *Where Is Boasting?*, 247–248. The bracketed words are mine.

Notice the main point about justification in verse 18: It happens to all
who are connected to Christ the same way condemnation happened to
those who were connected to Adam. How is that? Adam acted sinfully,
and because we were connected to him, we were condemned in him.
Christ acted righteously, and because we are connected to Christ we
are justified in Christ. Adam's sin is counted as ours. Christ's "act of
righteousness" is counted as ours.

> Verse 19 supports this by saying it another way to make sure we get
> the main point: "For as through the one man's disobedience the many
> were made (κατεστάθησαν, *katestathēsan*) sinners, even so through
> the obedience of the One the many will be made (κατασταθήσονται,
> *katastathēsontai*) righteous."[11]

After wrestling with the possible meanings of κατασταθήσονται,
I conclude that "the whole context calls for the common meaning
of καθίστημι (*kathistēmi*) in verse 19, namely, 'appoint.' Through
the obedience of the One, many will be appointed or counted
righteous."[12]

> Paul's point is that our righteousness before God, our justification, is
> not based on what we have done, but on what Christ did. His righteous
> act, his obedience, is counted as ours. We are counted, or appointed,
> righteous in him. It is a real righteousness, and it is ours, but it is ours
> only by imputation—or to use Paul's language from earlier in the letter,
> God "imputes righteousness" to us apart from works (4:6); or "righ-
> teousness is imputed" to those who believe (4:9).[13]

It is significant that Paul does not say in Romans 5:19 that "by the one
man's disobedience the many were made" *guilty*. That is true. But it is
important to see that what he actually says is: "By the one man's disobedience the many were made *sinners* [ἁμαρτωλοί]." This is important
because the imputation of Adam's sin is more than the imputation of a
"status." We are counted as having *sinned* in Adam. Therefore, when
Paul goes on to say, "so by the one man's obedience the many will be
made righteous," he does not mean only that Christ's *status* was imputed

---

[11]Piper, *Counted Righteous in Christ*, 107–108.
[12]Ibid., 109.
[13]Ibid., 110. Christ's obedience reaches its climax in the cross (Phil. 2:8), but it is not limited to
the cross. The obedience of dying on the cross is inseparable from his whole life of obedience *both*
because there could be no vicarious death without a comprehensively perfect sacrifice *and* because
there is no place you can draw a line before three o'clock on Good Friday before which the obedience
of Jesus would not be included in what we need from him.

to us. Rather, in Christ we are counted as having done all the righteousness that God requires. Imputation is not the conferring of a status without a ground of real imputed moral righteousness. It is the counting of an alien, real, moral, perfect righteousness, namely Christ's, as ours.

PHILIPPIANS 3:9

Philippians 3:9 speaks of a righteousness that Paul "has" (ἔχων) that is "not his own" (μη . . . ἐμὴν) and that "comes . . . from God" (τὴν ἐκ θεοῦ δικαιοσύνην) because we are "in Christ" (ἐν αὐτῷ).

> *I count everything as . . . rubbish, in order that I may gain Christ and be found in him, not having a righteousness of my own that comes from the law, but that which comes through faith in Christ, the righteousness from God that depends on faith. (Phil. 3:8–9)*

Notice that the righteousness Paul counts on having "from God" is pursued with a longing to "be found in Christ." The righteousness that he has is his because he is "found in Christ." This use of "in Christ" is positional. *In Christ by faith* is the place where God's righteousness counts as a righteousness I *have*, while not being "a righteousness of my own."[14] Thus, "being found in Christ" is the way to "have a righteousness not my own." True, this does not say explicitly that *Christ's* righteousness is *imputed* to us, but along with the other evidence pre-

---

[14]There is, of course, nothing new about emphasizing that justification happens to us by virtue of our union with Christ and no other way. For example, Andrew Fuller (the great "rope holder" of missionary pioneer William Carey), following his teachers John Owen and Jonathan Edwards, put it like this for the controversies of his own day:

> It is said to be 'of faith that it might be by grace' [Rom. 4:16]. There must, therefore, be something in the nature of faith which peculiarly corresponds with the free grace of the gospel; something which looks out of self, and receives the free gifts of Heaven as being what they are—pure undeserved favor. We need not reduce it to a mere exercise of the intellectual faculty [contra the intellectualistic Sandemanians of his day], in which there is nothing holy; but whatever holiness there is in it, it is not this, but the obedience of Christ, that constitutes our justifying righteousness. *Whatever other properties the magnet may possess, it is as pointing invariably to the north that it guides the mariner; and whatever other properties faith may possess, it is as receiving Christ, and bringing us into union with him, that it justifies"* [added emphasis]. . . . It is thus that justification stands connected, in the Scriptures, with the *union* with Christ: "Of him are ye *in* Christ Jesus, who of God is made unto us – righteousness" [1 Cor. 1:30].—"There is therefore now no condemnation to them that are *in* Christ Jesus" [Rom. 8:1].—"That I may be found *in* him, not having mine own righteousness which is of the law, but that which is through faith in Christ, the righteousness which is of God by faith" [Phil. 3:9]. From these and other passages we perceive that faith justifies, not in a way of merit, not on account of anything in itself, be it what it may, but as uniting us to Christ. (Andrew Fuller, *The Complete Works of Reverend Andrew Fuller*, ed. Joseph Belcher [Harrisonburg, VA: Sprinkle Publications, 1988], 1:281)

sented here and in *Counted Righteous in Christ*, it is a natural implication of this verse.[15]

1 CORINTHIANS 1:30[16]

Wright says of 1 Corinthians 1:30, "It is the only passage I know where something called 'the imputed righteousness of Christ,' a phrase more often found in post-Reformation theology and piety than in the New Testament, finds any basis in the text."[17] That concession is not insignificant, especially in view of the fact that Christ becomes our righteousness because we are "in Christ Jesus."

The reality of being "in Christ" is all-important for understanding justification. We will see below in 2 Corinthians 5:21 that "*in him* we become the righteousness of God" (ἐν αὐτῷ), and in Philippians 3:9, we "have" divine righteousness "in him" (ἐν αὐτῷ). Paul says explicitly in Galatians 2:17 that we are "justified *in Christ*" (δικαιωθῆναι ἐν Χριστῷ). The implication seems to be that our union with Christ is what connects us with divine righteousness. This truth raises the importance of 1 Corinthians 1:30.

> By [God's] doing you are in Christ Jesus [ἐξ αὐτοῦ δὲ ὑμεῖς ἐστε ἐν Χριστῷ Ἰησοῦ], who became to us wisdom from God, and righteousness, and sanctification, and redemption. (NASB)

Here is a clear statement that Christ "became for us righteousness [ἐγενήθη . . . ἡμῖν . . . δικαιοσύνη]." This is remarkable. In some sense, Christ has become our righteousness. Add to this that he becomes righteousness for us (ESV, "to us"; ἡμῖν) by virtue of our being *in him* (ἐν Χριστῷ Ἰησοῦ). And then add to that how Paul says explicitly in Galatians 2:17 that "justification" is "in Christ." This surely suggests strongly that Christ's "becoming" or "being" (as the verb ἐγενήθη can mean) righteousness for us is related to justification—our being counted righteous.

C. K. Barrett argues:

> The root of the thought is forensic: man is arraigned in God's court, and is unable to satisfy the judge unless righteousness, which he cannot

---

[15]This is argued at greater length in *Counted Righteous in Christ*, 83–84.
[16]This section is based on the material in *Counted Righteous in Christ*, 84–87.
[17]Wright, *What Saint Paul Really Says*, 123.

himself produce, is given to him. . . . Christ himself becomes righteousness for him (2 Cor. 5:21), and God the judge views him not as he is in himself but in Christ.[18]

One may object that Christ's becoming sanctification for us is not an imputed reality, but rather is worked in us, so why should we assume that Christ's becoming righteousness for us refers to an imputed righteousness? In answer, I don't *assume* it. Instead I note that the other passages that connect righteousness with being "in Christ" have to do with justification (Gal. 2:17) and speak of a righteousness that is "not our own" (Phil. 3:9) and that "we . . . become the righteousness of God" in the same way Christ became sin, that is, by imputation (see below on 2 Cor. 5:21).

Then I observe that there is no reason to think that Christ must "become" for us righteousness exactly the same way he becomes wisdom and sanctification and redemption. This is not said or implied.[19] In fact, it is plausible to see a natural progression in the four realities that Christ is for us. In our union with Christ, he becomes "wisdom" for us in overcoming the blinding and deadening *ignorance* that keeps us from seeing the glory of the cross (1 Cor. 1:24). Then he becomes righteousness for us in overcoming our *guilt and condemnation* (Rom. 8:1). Then he becomes sanctification for us in overcoming our *corruption and pollution* (1 Cor. 1:2; Eph. 2:10). Finally, he becomes redemption for us in overcoming, in the resurrection, all *the miseries, pain, futility, and death* of this age (Rom. 8:23).[20] There is no reason to force this text to mean that Christ becomes all these things for us in exactly the same way, namely, by imputation. He may become each of these things for us as each reality requires.

Whether Paul had this progression in mind or not, 1 Corinthians 1:30 stands as a signal pointing to the righteousness of Christ that becomes ours when we are united to him by God through faith. In connection with the other texts we have seen, it is therefore war-

---

[18]C. K. Barrett, *A Commentary on the First Epistle to the Corinthians* (New York: Harper and Row, 1968), 60.

[19]This is why Wright is incorrect when he says that if we claim 1 Corinthians 1:30 as a textual basis for imputed righteousness, then "we must also be prepared to talk of the imputed wisdom of Christ; the imputed sanctification of Christ; and the imputed redemption of Christ." Wright, *What Saint Paul Really Said*, 123.

[20]I have leaned here on John Flavel from his sermon on 1 Corinthians 1:30 in John Flavel, *The Method of Grace* (Grand Rapids, MI: Baker, 1977), 14.

ranted to speak of his righteousness being imputed to us by faith in him.

2 CORINTHIANS 5:21

Other texts in Paul point to the imputation of Christ's righteousness to the believer,[21] but we turn now to the one that has been viewed historically as pivotal but that is discounted by N. T. Wright in the unprecedented way he interprets it. This verse is one of the most compelling concerning the imputation of the divine righteousness to believers because of our union with Christ. "For our sake [God] made [Christ] to be sin who knew no sin, so that in him we might become the righteousness of God."

What is crucial to focus on here is the parallel between the two halves of the verse. Charles Hodge points to the parallel when he says, "His being made sin is consistent with his being in himself free from sin; and our being made righteous is consistent with our being in ourselves ungodly."[22] What is so illuminating here is specifically the parallel between Christ's being "made sin" and our "becoming righteous." George Ladd brings this out with its crucial implication for imputation.

> Christ was made sin for our sake. We might say that our sins were reckoned to Christ. He, although sinless, identified himself with our sins, suffered their penalty and doom—death. So we have reckoned to us Christ's righteousness even though in character and deed we remain sinners. It is an unavoidable logical conclusion that men of faith are justified because Christ's righteousness is imputed to them.[23]

"IN HIM WE BECOME GOD'S COVENANT FAITHFULNESS"?

Wright's interpretation of this verse is based on his reading the term δικαιοσύνη θεοῦ ("righteousness of God") "as a clear Pauline technical term meaning 'the covenant-faithfulness of [Israel's] God.'"[24] The term

---

[21]See Appendix 1 on Romans 10:4 and *Counted Righteous in Christ*, 87–90.
[22]Charles Hodge, *An Exposition of the Second Letter to the Corinthians* (Grand Rapids, MI: Eerdmans, n.d.), 149. Hodge admits that "Paul never expressly states that the righteousness of Christ is reckoned to believers" (148). But his conclusion shows that the absence of doctrinal explicitness and systematization in Paul may be no more problematic for the doctrine of the imputation of Christ's righteousness than it is for the doctrine of the Trinity.
[23]George Ladd, *A Theology of the New Testament*, revised edition, Donald Hagner, ed. (Grand Rapids, MI: Eerdmans, 1993), 491.
[24]Wright, "On Becoming the Righteousness of God," 203.

is ordinarily translated "righteousness of God" (" . . . so that in him we might become the *righteousness of God"*). The resulting translation with Wright's comments goes like this:

> "For our sake God made Christ, who did not know sin, to be a sin-offering for us, *so that in him we might become God's covenant-faithfulness.*" The "righteousness of God" in this verse is not a human status in virtue of which the one who has "become" it stands "righteous" before God. . . . It is the covenant faithfulness of the one true God, now active through the paradoxical Christ-shaped ministry of Paul, reaching out with the offer of reconciliation to all who hear his bold preaching.
>
> What the whole passage involves, then, is the idea of the covenant ambassador, who represents the one for whom he speaks in such a full and thorough way that he actually *becomes* the living embodiment of his sovereign.[25]

If this (as far as I know, unprecedented) interpretation were correct, 2 Corinthians 5:21 would obviously have nothing to say in support of the imputation of God's righteousness to us in Christ. But it is very unlikely that Wright's interpretation is correct.

His Three Arguments

His main arguments are, first, that the term δικαιοσύνη θεοῦ is a technical term and means "covenant faithfulness." Second, he argues that the context of 2 Corinthians 3–5 is a portrayal of Paul's apostleship as a minister of the new covenant (3:6), so that his interpretation gives a contextually fitting and pithy climax to the unit: "In his ministry, Paul becomes the righteousness of God, that is, the covenant faithfulness of God, the living embodiment of his sovereign extension of the new covenant in the world." Third, he says that the traditional interpretation would be "an aside, a soteriological statement thrown in here for good measure as though to explain how it is that people can in fact thus be reconciled."[26]

Remarkable Claims about This Passage

In regard to the more historic understanding of 2 Corinthians 5:21, Wright says (1) that this verse is a "detached statement." "The verse

---

[25]Ibid., 205–206.
[26]Ibid., 205.

has traditionally been read as a somewhat detached statement of atonement theology."[27] He says (2) that the traditional interpretation treats it as a "soteriological statement *thrown in here for good measure*."[28] And he adds (3) that the traditional view treats the verse as "an extra added comment about something other than the subject of the previous paragraph."[29] I find the first of these three statements unhelpful and the last two untrue. Consider the context leading up to 2 Corinthians 5:21.

In 2 Corinthians 5:14, Paul places the death of Christ squarely underneath his apostolic ministry as its foundational, controlling impulse: "For the love of Christ controls us, because we have concluded this: that one has died for all, therefore all have died." It is typical of Paul that he moves back and forth from personal testimony about his work to massively profound statements about Christ. In this case, he does not simply introduce the death of Christ as the controlling vision of his life ("the love of Christ controls us") but makes a stunning comment about the deep workings of the death of Christ: "One has died for all, therefore all have died." This statement is deeply connected to verse 21a: "For our sake he made him to be sin who knew no sin." They complement each other, for verse 14 does not mention sin, which verse 21 does; and verse 21 does not mention the death of Christ, which verse 14 does. And in both Paul thinks in terms of our profound identification with Christ in his death: When he died, we died in him, and the reason is that my sin was made his sin on the cross. This is the wider context of verse 21, and the concept of imputation is present well before we arrive at verse 21.

THE LINKS BETWEEN VERSE 21 AND THE SOTERIOLOGICAL ASPECTS OF THE CONTEXT

As we move through the paragraph, the contextual links with soteriological aspects of verse 21 abound. Paul draws the inference from Christ's death for us and our death with him (v. 14) that we should live for him and regard no one according to the flesh, and that in Christ we are a new creation (vv. 15–17). Two crucial links between verse 21 and

---

[27]Ibid., 203.
[28]Ibid., 205. Emphasis added. He multiplies labels by saying the verse is "not an *abstract, detached* statement." Ibid., 208. Emphasis added.
[29]Ibid., 207.

this complex of thought are the logic of the verse and the statement that "in him" we become the righteousness of God. The logic is that Christ was made sin for our sake "so that" (ἵνα) we might become the righteousness of God in him. This is the same logic that is working between verses 14 and 17. Christ died for all and all died in him *so that* in him we might become a new creation in Christ.

BECOMING RIGHTEOUSNESS IN HIM AND BECOMING A NEW CREATION IN CHRIST

And not only does the logic connect verse 21 to this context, but also the analogy between becoming a new creation "in Christ" and becoming the righteousness of God "in him."[30] Wright makes no comment about the words "in him" in verse 21. They are not a natural part of his interpretation. But they are *essential* in the traditional interpretation. "In him we . . . become the righteousness of God." Notice the close parallel with verse 17 ("If anyone is in Christ, he is a new creation"). This parallel inclines us not only to discount Wright's comments about a soteriological reading of verse 21 being "detached"; it also inclines us to give the phrase "become the righteousness of God" a meaning analogous to the phrase "become a new creation," which applies to *everyone* in Christ, not just the apostles as the embodiment of God's covenant faithfulness.

THE BRIGHTNESS THAT WRIGHT OBSCURES

As we continue to read in the context, we find the connection between verses 18 and 19 doing exactly what Wright obscures. He says the traditional interpretation implies that verse 21 is "thrown in . . . *as though* to explain how it is that people can in fact thus be reconciled" and that this would be "something *other than* the subject of the previous paragraph."[31] But Paul explicitly does what Wright denies. He "explains how it is that people can in fact thus be reconciled." That is the point of verse 19:

All this is from God, who through Christ reconciled us to himself and gave us the ministry of reconciliation; that is [ὡς ὅτι], in Christ God

---

[30]I don't mean to press this to imply that "become the righteousness of God" carries all the metaphysical implications of "become a new creation." I don't think that is so, since the closer parallel is in verse 21 with "made him to be sin," which implies imputation, not metaphysical transformation. I simply am pointing out, by way of analogy, a structural link with the context.
[31]Ibid., 205, 207. Emphasis added.

*was reconciling the world to himself, not counting their trespasses
against them, and entrusting to us the message of reconciliation.*

Of course, the paragraph is about Paul's *ministry* of reconciliation.
But it is also about *how* that reconciliation is possible. That is explicit
and unmistakable. Paul is jealous to draw attention to *the way reconciliation works* in verses 14, 17, 19, and 21. Moreover, when Paul says
in verse 19 that God was "not counting their trespasses against them,"
this begs for the explanation of verse 21 that "for our sake he made
him to be sin who knew no sin." That is how our sins might justly not
be counted against us. All of these connections are shrouded in Wright's
misleading comments about the verse being "abstract" and "detached"
when read "*as though* to explain how it is that people can in fact thus
be reconciled."

WHO ARE "HE" AND "HIM"?
The context becomes even more powerful when you consider that the
meaning of "he" and "him" in verse 21a ("For our sake *he* made *him*
to be sin . . .") must be taken from the immediately preceding words in
verse 20, which is Paul's plea for *others* to be reconciled. "We implore
you on behalf of *Christ*, be reconciled to *God*. For our sake *he* made
him to be sin who knew no sin." The implication of this close connection between verses 20 and 21 is that we should read verse 21 in closest
connection to the words "Be reconciled to God."

That would imply two things. One is that verse 21 is indeed about
how to be reconciled. And the other is that the point of the verse is for
the sake of those Paul is appealing to, not for the sake of describing his
own ministry. When Paul says "for *our* sake" God made Christ to be
sin, the most natural meaning is not "for the sake of me and my fellow
apostles" but rather "for the sake of all of us who trust Christ." The
"for us" (ὑπὲρ ἡμῶν) of verse 21 is most closely connected to the "for
all" (ὑπὲρ πάντων) in verses 14 and 15 and warrants the global "we
implore [everyone]"[32] in verse 20.

---

[32]Andreas Köstenberger argues compellingly that the absence of the direct object "you" after the
verb "we implore" in the original Greek signals Paul's intention not to address some unreconciled
component of the Corinthian church, but rather to state "the general nature of his apostolic message
of reconciliation" whenever he preaches it to all people: "We the apostles plead with our respective
audiences, 'Be reconciled to God.'" "We Plead on Christ's Behalf: 'Be Reconciled to God,'"in *The
Bible Translator,* Vol. 48, No. 3, 328-331.

δικαιοσύνη θεοῦ
Does Not Mean Covenant Faithfulness

Finally, Wright's assumption that the phrase δικαιοσύνη θεοῦ means "the covenant faithfulness of God," instead of the more traditional "the righteousness of God," is not warranted. I have tried to show why this is the case (see chapter 3). The meaning of δικαιοσύνη θεοῦ is most fundamentally the "righteousness of God" in reference to his unwavering commitment and follow-through to do what is right—which is to always uphold the worth of his glory. It is the opposite of *sin*, which is a *falling short of God's glory* (Rom. 3:23); and it is what God requires that all of us *must* have (Rom. 1:21), but that none of us *does* have: "None is righteous, no, not one" (Rom. 3:10).

Not surprisingly, Wright makes nothing of the coordination of "sin" in the first half of verse 21 and "righteousness" in the second half of the verse.

> For our sake he made him to be *sin* who knew no *sin*,
> so that in him we might become the *righteousness* of God.

The most natural way to think about "righteousness" in this verse is as the counterpart of "sin." This points most naturally to the understanding of righteousness as the attribute of loving and doing the opposite of sin, that is, loving and doing what is right.

Therefore, from this and all the contextual observations above, I conclude that Wright's novel interpretation is not correct, but the historic understanding of these words is warranted and crucial and precious.

Summarizing the Glory That Still Shines Through This Text

I do not know a better summary of the implications of 2 Corinthians 5:21 than the words of Charles Hodge:

> There is probably no passage in the Scriptures in which the doctrine of justification is more concisely or clearly stated than in [2 Cor. 5:21]. Our sins were imputed to Christ, and his righteousness is imputed to us. He bore our sins; we are clothed in his righteousness. . . . Christ bearing our sins did not make him morally a sinner . . . nor does Christ's

righteousness become subjectively ours, it is not the moral quality of our souls. . . . Our sins were the judicial ground of the sufferings of Christ, so that they were a satisfaction of justice; and his righteousness is the judicial ground of our acceptance with God, so that our pardon is an act of justice.[33]

In other words, this text gives us biblical warrant for believing that the divine righteousness that is imputed to believers in Romans 4:6 and 4:11[34] is the righteousness of Christ. Becoming the righteousness of God "*in him*" implies that our identity with Christ is the way God sees his own righteousness as becoming ours.[35]

---

[33]Hodge, *An Exposition of the Second Letter to the Corinthians*, 150–151.

[34]"David also speaks of the blessing of the one *to whom God counts [imputes] righteousness apart from works*" (Rom. 4:6). "[Abraham] received the sign of circumcision as a seal of the righteousness that he had by faith while he was still uncircumcised. The purpose was to make him the father of all who believe without being circumcised, so that *righteousness would be counted [imputed] to them as well*" (Rom. 4:11).

[35]Don Carson, defending a similar position, draws attention to verse 19: "The opening clause of verse 19 must not be overlooked: *God was in Christ* reconciling the world to himself, or *God* was reconciling the world to himself *in Christ*. . . . It is difficult to imagine why this righteousness should be understood to be 'the righteousness of God' and *not* the righteousness of Christ." D. A. Carson, "The Vindication of Imputation: On Fields of Discourse and Semantic Fields," in *Justification: What's at Stake in the Current Debates*, ed. Mark Husbands and Daniel Treier (Downers Grove, IL: InterVarsity Press, 2004), 69–70.

CONCLUSION

IS THE REFORMATION OVER?

In answer to the burning question *Is the Reformation Over?*[1] N. T. Wright's answer is optimistic on justification but pessimistic on other issues. "Not that there are not large and important problems in ecumenical relations. I am horrified at some of the recent Anglican/Roman statements, for instance, and on things like the Papacy, purgatory, and the cult of saints (especially Mary), I am as protestant as the next person, for (I take it) good Pauline reasons."[2] But on the issue of justification, Wright says that the entire debate between Protestantism and Roman Catholicism has been misconceived.

> Once we relocate justification, moving it from the discussion of how people become Christians to the discussion of how we know that someone is a Christian, we have a powerful incentive to work together across denominational barriers. One of the sad ironies of the last four hundred years is that, at least since 1541, we have allowed disputes about how people become Christians—that which we thought was denoted by the language of justification—to divide us, when the doctrine of justification itself, urging us to unite across our cultural divides, went unheard.[3]

So the upshot of Wright's view on justification for the Protestant-Catholic controversy is: Both your houses have missed the point. Justification is not about how a person becomes a Christian. So the issue is not as supercharged as you thought it was. "Justification by faith tells me that if my Roman neighbor believes that Jesus is Lord

---

[1]Mark Noll and Carolyn Nystrom, *Is the Reformation Over? An Evangelical Assessment of Contemporary Roman Catholicism* (Grand Rapids, MI: Baker Academic, 2005). For a significant, fair, and critical review see Scott Manetsch, "Discerning the Divide: A Review Article," in *Trinity Journal*, 28NS (2007): 62–63.
[2]Wright, "New Perspectives on Paul," 261.
[3]Ibid.

and that God raised him from the dead then he or she is a brother or sister, however much I believe them muddled, even dangerously so, on other matters."[4]

I do not think it is likely that the way the question has been framed for centuries will be abandoned easily. And one implication of this book is that this framing of the question *should not* be abandoned, but resolved. Justification is, in fact, part of the event of becoming a Christian. By justification we come into a right standing with God. And until we do, we are not saved, we are not Christians. And because of the abiding reality of this right standing, we are, and remain, Christians. "I, Paul, say to you that if you accept circumcision, Christ will be of no advantage to you" (Gal. 5:2). The faith that justifies continues to hold fast to Christ alone as the ground of our having God as our Father who is completely for us. Whether this right standing with God consists in the *imputation* of righteousness from beginning to end or consists partly in the *impartation* of righteousness is a crucial and necessary question.

THE REFORMERS WOULD NOT SAY IT IS OVER

Whatever the wobbling views of justification are among Protestants today, it seems clear to me that at least the views of the Reformers are fundamentally at odds with the official position of the Roman Catholic Church expressed today in the *Catholic Catechism*.[5] If, as I believe, the Reformers got it fundamentally right, then the Reformation is not over.

Among the positions on justification in the *Catholic Catechism* with which the Reformers would energetically disagree would be these:

> Justification is conferred in Baptism, the sacrament of faith. It conforms us to the righteousness of God, who makes us inwardly just by the power of his mercy.[6]

> Justification has been merited for us by the Passion of Christ. It is granted through Baptism. It conforms us to the righteousness of God, who justifies us. It has for its goal the glory of God and of Christ, and the gift of eternal life. It is the most excellent work of God's mercy.[7]

---

[4]Ibid., 261–262.
[5]*Catechism of the Catholic Church* (Vatican City: Libreria Editrice Vaticana, 1994).
[6]Ibid., 482, par. 1992.
[7]Ibid., 489, par. 2020.

In other words, in today's official Roman Catholicism, the act of justification is not the imputation of the obedience of Christ, as the Reformers believed,[8] but the infusion of righteousness. "Justification . . . conforms us to the righteousness of God." Thus "God's final verdict of justification is based on the Christian's *inherent* righteousness, acquired by grace through baptism and through meritorious good works freely performed in response to and in cooperation with God's grace. Christians are judged righteous (and receive eternal life) because they are truly righteous."[9]

THE CRITICAL PLACE OF OUR WORKS IN FUTURE JUDGMENT

Wright's statements about future justification[10] are so similar to this (even if his meaning isn't) that it is doubtful his paradigm will set Roman Catholics on a new conceptual playing field. It is more likely that his view will be co-opted as confirmation of the Catholic way.

One of the crucial things that has become clear in our study is that for N. T. Wright, and for the historic debate between Catholics and Protestants—indeed, for anyone who takes the Bible seriously and reads it carefully—the role of our own obedience in relationship to justification and final judgment is enormously important. It is not

---

[8]For Luther on imputation, see quotes in Bruce McCormack, "What's at Stake in Current Debates over Justification? The Crisis of Protestantism in the West," in *Justification: What's at Stake in the Current Debates?* 81–117. Luther said, for example, "This is a marvelous definition of Christian righteousness: it is a divine imputation of reckoning as righteousness or to righteousness, for the sake of our faith in Christ or for the sake of Christ." McCormack, p. 93; *Luther's Works*, Vol. 26, ed. Jaroslav Pelikan (St. Louis: Concordia, 1963), 231. See also Timothy George, "Modernizing Luther, Domesticating Paul: Another Perspective," in D. A. Carson, Peter T. O'Brien, and Mark A. Seifrid, *Justification and Variegated Nomism* (Grand Rapids, MI: Baker Academic, 2004), 437–464. Calvin said, "We explain justification simply as the acceptance with which God receives us into his favor as righteous men. And we say that it consists in the remission of sins and the imputation of Christ's righteousness. . . . You see that our righteousness is not in us but in Christ, that we possess it only because we are partakers in Christ; indeed, with him we possess all its riches. . . . To declare that by him alone we are accounted righteous, what else is this but to lodge our righteousness in Christ's obedience, because the obedience of Christ is reckoned to us as if it were our own?" John Calvin, *Institutes of the Christian Religion*, Vol. 1 (Philadelphia: Westminster, 1960), 727, 753. On Calvin's view of justification see also Anthony N. S. Lane, *Justification by Faith in Catholic-Protestant Dialogue: An Evangelical Assessment* (London: T&T Clark, 2002), 17–44.
[9]Manetsch, "Discerning the Divide: A Review Article," 57.
[10]Quoting from the Introduction to this book (p. 22 where the sources are given), "Wright makes startling statements to the effect that our future justification will be on the basis of works. 'The Spirit is the path by which Paul traces the route from justification by faith in the present to justification, *by the complete life lived*, in the future.' 'Paul has . . . spoken in Romans 2 about the final justification of God's people *on the basis of their whole life*.' 'Present justification declares, on the basis of faith, what future justification will affirm publicly (according to [Rom.] 2:14–16 and 8:9–11) *on the basis of the entire life*.'"

accidental that the title of this book has a double meaning. *The Future of Justification* draws attention not only to where the doctrine itself may be going, but also to the critical importance of God's future act of judgment when our justification will be confirmed. How will our obedience function in that Day?

With analysis and argumentation behind us,[11] it is time for affirmation and proclamation. My hope is that what follows as a final declaration will be a fresh statement of very old and wonderful truth. May the Lord use it not simply to commend a position, but also to mobilize missions. In the end, what is at stake is not simply a doctrine, but the strength and purity of the spring of love.

HERE I STAND

Our only hope for living the radical demands of the Christian life is that God is totally for us now and forever. Therefore, God has not ordained that living the Christian life should be the basis of our hope that God is for us. That basis is the death and righteousness of Christ, counted as ours through faith alone. On the cross Christ endured for us all the punishment required of us because of our sin. And in order that *God, as our Father, might be completely for us and not against us forever,* Christ has performed for us, in his perfect obedience to God, all that God required of us as the ground of his being totally for us forever.

This punishment and this obedience are completed and past. They can never change. Our union with Christ and the enjoyment of these benefits is secure forever. Through faith alone, God establishes our union with Christ. This union will never fail, because in Christ God is for us as an omnipotent Father who sustains our faith, and works all things together for our everlasting good. The one and only instrument through which God preserves our union with Christ is faith in Christ—the purely *receiving* act of the soul.

THE PLACE OF OUR GOOD WORKS IN GOD'S PURPOSES

Our own works of love do not create or increase God's being for us as a Father committed to bringing us everlasting joy in his presence.

---

[11]Besides the arguments in this book, I have addressed this issue in *Counted Righteous in Christ*, in *Future Grace*, and in many sermons arranged by text and topic at www.desiringGod.org.

That fatherly commitment to be for us in this way was established once for all through faith and union with God's Son. In his Son, the perfection and punishment required of us are past and unchangeable. They were performed by Christ in his obedience and death. They cannot be changed or increased in sufficiency or worth.

Our relationship with God is with One who has become for us an omnipotent Father committed to working all things together for our everlasting enjoyment of him. This relationship was established at the point of our justification when God removed his judicial wrath from us, and imputed the obedience of his Son to us, and counted us as righteous in Christ, and forgave all our sins because he had punished them in the death of Jesus.

Therefore, the function of our own obedience flowing from faith (that is, our own good works produced as the fruit of the Holy Spirit) is to make visible the worth of Christ and the worth of his work as our substitute-punishment and substitute-righteousness. God's purpose in the universe is not only to *be* infinitely worthy, but to be *displayed* as infinitely worthy. Our works of love, flowing from faith, are the way Christ-embracing faith shows the value of what it has embraced. The sacrifices of love for the good of others show the all-satisfying worth of Christ as the one whose blood and righteousness establish the fact that God is for us forever.

All the benefits of Christ—all the blessings that flow from God being for us and not against us—rest on the redeeming work of Christ as our Substitute. If God is for us, who can be against us? With this confidence—that God is our omnipotent Father and is committed to working all things together for our everlasting joy in him—we will love others. God has so designed and ordered things that invisible faith, which embraces Christ as infinitely worthy, gives rise to acts of love that make the worth of Christ visible. Thus our sacrifices of love do not have any hand in establishing the fact that God is completely for us, now and forever. It's the reverse: the fact that God is for us establishes our sacrifices of love. If he were not totally for us, we would not persevere in faith and would not therefore be able to make sacrifices of love.

If we make the mistake of thinking that our works of love (the fruit of God's Spirit) secure or increase God's commitment to be completely for us, now and in the last judgment, we compromise the very reason that these works of love exist, namely, to display the infinite worth of Christ and his work as our all-sufficient obedience and all-sufficient sacrifice.

Our mind-set toward our own good works must always be: These works depend on God being totally for us. That's what the blood and righteousness of Christ have secured and guaranteed forever. Therefore, we must resist every tendency to think of our works as establishing or securing the fact that God is for us forever. It is always the other way around. Because he is for us, he sustains our faith. And through that faith-sustaining work, the Holy Spirit bears the fruit of love.

THE DOUBLE TRAGEDY

There would be a double tragedy in thinking of our works of love as securing the fact that God is completely for us. Not only would we obscure the very reason these works exist—namely, to display the beauty and worth of Christ, whose blood and righteousness is the only and all-sufficient guarantee that God is for us—but we would also undermine the very thing that makes the works of love possible—namely, the assurance that God is totally for us, from which flows the freedom and courage to make the sacrifices of love.

Let us make no mistake: Our works of love are *necessary*. There is a holiness without which we will not see the Lord (Heb. 12:14). Our works of love—the fruit of the Holy Spirit—are as necessary as the purpose of God to make the worth of his Son visible in the world. Therefore, the necessity that God has established is of such a kind that it will never compromise the worth of his Son. It will never compromise the total sufficiency of his Son's work in providing all the obedience and all the suffering required in order for God to be for us in Christ. The necessity of our obedience is of such a nature that it always highlights and confirms this truth: The fact that God is completely for us as an omnipotent Father is secured and guaranteed solely by the all-sufficient obedience and suffering of Christ.

When the Bible says that we will not inherit the kingdom of God without the fruit of the Holy Spirit (Gal. 5:21), it does not mean that we add anything to what Christ has done to secure the fact that God is totally for us. It means that God has established his Son's perfect obedience and suffering as the completely sufficient spring of our necessary obedience. This obedience—admittedly imperfect—*will* come to pass in the lives of those who count on Christ's obedience and sacrifice as the guarantee of God's being for them.

Our obedience does not *add to* the perfection and beauty and all-sufficiency of Christ's obedience in securing the reality that God is for us; it *displays* that perfection and beauty and all-sufficiency. Our works of love are as necessary as God's purpose to glorify himself. That is, they are necessary because God is *righteous*—he has an eternal and unwavering commitment to do the ultimately right thing: to make the infinite value of his Son visible in the world.

WHY THIS BOOK?

My ultimate reason for writing this book is to avert the double tragedy that will come where the obedience of Christ, imputed to us through faith alone, is denied or obscured. Inevitably, in the wake of that denial, our own works—the fruit of the Holy Spirit—begin to take on a function that contradicts the very reason these good works exist. They exist to display the beauty and worth of Christ whose sacrifice and obedience (counted as ours through faith alone) are the only and all-sufficient security of the fact that God is completely for us. That's the first tragedy: In our desire to elevate the importance of the beautiful works of love, we begin to nullify the very beauty of Christ and his work that they were designed to display.

The other tragedy that I pray we can avert is the undermining of the very thing that makes the works of love possible. What makes radical, risk-taking, sacrificial, Christ-exalting works of love possible is the fact that Christ's perfect obedience (counted as our righteousness) and Christ's perfect sacrifice (counted as our punishment) secured completely the glorious reality that God is for us as an omnipotent Father who works all things together for our everlasting joy in him. If we begin to deny or minimize the importance of the obedience of Christ, imputed to us through faith alone, our own works will begin to assume the role that should have been Christ's. As that happens, over time (perhaps generations), the works of love themselves will be severed from their root in the Christ-secured assurance that God is totally for us. In this way, for the sake of exalting the importance of love, we will undermine the very thing that makes them possible.

Yet the freedom and courage to love is what the world desperately needs to see in the church and from the church. The world does not need to see strident, triumphalistic evangelicals laying claim on their rights. The world needs to see the radical, risk-taking, Christ-exalting sacrifice of humble love that makes us willing to lay down our lives for the good of others, without the demand of reward on this earth. For the sake of this display of the glory of Christ, I plead for our allegiance to a robust, biblical, historic vision of Christ whose obedience is counted as ours through faith alone.

A Note on the Purpose of the Appendices

THESE APPENDICES WERE NOT written in response to the work of N. T. Wright. Most of them were written before I had read Wright's work. They do not interact with his work. The reason for their presence here is to give some windows into my wider understanding of justification and related exegetical issues.

In my interaction with Wright by e-mail, he questioned me about my own understanding of the bigger picture and some texts in particular. Most of my responses to that interaction were built into the book as it grew to twice the size it was before that interaction. But it seemed to me that even though I could not afford to write another whole book of constructive exegesis on justification, I could perhaps offer some exegetical glimpses into what such a book might look like.

These appendices are not interwoven. They are self-standing. The reader may be selective according to interest, or pass over them entirely. They are not part of the substance of my critique of Wright. I hope that they will be helpful for some readers in leading toward a coherent understanding of Paul's vision of justification through the imputation of the obedience of Christ to sinners through faith alone.

What Does It Mean That Israel Did Not "Attain The Law" Because She Pursued It "Not By Faith But as Though It Were by Works"?

Thoughts on Romans 9:30–10:4

What shall we say, then? That Gentiles who did not pursue righteousness have attained it, that is, a righteousness that is by faith; 31 but that Israel who pursued a law that would lead to righteousness did not succeed in reaching that law. 32 Why? Because they did not pursue it by faith, but as if it were based on works. They have stumbled over the stumbling stone, 33 as it is written, "Behold, I am laying in Zion a stone of stumbling, and a rock of offense; and whoever believes in him will not be put to shame." 10:1 Brothers, my heart's desire and prayer to God for them is that they may be saved. 2 For I bear them witness that they have a zeal for God, but not according to knowledge. 3 For, being ignorant of the righteousness of God, and seeking to establish their own, they did not submit to God's righteousness. 4 For Christ is the end of the law for righteousness to everyone who believes.

THESIS: ROMANS 9:32A ("Because they did not pursue it by faith, but as if it were based on works") teaches us that the long-term aim and end (τέλος) of the Mosaic law was and is "Christ for righteousness to everyone who believes" (10:4, my translation). The aim and end of the law was not to help us establish our own righteousness (10:3). To say it another way, submitting to the righteousness of God (10:3) is not accomplished by "works" (9:32), but by faith in Christ, which is the overall, long-term aim of the law. Therefore, Romans 9:32a does not exclude the meaning that there is a *subordinate, short-term* aim of the law that may suitably be described as "not of faith," as in Galatians 3:12 ("But the law is not of faith, rather 'The one who does them shall live by them'").

1. The situation in view in Romans 9:30–32 is Paul's contemporary situation described in 9:24 (". . . even us whom he has called, not from the Jews only but also from the Gentiles"). Jews and Gentiles are being called by God as vessels of mercy. But the problem of 9:1–5 lingers: While Gentiles are being saved, some Jews stumble over the stumbling stone of Christ (9:33) and are not saved (10:1), but are accursed and cut off from Christ (9:3). Paul was wrestling in Romans 9:6–13 with why his Jewish kinsmen were accursed in view of God's promises to Israel. He continues to wrestle with the stumbling and lostness of Israel in Romans 9:30–10:4. In 9:6–29, Paul answers the problem of Israel's perishing with the doctrine of election: Not all Israel is Israel (9:6). Here in 9:30–10:4, he answers the problem with Israel's unbelief and their rejection of the true, long-term aim of the Torah, namely, the Messiah (Christ) as their righteousness.

2. Even though the Gentiles have not been engaged in the pursuit of righteousness, many of them have laid hold of it, namely, the "righteousness that is by faith" (δικαιοσύνην δὲ τὴν ἐκ πίστεως). They may not even know about the law, but when they hear of Christ, who is the aim of the law (10:4), they believe on him, so that he becomes their righteousness (the aim of the law is "Christ . . . for righteousness to everyone who believes," even for those who do not know the law, 10:4).

On the other hand, Israel in Paul's day does know the law and is "pursuing a law [of] righteousness" (διώκων νόμον δικαιοσύνης, 9:31, author's translation). But they do not arrive at that law (εἰς νόμον οὐκ ἔφθασεν, 9:31). What does this mean—"pursue but fail to arrive at the law"? It may mean something general like: pursue and fail to keep the law's statutes. Or it may mean: pursue and fail to arrive at the overall, long-term aim of the law.

For example, if I said, "I pursued my diet but failed to attain it," I might mean: "I failed to eat the right things." Or I might mean: "I failed to lose weight." The context supports the second meaning in verse 31, namely, Israel, as a group in Paul's day, failed to attain the overall, long-term aim of the law, that is, "Christ for righteousness to everyone who believes" (Χριστὸς εἰς δικαιοσύνην παντὶ τῷ πιστεύοντι, 10:4).[1] In other words, Paul is not dealing here with a programmatic analysis of the law in all of its aspects; rather, he is specifically discussing the long-term aim of the law: Christ for righteousness to all who believe.

3. The clearest evidence for this (that Israel's failure to "attain the law" refers to her failure to attain the overall, long-term aim of the law: "Christ for righteousness") is that the *explanation* for Israel's failure to "attain the law" is that "they have stumbled over the stumbling stone" (9:32b). The stumbling stone is Christ, which is made clear in 9:33, since believing on him is the opposite of stumbling over the stone ("As it is written, 'Behold, I am laying in Zion a stone of stumbling, and a rock of offense; and whoever believes in him will not be put to shame.'"). So Israel failed to "attain the law" (v. 31b) because they stumbled over Christ by failing to believe on him "for righteousness," but sought to establish their own (10:3). Thus, "pursuing the law and not attaining it" refers to pursuing the overall, long-term aim of the law, namely, righteousness, which Paul argues is "Christ . . . for righteousness to everyone who believes" (10:4).

4. Another reason for saying that failure to "attain the law" (9:31) refers to failure to trust Christ for righteousness is the close parallel in

---

[1]Though my point in this appendix does not entirely depend on it, I am construing τέλος to be the subject of the sentence in Romans 10:4. It seems to me that nothing stands in the way of bringing the Greek words over into English in almost the exact order that they stand in the original:
τέλος γὰρ νόμου Χριστὸς εἰς δικαιοσύνην παντὶ τῷ πιστεύοντιx
For the goal of the law is Christ for righteousness to everyone who believes.
As I have considered the relevant sections in Daniel B. Wallace's *Greek Grammar Beyond the Basics* (Grand Rapids, MI: Zondervan, 1996), concerning the predicate nominative, and particularly the section titled "How to Distinguish Subject from Predicate Nominative" (42–46) and the section on Colwell's Construction, especially the appendix "When the Verb Is Absent" (269–270), it has seemed to me that no general rule can answer the question whether τέλος or Χριστὸς is the subject or the predicate nominative of this sentence. But Wallace makes one observation that inclines me toward construing τέλος as the subject: Concerning Colwell's rule about anarthrous definite predicate nouns (257), when there is no verb present (as in Romans 10:4), Wallace says, "By placing the PN [predicate nominative] before the subject, an author is making the PN emphatic and if emphatic, then either qualitative or definite" (270). Τέλος is before *Christos* in Romans 10:4. But it seems to me that Paul's intention in this verse is *not* to make τέλος emphatic, but to make *Christ* emphatic. In other words, the emphasis should be as follows: Not: Christ is *the goal of the law*, but: The goal of the law is *Christ*. What is surprising and emphatic in the flow of Paul's thought is not the introduction of the τέλος of the law, but the introduction of *Christ* as the τέλος of the law. Therefore, according to Wallace's comment, τέλος would not naturally be thought of as the predicate nominative, coming first for emphasis, but as the subject of the sentence. But again, I would say that the argument of this appendix does not depend on whether τέλος or Χριστὸς is the subject. More important is the fact that in the natural flow of the sentence, "Christ" belongs closely with the phrase "for righteousness to everyone who believes."

thought between 9:31 and 10:3. In 9:31 Paul says of Israel, "pursuing a law of righteousness, they did not attain the law." In 10:3 he says of Israel, "seeking to establish their own [righteousness] they did not submit to the righteousness of God." The "seeking" and "pursuing" in these two verses are very similar and probably refer to the same striving. Then in 10:4, Paul explains and supports (γὰρ) what he means by not submitting to "the righteousness of God." It refers to Israel's failure to embrace "Christ for righteousness to everyone who believes." This was the overall, long-term aim (τέλος 10:4a) of the law—to submit to God's righteousness, that is, to believe on Christ for righteousness. This is what Israel failed to attain because they did not believe on Christ for their righteousness.

5. This understanding of Israel's failure to "attain the law" (9:31) is confirmed by another parallel, this time between 9:32 and 10:3. Romans 9:32 says that the reason Israel failed to "attain the law" was because they went about this pursuit "not from faith but as from works" (οὐκ ἐκ πίστεω ἀλλ᾽ ὡς ἐξ ἔργων). The parallel in 10:3 says that the reason Israel failed to submit to God's righteousness is that they "sought to establish their own [righteousness]" (τὴν ἰδίαν δικαιοσύνην· ζητοῦντέ στῆσαι). Thus, the parallel is between seeking to establish one's own righteousness rather than submitting to God's righteousness, on the one hand (10:3), and pursuing the law "as from works," rather than "from faith," on the other hand (9:32). But 10:4 makes clear that the failure to submit to God's righteousness is equivalent to failing to embrace "Christ for righteousness" as the overall, long-term aim (τέλος) of the law.

The implication of this parallel is that "pursuing the law . . . as from works" (9:31–32) refers to pursuing the overall, long-term aim of the law, namely, "Christ for righteousness to everyone who believes," "as by works." Simply put, Israel stumbled over the stumbling stone, Christ, because they sought the overall, long-term aim of the law, namely, righteousness, "as from works," when, in fact, that aim (τέλος) was not "from works" but "by faith," namely, by faith in "Christ for righteousness to everyone who believes."

6. The upshot of this interpretation for what Romans 9:32 teaches about the law is this: Its long-term aim was and is "Christ for righ-

teousness to everyone who believes," and this long-term aim of the law was and is to be attained "by faith" and not "as by works."

7. A corollary of this conclusion is that Romans 9:32 views the law as it points to and aims at "Christ for righteousness," not in *all* the law's designs and relations to faith. Therefore, it would be a mistake to use Romans 9:32 to deny, for example, that there is a short-term aim of the law that may suitably be described as "not of faith" as in Galatians 3:12 ("But the law is not of faith, rather 'The one who does them shall live by them'"). I myself have argued in the past, for example, without careful distinction, that "the law teaches faith" because Romans 9:32 says that you don't "attain the law" if you fail to pursue it "by faith," but pursue "as from works." But the distinction that must be made is whether we are talking about the overall, long-term aim of the law, which is in view in Romans 9:32, or whether we are making a sweeping judgment about all the designs of the law. We would go beyond what Romans 9:32 teaches if we made such a sweeping judgment, so as to deny that there is a short-term design of the law not easily summed up in the phrase "the law teaches faith" but fairly described in the words "the law is not of faith" (Gal. 3:12).

For example, one short-term aim of the law was to "imprison everything under sin, so that the promise by faith in Jesus Christ might be given to those who believe" (Gal. 3:22). That is, the law functions, in a subordinate, short-term way, to keep people in custody, awaiting the fullness of time, which is a time of faith, as Galatians 3:23 says, "Now before faith came, we were held captive under the law, imprisoned until the coming faith would be revealed." If, in some sense, "faith" had not yet come, but was "to be later revealed," then it would not be strange to say "the law is not of faith" if the faith being referred to is the faith of Galatians 3:23, that is, faith in the Son of God who has come in the fullness of time (Gal. 4:4). This is probably what Paul means when he says in Galatians 3:12, "The law is not of faith." The faith that was to come—to which the law was leading Israel, as it held them in custody—is faith that is consciously in Christ, "the end of the law for righteousness for all who believe."

THOUGHTS ON LAW AND FAITH
IN GALATIANS 3

1. THE LAW, IN ITS NARROW, short-term design, demands perfectly doing the 613[1] commandments of the Pentateuch in order to have life (Gal. 3:10, 12; 5:3; 6:13; Rom. 4:2; 10:5). This is not a kind of legal arrangement that excludes reliance on God for enabling power. There is no thought in this arrangement of man being required to give to God what he has not first given to man (Rom. 11:35–36). This narrow, short-term design of the law holds up an absolute standard of child-like, humble, God-reliant, God-exalting perfection, and thus provides the moral backdrop without which the sin-atoning provisions of the Pentateuch and the work of Christ would make no sense.[2]

2. The recipients of this law (Israel and, indirectly, all the Gentiles) are uniformly sinful and hostile to God. They do not submit to God and cannot (Rom. 8:7).

3. Therefore, the effect of this law on sinful Israel, when she is confronted with hundreds of commandments, is (a) the awareness of latent sin (Rom. 7:7); (b) the increase of sin by its becoming exceedingly sinful (Rom. 5:20; 7:13); and (c) the multiplication of transgressions (Rom. 5:20; 4:15). This effect was part of God's design for the law: "[The law] was added because of transgressions" (Gal. 3:19); "The law came in to increase the trespass" (Rom. 5:20). The Mosaic law itself shows that its aim is indictment in the short run—Deuteronomy 31:26–27: "Take this Book of the Law and put it by the side of the ark of the covenant

---

[1]See John Sailhamer, *The Pentateuch as Narrative* (Grand Rapids, MI: Zondervan, 1992), 481, for the explanation of the origin of the number 613.
[2]On the underlying biblical demand for perfection see above, chapter 8, footnote 15.

of the LORD your God, that it may be there for a witness against you. For I know how rebellious and stubborn you are."

4. This narrow, short-term design of the law is expressed in Galatians 3:22: "The Scripture imprisoned everything under sin." The effect of this design of the law is to kill rather than to make alive. Paul says he is the servant "of a new covenant, not of the letter but of the Spirit. For the letter kills, but the Spirit gives life" (2 Cor. 3:6). The old covenant, the letter, is the Mosaic covenant, the law (Gal. 3:17–19; Rom. 7:6) which was different from the "new covenant," especially in that the old covenant could not "give life" the way the Spirit could. Paul says this in Galatians 3:21: "If a law had been given that could *give life*, then righteousness would indeed be by the law." The law could not give life. It could only kill, because it shut people up to sin and multiplied transgressions. Or, as Paul says in Romans 3:20, this narrow, short-term design of the law is not that anyone be justified but that the "knowledge of sin" be awakened: "By works of the law no human being will be justified in his sight, since through the law comes knowledge of sin."

5. All of this deadly design of the law is sufficient to warrant the statement in Galatians 3:12: "The law is not of faith." The point of this statement is not to say that the demand of the law for perfect obedience excluded reliance on God for enabling (see #1). The context of Galatians 3 makes clear that the point of saying "the law is not of faith" is that the design of the law was not to give life to the faith of the new covenant that would arrive with the coming of Christ. "The law is not of faith" means: The narrow, short-term design of the law is imprisonment to sin, multiplied transgressions, and death, all of which happen because the law is primarily "commandments" (Rom. 7:8–13; 13:8–9; Eph. 2:15, see below #12), demanding perfect obedience without giving the Spirit who "gives life" (Gal. 3:21; 2 Cor. 3:6).

6. This all-important context of Galatians 3 speaks of faith in a striking way: Faith is the way Abraham was justified when he received the promise by faith (3:6–8); and faith is something "later to be revealed" (after the law). It is something that does not "come" until Christ comes. The law "was added," Paul says, 430 years after Abraham, "until the offspring should come to whom the promise had been made" (Gal. 3:19). When Christ, the offspring, comes, then, the

deadly, old-covenant work of the law will pass away, and the time for the Spirit and life and justification by faith in Christ will have arrived. In Paul's way of thinking, the faith he has in view "has come," and the role of the law as a tutor to bring us to Christ is over:

> Now before faith came, we were held captive under the law, imprisoned until the coming faith would be revealed. So then, the law was our guardian until Christ came, in order that we might be justified by faith. But now that faith has come, we are no longer under a guardian. (Gal. 3:23–25)

7. The upshot of #6 is that there is another design of the law besides the narrow, short-term design of sin, transgression, unbelief, and death. There is an overall, long-term design for the law, namely, to lead Israel to Christ "in order that we might be justified by faith" (Gal. 3:24). God's design is that the outpouring of the Spirit (Gal. 4:6) and the giving of life and the act of justification by faith be clearly attached to the work of Christ. That is why, until Christ came, God restrained the Spirit and the gift of life and the work of faith.

8. In view of these two designs of the law (short-term to kill and long-term to lead to Christ who gives life), we can understand Paul's argument for why the law is not against the promise (Gal. 3:21) and therefore not against faith (Rom. 3:31). In Galatians 3:21 Paul asks, "Is the law then contrary to the promises of God?" His answer is an emphatic "Certainly not!" But the reason he gives is remarkable. To understand it, the rest of verse 21 and verse 22 must be taken together. He says:

> [21] [The promise and the law are not contrary because] if a law had been given that could give life, then righteousness would indeed be by the law. [22] But the Scripture imprisoned everything under sin, so that the promise by faith in Jesus Christ might be given to those who believe.

In other words, the reason the law is not against the promise is precisely that it was designed *not* to give life but to hold under sin and lead to Christ who gives life. Paul says that *if* the law had given life, then it would have been against the promise. It would have short-circuited the purpose of the promise to make Christ the basis of life and righteousness. It would have played into the hands of those who want to make their own doing (enabled by life-giving law) the basis of their right standing with God. But the law does not do that. It holds under sin and leads to Christ. Thus its aim (τέλος) is "Christ . . . for righteousness to everyone who believes" (Rom. 10:4). The short-term design of the law (to hinder life and faith and righteousness) serves the long-term design of the law (to base life and faith and righteousness on Christ). In this way, the fact that the law is "not of faith" serves faith in Christ. And the (non-life-giving) law prevents life and justification from being "by the law" (Gal. 3:21).

9. Now we need an explanation of Galatians 3:18. "If the inheritance comes by the law, it no longer comes by promise." This statement made the question in verse 21 very pressing: "Is the law then contrary to the promises?" Verse 18 surely sounds like law and promise are contrary, because it denies that they could both be the basis of the inheritance. Law and promise are antithetical foundations for the inheritance. Paul's argument in verses 21–22 (see #8) helps us understand why promise and law cannot both be the basis of the inheritance, and yet promise and law are not contrary.

Paul says that the law would indeed be contrary to the promise if it "gave life" ("If a law had been given that could give life, then righteousness would indeed be by the law"), but since the law doesn't give life, it will instead bring Israel to Christ in whom the blessing (inheritance) of Abraham comes to the Gentiles by faith (3:14). How then are we to understand the apparent antithesis between promise and law in verse 18? We understand the antithesis as potential: The law *would* have put the inheritance on another footing *if* God had ordained for the law to give life and thus enable people to attain righteousness without Christ. Thus the phrase "inheritance comes by the law" in verse 18 refers to the use of the law—not legalistically, but in the life-giving power of God—to attain a righteousness that would be acceptable to God without need of the work of Christ. This *would* be contrary to the promise that says, "In Christ Jesus [the offspring, 3:16] the blessing of Abraham [will] come to the Gentiles" (3:14). But the law is not contrary to the promise, since it was not added as another way of getting right with God without Christ, but "because of transgressions [to hold

Israel under sin] until the offspring should come to whom the promise had been made" (Gal. 3:19).

12. So "the law is not of faith" may mean that the law, in the narrow and short-term sense, was not designed to produce faith, *even though* it may call for faith when understood in its larger Pentateuchal context. Its narrow and short-term design is to be "letter," not "Spirit," and so to kill rather than give life (2 Cor. 3:6), that is, "to imprison everything under sin" (Gal. 3:22, 19; Rom. 5:20; 7:8, 13). It does this by (a) putting commandments in the dominant place rather than God's redeeming Substitute and enabling grace and thus awakening the "knowledge of sin" (Rom. 3:20; 7:7); (b) by commanding perfect obedience (Gal. 3:10; 5:3; 6:13); and (c) by not providing the new heart of the new covenant that enables the fulfillment of the law in a life of love (Deut. 5:29; 29:4; Gal. 3:21, 23; Rom. 8:3–4).

THOUGHTS ON GALATIANS 5:6 AND THE RELATIONSHIP BETWEEN FAITH AND LOVE

For in Christ Jesus neither circumcision nor uncircumcision counts for anything, but only faith working through love.

ἐν γὰρ Χριστῷ 'Ιησοῦ οὔτε περιτομή τι ἰσχύει οὔτε ἀκροβυστία ἀλλὰ πίστις δι' ἀγάπης ἐνεργουμένη

AS WE WILL SEE, much of the Reformation division between Rome and Protestantism was over how to understand this verse. The observation has been made to me, for example, "In Galatians 5:6, Paul doesn't say, 'the kind of faith which works through love avails everything (including justification),' but he does say that 'faith expressing itself in love avails everything (including justification).'" The implication of this observation is that the faith that justifies is not merely the kind of faith that produces the new activity of love, but rather that the new activity of love is a form of faith.

It is possible that the nuance of ἐνεργουμένη ("working") falls on the self-extension of faith, so that "faith working through love" means that faith extends itself in the form of love. But that is not obvious either from the grammar or the nearest parallels in the New Testament.

One might put a "self-expressive" twist on the middle voice of ἐνεργουμένη that it need not have in any of its uses in the New Testament and cannot have in several. In Paul's use of ἐνεργεῖν in the active voice, the verb generally has a personal subject and a direct object and means "to effect or bring about" (e.g., 1 Cor. 12:6, 11; Gal.

3:5; Eph. 1:11, 20; Phil. 2:13). But wherever he uses ἐνεργεῖν in the middle voice, the subject is not a person, and there are no direct objects. The meaning is simply "become effective" (Rom. 7:5; 2 Cor. 1:6; 4:12; Eph. 3:20; Col. 1:29; 1 Thess. 2:13; 2 Thess. 2:7). That is the basic difference between the active and middle voice: In the active voice, someone effects something; in the middle voice, something "becomes effective." There is no necessary implication in the middle voice of the subject extending itself as a new form.

On the contrary, several parallels show that this is not likely. For example, in 1 Thessalonians 2:13 Paul says, "You accepted [the word of God] not as the word of men but as what it really is, the word of God, which is at work in you believers" (ὃς καὶ ἐνεργεῖται ἐν ὑμῖν τοῖς πιστεύουσιν). Here "the word of God" is the subject of the middle voice ἐνεργεῖται ("is at work"). The point is that the word of God is "becoming effective" in producing bold and patient Christians under affliction (as 2:14 makes plain). So the effect of the word is not a self-extension of the word itself, but rather is patience in affliction. The word of God is not "extending itself" in patience. The word of God and patient endurance are different realities. The word effects or brings about the endurance, but does not become a form of endurance.

Another example, James 5:16, is the closest parallel in the New Testament to Paul's use of ἐνεργουμένη here. Recall the form of Galatians 5:6 (ἐν γὰρ Χριστῷ Ἰησοῦ οὔτε περιτομή τι ἰσχύει οὔτε ἀκροβυστία ἀλλὰ πίστις δι᾽ ἀγάπης ἐνεργουμένη). James says, "The prayer of a righteous person has great power as it is working" (πολὺ ἰσχύει δέησις δικαίου ἐνεργουμένη). What makes this parallel so close to Galatians 5:6 is (1) the use of the verb ἰσχύει ("counts" in Gal. 5:6; "has great power" in Jas. 5:16) both here and in Galatians 5:6; (2) the anarthrous noun as subject (δέησις and πίστις); (3) the anarthrous identical form of ἐνεργουμένη ending the sentence; and (4) a modifier separating the subject (δέησις) and the final participle (ἐνεργουμένη), namely, δι᾽ ἀγάπης in Galatians 5:6 and δικαίου in James 5:16.

A literal rendering of James 5:16 would be: "The prayer of a righteous man, becoming effective, avails much." This corresponds in Galatians 5:6 to "The faith becoming effective through love avails [justification]." The only point I want to make is that prayer is not rain. That is, when James says that Elijah prayed and it "became effective" in drought and rain, he was not saying that prayer "expressed itself" in drought and rain. He was saying that prayer had the effect of producing drought and rain. That is analogous to how faith relates to love.

I conclude therefore that the use of ἐνεργουμένη in the middle voice does not have the nuance implication of extending itself, with the implication that the love in which this self-extension happens is part of what faith is. That cannot be shown from the words as they are used.

Moreover the grammar of the verse suggests that Paul is saying that justifying faith is the kind of faith that produces love. The anarthrous participle (ἐνεργουμένη) following an anarthrous noun (πίστις) is naturally construed as having an attributive relationship. That is, the natural way to read it is: "faith, which through love becomes effective." "The attributive participle stands both with and without the article and is equivalent to a relative clause."[1]

Therefore, even though it is possible that ἐνεργουμένη is adverbial ("faith, by means of becoming effective through love, avails justification"), this is not obvious. In fact, the effect of this unnecessary translation is to make love "the instrument of the instrument" of justification (justification is by faith by love). This translation is then used as an argument that justification is not by faith alone apart from works of love, but rather that justification is by faith by means of works of love. This, I think is the opposite of what Paul teaches in Romans 3:28; 4:4–6; 5:1; 10:3–4; Philippians 3:8–9; Galatians 2:16; 3:8, 24.

In one sense, the Reformation hinges on how love and faith are related in Galatians 5:6. Luther summed up the battleground this way in reference to Galatians 5:6: "This place the schoolmen do wrest unto their own opinion, whereby they teach that we are justified by charity or works. 'For they say that faith, even though it be infused from above . . . justifieth not, except it be formed by charity."[2] In other words, what Luther was willing to fight over was whether δι' ἀγάπης ἐνεργουμένη was attributive, defining the kind of faith that justifies (his own view), or was doubly adverbial, explaining how faith justifies. Thus (1) ἐνεργουμένη is adverbial in that it implies that faith justifies by means of extending itself through love. And (2) δι' ἀγάπης has an

[1] J. H. Moulton, A Grammar of the Greek New Testament, 3 vols. (Edinburgh: T&T Clark, 1963), 3:152.
[2] Martin Luther, Commentary on St. Paul's Epistle to the Galatians (Westwood, NJ: Fleming H. Revell, 1953), 464.

adverbial force in that it implies that the essentially justifying instrument is faith formed by love—that is, faith in the form of love.

I would argue that we stay closer to the mind of Paul by giving δι' ἀγάπης ἐνεργουμένη a simple attributive meaning. "Faith, which becomes effective through love, avails justification." The clause "which becomes effective through love" is an adjectival modifier of faith. It tells what kind of faith avails justification. Therefore, love as an expression of faith is not the instrument of justification—it does not unite us to Christ who is our perfection. Only faith does. But this faith is the kind of faith that inevitably gives rise to love.[3]

---

[3]My effort to explain why and how justifying faith has this effect is found in *Future Grace*.

USING THE LAW LAWFULLY

Thoughts on 1 Timothy 1:5–11

⁵ The aim of our charge is love that issues from a pure heart and a good conscience and a sincere faith. ⁶ Certain persons, by swerving from these, have wandered away into vain discussion, ⁷ desiring to be teachers of the law, without understanding either what they are saying or the things about which they make confident assertions. ⁸ Now we know that the law is good, if one uses it lawfully, ⁹ understanding this, that the law is not laid down for the just but for the lawless and disobedient, for the ungodly and sinners, for the unholy and profane, for those who strike their fathers and mothers, for murderers, ¹⁰ the sexually immoral, men who practice homosexuality, enslavers, liars, perjurers, and whatever else is contrary to sound doctrine, ¹¹ in accordance with the gospel of the glory of the blessed God with which I have been entrusted.

FIRST TIMOTHY 1:5 TEACHES THAT "the aim of our charge is love from a pure heart and a good conscience and a sincere faith." So Paul's gospel preaching aims at a certain kind of lifestyle. Love. That is what accords with his instruction.

This love flows "from a pure heart and a good conscience and a sincere faith" (v. 5). So the way to teach and awaken this love is by focusing on the transformation of the heart and the conscience and the awakening and strengthening of faith.

However, according to verses 6–7, "certain persons, by swerving from these, have wandered away into vain discussion, desiring to be *teachers of the law, without understanding either what they are saying* or the things about which they make confident assertions." So their error is that they misuse the law. They are trying to teach the law, but they are turning aside from matters of the *heart* and *conscience* and *faith*. And so they are not arriving at love. In this way, they are making the law an instrument of something other than love.

But in Romans 13:8 and Galatians 5:14, Paul says that the law is fulfilled by love. So these men do not know what they are doing. Is the law then the problem?

No. Paul absolves the law by saying in verse 8, "Now we know that the law is good, if one uses it lawfully." The "lawful" use of the law is to use it now as a pointer to the *gospel*, which is the way to awaken love (as Paul shows in the rest of the passage). Paul says in verse 9, "The law is not laid down for the just but for the lawless." Then he lists several kinds of lawless people that he says the law is meant to confront (ungodly and sinners, the unholy and profane, those who strike their fathers and mothers, murderers, the sexually immoral, men who practice homosexuality, enslavers, liars, perjurers).

Then, in a decisive and sweeping statement, he says that the law is meant to confront and expose not only this long list of ungodly people but also "whatever else is contrary to sound doctrine, in accordance with the gospel of the glory of the blessed God." This is remarkable. To use the law lawfully (v. 8) is to understand that it is designed to lead people to the gospel of Christ and to indict what is not in accord with the gospel. In this way, the lawful use of the law leads to the transformation of the heart through "sincere faith" (v. 5) and thus leads to love, which is in turn the aim of Paul's preaching (v. 5) and the fulfilling of the law (Rom. 13:8). *The* key defining criterion of the life-change that Paul is pursuing is whether it is "in accordance with the gospel of the glory of the blessed God" (v. 11). Using the law lawfully means using it to *convict people of living out of accordance with the gospel.* "The law is for . . . [convicting people of] whatever is contrary to sound teaching . . ." (v. 10, author's translation), that is, whatever does not "accord with the glorious gospel" (v. 11).

And so Paul's focus is on what the gospel does to people in heart and conscience and faith (v. 5). This gives rise to love (v. 5). But if we turn it around and start using the law as the direct and decisive means of sanctification, it will be misused and will abort. We will fall under the criticism of verse 7: "[They have wandered into vain discussion] desiring to be teachers of the law, without understanding either what

they are saying or the things about which they make confident assertions." In other words, there are moralists who use simple teachings
about right and wrong—even from the Bible—to get people to change
behavior, but do not know what they are doing. They do not know that
what they are doing is profoundly out of sync (κατὰ, v. 11) with the
gospel. They don't understand the way the gospel works. They don't
understand Romans 7:4: "My brothers, you also have died to the law
through the body of Christ, so that you may belong to another, to him
who has been raised from the dead, in order that we may bear fruit
for God."

We bear fruit for God (love) by being joined through faith to Jesus,
not through the law. That is what the law was ultimately designed to
show.

Does the Doctrine of the Imputation of Christ's Righteousness Imply That the Cross Is Insufficient for Our Right Standing with God?

WHEN WE TEACH THAT our right standing with God is attained through the imputation of Christ's obedience to our account (2 Cor. 5:21; Rom. 4:6, 11; 5:19; 10:3), does this imply that the work of Christ on the cross—his final suffering and death—are insufficient for our justification?

This question arises in part because of texts that connect the cause of justification specifically to the cross of Christ. For example:

- Romans 3:24–25: "[They] are justified by his grace as a gift, through the redemption that is in Christ Jesus, whom God put forward as a propitiation by his blood."
- Romans 4:25: "[He] was delivered up for our trespasses and raised for our justification."
- Romans 5:9: "Since, therefore, we have now been justified by his blood, much more shall we be saved by him from the wrath of God."
- Galatians 2:21: "I do not nullify the grace of God, for if righteousness were through the law, then Christ died for no purpose."

To see the answer, we might ask a similar question concerning the forgiveness of sins. In other words: Does the insistence upon Jesus' sinless life imply that the work of Christ as the spotless Lamb of God on the cross is insufficient for the canceling of the debt of our sins? Our sins being canceled and forgiven is connected most directly to the death of Christ. For example:

- Colossians 2:14: "[He forgave] by canceling the record of debt that stood against us with its legal demands. This he set aside, nailing it to the cross."
- 1 Corinthians 15:3: "I delivered to you as of first importance what I also received: that Christ died for our sins in accordance with the Scriptures."
- Isaiah 53:5: "He was wounded for our transgressions; he was crushed for our iniquities."
- 1 Peter 2:24: "He himself bore our sins in his body on the tree."
- Revelation 1:5: "To him who loves us and has freed us from our sins by his blood."
- 1 John 1:7: "The blood of Jesus his Son cleanses us from all sin."

Is the death of Jesus sufficient to cleanse us from all our sins? Yes, but only *as the climax of a sinless life*. The book of Hebrews is most explicit about the necessity of the Son of God being perfect and without sin so that he can bear our sins once for all.

- Hebrews 4:15: "We do not have a high priest who is unable to sympathize with our weaknesses, but one who in every respect has been tempted as we are, *yet without sin*."
- Hebrews 7:27–28: "He has no need, like those high priests, to offer sacrifices daily, *first for his own sins* and then for those of the people, since he did this once for all when he offered up himself. For the law appoints men in their weakness as high priests, but the word of the oath, which came later than the law, appoints *a Son who has been made perfect forever*."
- Hebrews 2:10: "It was fitting that he, for whom and by whom all things exist, in bringing many sons to glory, should *make the founder of their salvation perfect* through suffering."
- Hebrews 5:9: "And *being made perfect*, he became the source of eternal salvation to all who obey him."

So the death of the Son of God is sufficient to cover all our sins *as the climax of a sinless life*. This is no disparagement to the cross. It is not adding to the cross. The New Testament writers saw the death of Christ as the climax of his life. His whole life was designed to bring him to the cross (Mark 10:45; John 12:27; Heb. 2:14). That is why he was born, and why he lived. To speak of the saving effect of his death was therefore to speak of his death *as the sum and climax of his sinless life.*

Similarly, the final obedience of Christ in his death is sufficient to justify his people *as the climax of a sinless life.* It is not likely that the apostles thought of Jesus' obedience on the cross as separate from his obedience leading to the cross. Where would one draw the line between his life of sinless obedience and the final acts of obedience? Any line would be artificial. Do we draw it at the point where he submitted to the piercing of his hands? Or at the point when he submitted to his arrest in the garden? Or at the point where he endured Judas' departure from the supper? Or at the point where he planned his final entry to Jerusalem? Or at the point where he "set his face to go to Jerusalem" (Luke 9:51)? Or at the point of his baptism where he said, "It is fitting for us to fulfill all righteousness" (Matt. 3:15)?

It is more likely that when Paul spoke of Jesus' obedience as the cause of our justification he meant not merely the final acts of obedience on the cross, but rather the cross *as the climax of his obedient life.* This seems to be the way Paul is thinking in Philippians 2:7–8: "[He] made himself nothing . . . being born in the likeness of men. And being found in human form, he humbled himself by becoming *obedient to the point of death, even death on a cross.*" Notice the sequence of thought: He became a human. That is, he was found in human form. > He humbled himself. > The way he humbled himself was by becoming obedient. > This obedience was so complete that it willingly embraced death. > Even death in the most painful and shameful way—on a cross.

What this text shows is that between "being born in the likeness of men" at one end of his life and "even death on a cross" at the other end of his life was a life of self-humbling obedience. The fact that it came to its climax on the cross in the most terrible and glorious way is probably what causes Paul to speak of the cross as the sum and climax of all his obedience. But it is very unlikely that Paul would have separated the obedience of the final hours from the obedience that designed, planned, pursued, and embraced those final hours.

Thus when Paul says in Romans 5:18, "*One act of righteousness* [δι᾽ ἑνὸς δικαιώματος] leads to justification and life," and when he says in Romans 5:19, "By the *one man's obedience* [διὰ τῆς ὑπακοῆς τοῦ ἑνός] the many will be made righteous," there is little reason to think he meant to separate the final obedience of Jesus from the total obedience of Jesus. In Adam's case, it only took one sin to completely fail. In Christ's case, it took an entire life to completely succeed. That is how their disobedience and obedience correspond to each other.

Thus when Paul compares the "one trespass" of Adam to Christ's "one act of righteousness" (Rom. 5:18), there is no single act in Christ's life that corresponds to the eating of the forbidden fruit. Rather, his whole life of obedience was necessary so that he would not be a second *failing* Adam. *One single sin* would have put him in the category of a failing Adam. But it took *one entire life of obedience* to be a successful second Adam. That this complete life of obedience came to climax in the freely embraced death of Christ made such an overwhelming impression on his followers that they looked upon the "cross" or the "death" as the climax and sum of his obedience, but not separate from his cross-pursuing life.

So back to our initial question: "Does the doctrine of the imputation of Christ's righteousness imply that the cross is insufficient for our right standing with God?" The answer is no. Just as the perfectly obedient life of Christ is essential to the death of Christ as a covering for our sin, so the perfectly obedient life of Christ is essential to the death of Christ as the supreme act of obedience by which we are appointed righteous in him. The death of Christ is sufficient for covering our sins *as the climax of a sinless life.* And the death of Christ is sufficient for our justification *as the climax of a sinless life.*

TWELVE THESES ON WHAT IT MEANS TO FULFILL THE LAW

With Special Reference to Romans 8:4

¹ There is therefore now no condemnation for those who are in Christ Jesus. ² For the law of the Spirit of life has set you free in Christ Jesus from the law of sin and death. ³ For God has done what the law, weakened by the flesh, could not do. By sending his own Son in the likeness of sinful flesh and for sin, he condemned sin in the flesh, ⁴ in order that the righteous requirement of the law might be fulfilled in us, who walk not according to the flesh but according to the Spirit. ⁵ For those who live according to the flesh set their minds on the things of the flesh, but those who live according to the Spirit set their minds on the things of the Spirit. (Rom. 8:1–5)

WHAT DOES PAUL MEAN IN Romans 8:4 when he says that the aim of Christ's death is "that the righteous requirement of the law might be fulfilled in us, who walk not according to the flesh but according to the Spirit"?

Some take this to mean that Christ fulfilled the law *for* us when he obeyed it perfectly and died as the perfect sacrifice on our behalf.[1] Thus in him we are perfect with his perfection, and in him we are pardoned by his blood. I believe that is true in reality, and that it is foundational for a right understanding of Paul and for a life fully conformed to Christ's work. But I don't think that is the point of verse 4.

---

[1] Moo, *The Epistle to the Romans*, 483. "First, the passive verb 'might be fulfilled' points not to something that we are to do but something that is done in and for us. Second, the always imperfect obedience of the law by Christians does not satisfy what is demanded by the logic of the text." I stand with Moo theologically, but on this verse, not exegetically.

The reason I disagree with this interpretation is that it doesn't fit the wording of the text very well. Verse 4 says the aim of Christ's death is "that the righteous requirement of the law might be fulfilled *in* us." It does not say that the law is to be fulfilled *for* us. Again, I believe that the law is indeed fulfilled for us by Christ. I believe that is implied in Romans 5:19 and in the entire picture that unfolds when all the relevant texts make their contribution. But that does not seem to be the point here. In the next verse (v. 5), Paul focuses specifically on *our walking*—that is, our living—as the way the fulfillment of the righteous requirement of the law will happen: ". . . that the righteous requirement of the law might be fulfilled *in* us, who *walk . . . according to the Spirit*."[2]

So my question is: What does it mean to fulfill the requirement of the law? And specifically, how can any of my "walking" by the Spirit—which is always imperfect in this life—be said to fulfill God's law, which is holy and just and good? God's divine standard does not say, "Pretty good will do." I will try to answer this question with a summary of the relationship of the Christian to the law in twelve theses.

1. Fulfilling the righteous requirement of the law in Romans 8:4 refers to a life of real love for people (Rom. 13:8–10; Gal. 5:13–18; Matt. 7:12; 22:37–40).[3]

> *Owe no one anything, except to love each other, for the one who loves another has fulfilled the law. For the commandments, "You shall not commit adultery, You shall not murder, You shall not steal, You shall not covet," and any other commandment, are summed up in this word:*

---

[2] N. T. Wright sees the term in Romans 8:4 translated in the ESV "righteous requirement" (τὸ δικαίωμα τοῦ νόμου) *not* as a reference to behavior that the law requires, but as a reference to the decree of "resurrection life" that the law intended to give us, but could not because it was weak through the flesh (Rom. 7:10). Wright, *The Letter to the Romans*, 577–580. I don't see his arguments for this as compelling, but I don't want to make more of this than is necessary. In the end, he says that his view "does not, of course, exclude" the view I am taking, namely, that Paul is saying God condemned sin in the flesh of Jesus so that the "righteous requirement of the law" (meaning the way of life that the law required) might be fulfilled in us (580). And when he gets to Romans 13:8–10, he says, "People who love their neighbors thus 'fulfill Torah,' both in the immediate sense that they will never do any of the things that Torah forbids, and in the wider sense that through them God's way of life will be seen to advantage" (725).
[3] From the list of some of the Ten Commandments in Romans 13:8–10 we may infer that the law that love fulfills is primarily thought of as the *moral* law of God, which finds its chief historical summary in the Ten Commandments, which are tailored for Israel's situation. The focus of our fulfilling the law is not on all the Jewish-specific laws, such as circumcision and sacrifices and food laws and feast days. However, when Jesus says in Matthew 22:40 that "*all* the Law and the Prophets" hang on the love commands, he may indeed see love as, in some sense, the source and goal of even the more Jewish-specific laws. Either way, the point is that the law was pointing to Christ and to a life of love lived in dependence on him.

"You shall love your neighbor as yourself." Love does no wrong to a neighbor; therefore love is the fulfilling of the law. (Rom. 13:8–10)

You were called to freedom, brothers. Only do not use your freedom as an opportunity for the flesh, but through love serve one another. For the whole law is fulfilled in one word: "You shall love your neighbor as yourself." But if you bite and devour one another, watch out that you are not consumed by one another. But I say, walk by the Spirit, and you will not gratify the desires of the flesh. For the desires of the flesh are against the Spirit, and the desires of the Spirit are against the flesh, for these are opposed to each other, to keep you from doing the things you want to do. But if you are led by the Spirit, you are not under the law. (Gal. 5:13–18)

Whatever you wish that others would do to you, do also to them, for this is the Law and the Prophets. (Matt. 7:12)

[Jesus] said to him, "You shall love the Lord your God with all your heart and with all your soul and with all your mind. This is the great and first commandment. And a second is like it: You shall love your neighbor as yourself. On these two commandments depend all the Law and the Prophets." (Matt. 22:37–40)

2. Our fulfilling God's law in loving others is *not* the ground of our justification. The ground of justification is the sacrifice and obedience of Christ alone, appropriated through faith alone before any other acts are performed. Our fulfilling the law is the fruit and evidence of being justified by faith (Rom. 3:20–22, 24–25, 28; 4:4–6; 5:19; 8:3; 10:3–4; 2 Cor. 5:21).

By works of the law no human being will be justified in his sight, since through the law comes knowledge of sin. But now the righteousness of God has been manifested apart from the law, although the Law and the Prophets bear witness to it—the righteousness of God through faith in Jesus Christ for all who believe. (Rom. 3:20–22)

[Those who are in Christ] are justified by his grace as a gift, through the redemption that is in Christ Jesus, whom God put forward as a propitiation by his blood, to be received by faith. This was to show God's righteousness, because in his divine forbearance he had passed over former sins. (Rom. 3:24–25)

*We hold that one is justified by faith apart from works of the law.
(Rom. 3:28)*

*To the one who works, his wages are not counted as a gift but as his
due. And to the one who does not work but trusts him who justifies
the ungodly, his faith is counted as righteousness, just as David also
speaks of the blessing of the one to whom God counts righteousness
apart from works. (Rom. 4:4–6)*

*As by the one man's disobedience the many were made sinners, so by the
one man's obedience the many will be made righteous. (Rom. 5:19)*

*God has done what the law, weakened by the flesh, could not do. By
sending his own Son in the likeness of sinful flesh and for sin, he condemned sin in the flesh. (Rom. 8:3)*

*Being ignorant of the righteousness of God, and seeking to establish
their own, they did not submit to God's righteousness. For Christ
is the end of the law for righteousness to everyone who believes.
(Rom. 10:3–4)*

*For our sake he made him to be sin who knew no sin, so that in him we
might become the righteousness of God. (2 Cor. 5:21)*

(See also Phil. 3:8–9; 1 Cor. 1:30; Tit. 3:5; Gal. 2:16, 21; 3:10;
5:2–3.)

3. This fulfilling of God's law in loving others is rendered not in our
own strength but by the presence and power of the Holy Spirit (Rom.
8:4; Gal. 5:13–16, 22–23).

*[God condemned sin in Christ's flesh] in order that the righteous
requirement of the law might be fulfilled in us, who walk not according
to the flesh but according to the Spirit. (Rom. 8:4)*

*You were called to freedom, brothers. Only do not use your freedom
as an opportunity for the flesh, but through love serve one another. For
the whole law is fulfilled in one word: "You shall love your neighbor as
yourself." But if you bite and devour one another, watch out that you
are not consumed by one another. But I say, walk by the Spirit, and you
will not gratify the desires of the flesh. (Gal. 5:13–16)*

The fruit of the Spirit is love, joy, peace, patience, kindness, goodness,
faithfulness, gentleness, self-control; against such things there is no law.
(Gal. 5:22–23)

4. This fulfilling of God's law in loving others through the Spirit
is rendered by faith, that is, by being satisfied with all that God is for
us in Christ and him crucified—the perseverance of the same faith that
justifies (Gal. 3:5; 5:6; 1 Tim. 1:5; Heb. 11:6, 24–26; 10:34).

Does he who supplies the Spirit to you and works miracles among you
do so by works of the law, or by hearing with faith? (Gal. 3:5)

In Christ Jesus neither circumcision nor uncircumcision counts for
anything, but only faith working through love. (Gal. 5:6)

The aim of our charge is love that issues from a pure heart and a good
conscience and a sincere faith. (1 Tim. 1:5)

Without faith it is impossible to please him, for whoever would draw
near to God must believe that he exists and that he rewards those who
seek him. (Heb. 11:6)

By faith Moses, when he was grown up, refused to be called the son of
Pharaoh's daughter, choosing rather to be mistreated with the people
of God than to enjoy the fleeting pleasures of sin. He considered the
reproach of Christ greater wealth than the treasures of Egypt, for he
was looking to the reward. (Heb. 11:24–26)

You had compassion on those in prison, and you joyfully accepted the
plundering of your property, since you knew that you yourselves had a
better possession and an abiding one. (Heb. 10:34)

5. This fulfilling of God's law in loving others through the Spirit
by faith is not a perfect love in this life (Rom. 7:15, 19, 23–25; Phil.
3:12).

I do not understand my own actions. For I do not do what I want, but
I do the very thing I hate. (Rom. 7:15)

I do not do the good I want, but the evil I do not want is what I keep
on doing. (Rom. 7:19)

I see in my members another law waging war against the law of my mind and making me captive to the law of sin that dwells in my members. Wretched man that I am! Who will deliver me from this body of death? Thanks be to God through Jesus Christ our Lord! So then, I myself serve the law of God with my mind, but with my flesh I serve the law of sin. (Rom. 7:23–25)

Not that I have already obtained this or am already perfect, but I press on to make it my own, because Christ Jesus has made me his own. (Phil. 3:12)

6. But this fulfilling of God's law in loving others through the Spirit by faith will become perfect when we die or when Christ returns, and we will live in the perfection of love forever (Rom. 8:30; Phil. 1:6; Heb. 12:22–23).

Those whom he predestined he also called, and those whom he called he also justified, and those whom he justified he also glorified. (Rom. 8:30)

I am sure of this, that he who began a good work in you will bring it to completion at the day of Jesus Christ. (Phil. 1:6)

You have come to Mount Zion and to the city of the living God, the heavenly Jerusalem, and to innumerable angels in festal gathering, and to the assembly of the firstborn who are enrolled in heaven, and to God, the judge of all, and to the spirits of the righteous made perfect. (Heb. 12:22–23)

7. Even though we will one day be perfected in love, the totality of our existence, from conception to eternity, will never be a perfect one, because it will always include the first chapter of our fallen life. We will always be forgiven—that is, we will always be those who have sinned. We will always be in need of an imputed, alien righteousness and a sin-bearing Substitute for our right standing before God. In this way, Christ will be glorified forever in our salvation. We will forever lean on his righteousness and his sacrifice (Heb. 7:25; Rev. 5:9–10; 15:3).

[Jesus] is able to save to the uttermost those who draw near to God through him, since he always lives to make intercession for them. (Heb. 7:25)

> They sang a new song, saying, "Worthy are you to take the scroll and to open its seals, for you were slain, and by your blood you ransomed people for God from every tribe and language and people and nation, and you have made them a kingdom and priests to our God, and they shall reign on the earth." (Rev. 5:9–10)

> They sing the song of Moses, the servant of God, and the song of the Lamb. (Rev. 15:3)

8. Even though imperfect, this Spirit-dependent, Christ-exalting love (which is essentially self-sacrificing gladness in the temporal and eternal good of others, 2 Cor. 8:1–2, 8) is the true and real direction of life that God's law requires. In this life, we have new direction, not full perfection. This direction *is* what the law demands on the way to perfection (cf. texts under #1).

9. This fulfilling of the Old Testament law in the loving of others through the Spirit by faith is sometimes called "the law of liberty" (James 1:25; 2:12) and "the law of Christ" (1 Cor. 9:21; Gal. 6:2).

9.1 When the fulfilling of the law is called "the law of liberty," it means that, in the pursuit of love, Christians are free from law-keeping as the ground of our justification and as the power of our sanctification. Instead, we pursue it by the "law of the Spirit of life . . . in Christ Jesus" (Rom. 8:2). We look to the Spirit of Christ for transformation so that love flows by power from within, not pressure from without. We are dead to law-keeping and therefore at liberty to bear fruit for God in the newness of the Spirit (Rom. 7:4, 6). The law of liberty is the leading of the Spirit, and "where the Spirit of the Lord is, there is freedom" (2 Cor. 3:17) (Jas. 1:25; 2:10–12; Gal. 5:1; Rom. 7:4, 6; 2 Cor. 3:17–18).

> The one who looks into the perfect law, the law of liberty, and perseveres, being no hearer who forgets but a doer who acts, he will be blessed in his doing. (Jas. 1:25)

> Whoever keeps the whole law but fails in one point has become accountable for all of it. For he who said, "Do not commit adultery," also said, "Do not murder." If you do not commit adultery but do murder, you have become a transgressor of the law. So speak and so act as those who are to be judged under the law of liberty. (Jas. 2:10–12)

For freedom Christ has set us free; stand firm therefore, and do not submit again to a yoke of slavery. (Gal. 5:1)

My brothers, you also have died to the law through the body of Christ, so that you may belong to another, to him who has been raised from the dead, in order that we may bear fruit for God. . . . But now we are released from the law, having died to that which held us captive, so that we serve in the new way of the Spirit and not in the old way of the written code. (Rom. 7:4, 6)

The Lord is the Spirit, and where the Spirit of the Lord is, there is freedom. And we all, with unveiled face, beholding the glory of the Lord, are being transformed into the same image from one degree of glory to another. For this comes from the Lord who is the Spirit. (2 Cor. 3:17–18)

9.2 When the fulfilling of the law is called "the law of Christ," it means that our pursuit of love is guided and enabled by the life, word, and Spirit of Jesus Christ. The law of Christ is not a new list of behaviors on the outside, but a new Treasure, Friend, and Master on the inside. He *did* give us "a new commandment" ("A new commandment I give to you, that you love one another, even as I have loved you, that you also are to love one another," John 13:34). But this standard of love is the life and power of a person who indwells us by his Spirit (Rom. 7:4; 8:11). We pursue love as "the law of Christ" by looking to Christ as our sin-covering sacrifice, our all-sufficient righteousness, our all-satisfying Treasure, our all-providing Protection and Helper, and our all-wise counselor and guide (Rom. 7:4; 8:9, 12–14; 1 Cor. 9:21; Gal. 2:20; 6:2).

My brothers, you also have died to the law through the body of Christ, so that you may belong to another, to him who has been raised from the dead, in order that we may bear fruit for God. (Rom. 7:4)

Anyone who does not have the Spirit of Christ does not belong to him. . . . So then, brothers, we are debtors, not to the flesh, to live according to the flesh. For if you live according to the flesh you will die, but if by the Spirit you put to death the deeds of the body, you will live. For all who are led by the Spirit of God are sons of God. (Rom. 8:9, 12–14)

To those outside the law I became as one outside the law (not being outside the law of God but under the law of Christ) that I might win those outside the law. (1 Cor. 9:21)

I have been crucified with Christ. It is no longer I who live, but Christ who lives in me. And the life I now live in the flesh I live by faith in the Son of God, who loved me and gave himself for me. (Gal. 2:20)

Bear one another's burdens, and so fulfill the law of Christ. (Gal. 6:2)

10. The Old Testament law can be understood narrowly as a set of commandments, or more broadly as the entire teaching of the Pentateuch, or even as all the instruction of God in the Old Testament wherever he gives it.

10.1 In the narrow sense, one may think of the law as commanding perfect obedience that, if we could perform it (the way Adam should have) by depending on God's help, would be our righteousness and the ground of our justification. But, because of our sin, the law does not lead to life in this way (Gal. 3:21), but shuts us up to look away from law-keeping to Christ so that we might be justified through faith in him (Gal. 3:21–25).

Is the law then contrary to the promises of God? Certainly not! For if a law had been given that could give life, then righteousness would indeed be by the law. But the Scripture imprisoned everything under sin, so that the promise by faith in Jesus Christ might be given to those who believe. Now before faith came, we were held captive under the law, imprisoned until the coming faith would be revealed. So then, the law was our guardian until Christ came, in order that we might be justified by faith. But now that faith has come, we are no longer under a guardian. (Gal. 3:21–25)

10.2. In the broader sense of the whole Pentateuch or the whole Old Testament, we may think of the law not merely as making demands, but also as offering justification through faith by pointing forward to a Redeemer who would provide the ground of that justification, and in whom Jews and Gentiles would be counted righteous because of his blood and righteousness (Gen. 15:6; Rom. 4:3; Rom. 3:19–22).

[Abraham] believed the LORD, and he counted it to him as righteousness. (Gen. 15:6)

What does the Scripture say? "Abraham believed God, and it was counted to him as righteousness." (Rom. 4:3; cf. Gal. 3:6)

We know that whatever the law says it speaks to those who are under the law, so that every mouth may be stopped, and the whole world may be held accountable to God. For by works of the law no human being will be justified in his sight, since through the law comes knowledge of sin. But now the righteousness of God has been manifested apart from the law, although the Law and the Prophets bear witness to it—the righteousness of God through faith in Jesus Christ for all who believe. (Rom. 3:19–22)

11. When the law is understood in its entirety, its aim is that Jesus Christ get the glory as the one who provides the only ground for our imputed righteousness through faith (justification) and the only power for our imparted righteousness through faith (sanctification) (Rom. 5:19; 10:4; 2 Cor. 5:21; Phil. 1:11; 3:8–9).

As by the one man's disobedience the many were made sinners, so by the one man's obedience the many will be made righteous. (Rom. 5:19)

Christ is the end of the law for righteousness to everyone who believes. (Rom. 10:4)

For our sake he made him to be sin who knew no sin, so that in him we might become the righteousness of God. (2 Cor. 5:21; cf. texts under #2)

[I pray that you may be] filled with the fruit of righteousness that comes through Jesus Christ, to the glory and praise of God. (Phil. 1:11)

I count everything as loss because of the surpassing worth of knowing Christ Jesus my Lord. For his sake I have suffered the loss of all things and count them as rubbish, in order that I may gain Christ and be found in him, not having a righteousness of my own that comes from the law, but that which comes through faith in Christ, the righteousness from God that depends on faith. (Phil. 3:8–9)

12. Therefore, I give a summarizing three-part answer to the question, "How can our imperfect obedience and love fulfill the perfect law of God?"

12.1 First, our imperfect love is, nevertheless, real, God-dependent, Spirit-enabled, Christ-exalting love that *flows from* our justification and is not *a means* to it. And therefore it is the new direction that the law was aiming at and what the new covenant promised. In short, *Christ-exalting love as the fruit of faith* is what the law was aiming at.

12.2 Second, our imperfect love is the firstfruits of a final perfection that Christ will complete in us at his appearing. Romans 8:4 does not say that the entire fulfillment of the law happens in us *now*. But our walk by the Spirit *begins* now, and so does our fulfillment of the righteous requirement of the law.

12.3 Finally, our imperfect love is the fruit of our faith in Jesus who is himself our only justifying perfection before God. In other words, the only law-keeping we depend on as the ground of our justification is Jesus' law-keeping. His was perfect. Ours is imperfect. And so we will never (even in eternity) have a whole life of perfection to offer God. The acceptability of our lives to all eternity will always depend on the perfection of Jesus offered in our place. Our imperfect love now and our perfect love later will always be the fruit of faith that looks to Jesus as our only complete perfection. In the end, the law is fulfilled in us everlastingly because it was fulfilled in him from everlasting to everlasting. Our imperfection and need is a pointer to his perfection and all-sufficiency; and that pointing—that exaltation of Christ—is the aim of the law.

WORKS BY N. T. WRIGHT
CITED IN THIS BOOK

BOOKS

The Climax of the Covenant: Christ and the Law in Pauline Theology (Edinburgh: T&T Clark, 1991).

Jesus and the Victory of God (Minneapolis: Fortress, 1996).

The Last Word: Beyond the Bible Wars to a New Understanding of the Authority of Scripture (San Francisco: HarperSanFrancisco, 2005).

The Letter to the Romans, in *The New Interpreter's Bible*, Vol. X (Nashville: Abingdon Press, 2002), 393–770.

The New Testament and the People of God (Minneapolis: Fortress Press, 1992).

Paul for Everyone: Galatians and Thessalonians (Louisville: Westminster John Knox, 2004).

Paul in Fresh Perspective (Minneapolis: Fortress, 2005).

What Saint Paul Really Said: Was Saul of Tarsus the Real Founder of Christianity? (Grand Rapids, MI: Eerdmans, 1997).

ESSAYS, INTERVIEWS, AND LECTURES

"4QMMT and Paul: Justification, 'Works,' and Eschatology," in *History and Exegesis: New Testament Essays in Honor of Dr. E. Earle Ellis for His 80th Birthday*, ed. Aang-Won (Aaron) Son (New York and London: T&T Clark, 2006), 104–132.

"The Cross and the Caricatures: A Response to Robert Jenson, Jeffrey John, and a New Volume Entitled *Pierced for Our Transgressions*," http://www.fulcrum-anglican.org.uk/news/2007/20070423wright.cfm?doc=205.

"The Letter to the Galatians: Exegesis and Theology," in *Between Two Horizons: Spanning New Testament Studies and Systematic Theology*, ed. J. B. Green and M. Turner (Grand Rapids, MI: Eerdmans, 2000), 205–236.

"New Perspectives on Paul," in *Justification in Perspective: Historical Developments and Contemporary Challenges*, ed. Bruce L. McCormack (Grand Rapids, MI: Baker Academic, 2006), 243–264.

"On Becoming the Righteousness of God," in *Pauline Theology*, Volume II: *1 & 2 Corinthians*, ed. David M. Hay (Minneapolis: Fortress, 1993), 200–208.

"Paul in Different Perspectives: Lecture 1: Starting Points and Opening Reflections," at the Pastors Conference of Auburn Avenue Presbyterian Church, Monroe, Louisiana (January 3, 2005); http://www.ntwrightpage.com/ Wright_Auburn_Paul.htm.

"Righteousness," in *New Dictionary of Theology*, ed. David F. Wright et. al. (Downers Grove, IL: InterVarsity Press, 1988), 590–592.

"The Shape of Justification" (2001), http://www.thepaulpage.com/Shape.html.

Travis Tamerius, "An Interview with N. T. Wright," *Reformation & Revival Journal* 11, Nos. 1 and 2 (Winter and Spring 2003). Available online at http://www.hornes.org/theologia/content/travis_tamerius/interview_with_ n_t_wright.htm.

SCRIPTURE INDEX

PERSON INDEX

SUBJECT INDEX

⊞ desiringGod

If you would like to ponder further the vision of God and life presented in this book, we at Desiring God would love to serve you. We have produced hundreds of resources to help you grow in your passion for God and help you spread that passion to others.

At our website, desiringGod.org, you'll find almost all of the resources John Piper has written and preached, including more than 30 books. We've made over 25 years of his sermons available free for you to read, listen to, download, and in some cases watch online. In addition, you can access hundreds of articles, listen to our daily internet radio program, find out where John Piper is speaking, learn about our conferences, discover our God-centered children's curricula, and browse our online store.

John Piper receives no royalties from the books he writes and no remuneration from Desiring God. These funds are all reinvested into our gospel-spreading efforts. DG also has a whatever-you-can-afford policy for the materials we sell, designed for individuals with limited discretionary funds. If you'd like more information about this policy, please contact us at the address or phone number below.

We exist to help you treasure Jesus Christ above all things because he is most glorified in you when you are most satisfied in him. Let us know how we can serve you!

Desiring God
2601 East Franklin Avenue
Minneapolis, MN 55406-1103

888.346.4700 (phone)
612.338.4372 (fax)
Email: mail@desiringGod.org
Web: www.desiringGod.org